J.R.R. Tolkien and His Literary Resonances

J.R.R. Tolkien and His Literary Resonances

Views of Middle-earth

Edited by
George Clark and Daniel Timmons

Contributions to the Study of Science Fiction and Fantasy, Number 89
C. W. Sullivan, III, Series Adviser

GREENWOOD PRESS
Westport, Connecticut • London

Library of Congress Cataloging-in-Publication Data

J.R.R. Tolkien and his literary resonances : views of Middle-earth / edited by George
    Clark and Daniel Timmons.
        p.   cm.—(Contributions to the study of science fiction and fantasy, ISSN 0193–6875 ;
    no. 89)
    Includes bibliographical references and index.
    ISBN 0–313–30845–4 (alk. paper)
    1. Tolkien, J.R.R. (John Ronald Reuel), 1892–1973—Criticism and interpretation. 2.
Fantasy fiction, English—History and criticism. 3. Middle Earth (Imaginary place) I.
Clark, George, 1932– II. Timmons, Daniel, 1961– III. Series.
PR6039.O32 Z6618   2000
823′.912—dc21   99–056047

British Library Cataloguing in Publication Data is available.

Library of Congress Catalog Card Number: 99–056047
ISBN: 0–313–30845–4
ISSN: 0193–6875

First published in 2000

Greenwood Press, 88 Post Road West, Westport, CT 06881
An imprint of Greenwood Publishing Group, Inc.
www.greenwood.com

Printed in the United States of America

The paper used in this book complies with the
Permanent Paper Standard issued by the National
Information Standards Organization (Z39.48–1984).

10 9 8 7 6 5 4 3 2

Contents

Introduction

Daniel Timmons

> I rarely remember a book about which I have had such violent arguments. Nobody seems to have a moderate opinion: either, like myself, people find it a masterpiece of its genre or they cannot abide it, and among the hostile there are some, I must confess, for whose judgement I have great respect. . . . . In most cases, however, the objection must go far deeper. I can only suppose that some people object to Heroic Quests and Imaginary Worlds on principle. . . . . That a man like Mr. Tolkien, the English philologist who teaches at Oxford, should lavish such incredible pains upon a genre which is, for them, trifling by definition, is, therefore, very shocking.

From the time when W. H. Auden made these remarks in his review of *The Lord of the Rings* (*LR*) in 1956 (5) to the present, a prominent and perennial view has been that J.R.R. Tolkien is seldom read with indifference. *The Hobbit* has received essentially high praise since its initial publication, but *LR* and *The Silmarillion* (*Silm*) are another matter. Commentators have taken strong positions for and against these books. C.S. Lewis hailed *The Fellowship of the Ring* (*FR*) as a work of genius (1082), whereas Peter Green declared that he could not take the book "seriously" (8). Richard Hughes called Tolkien's work a "very remarkable achievement" (408), while Edmund Wilson labelled it "juvenile trash" (332). William Blissett regarded *LR* as "perhaps the last literary masterpiece of the Middle Ages" (449); Mark Roberts claimed that the work "is not moulded by some controlling vision of things which is at the same time its *raison d'être*" (459). So, at the outset of *LR*'s reception, admirers and detractors of Tolkien apparently had formed opposing camps or factions.

Commentary on the Middle-earth tales indeed contains both positive criticism and negative remarks. In the 1960s, Marion Zimmer Bradley noted that love was "the dominant emotion" in *LR*, not only love of honor and country, but "Gandalf's paternal and Goldberry and Galadriel's maternal love" (109); Catharine Stimpson thought that Tolkien displays "subtle contempt and hostility toward women" and that unlike "many very good modern writers, he is no homosexual" (19, 20). In the 1970s, W. R. Irwin called *LR* "the most impressive" work of its kind of the twentieth century (161); conversely, C. N. Manlove judged it to be "facile and weak" (206). With regard to *Silm*, in 1977 John Gardner considered Tolkien's vision to be "philosophically and morally powerful" (39), whereas Christopher Booker called the book "one long, self-indulgent, pseudo-mythical whiffle" (18). In the 1980s, Ursula K. Le Guin stated that Tolkien's style was "outstanding" (79), while Michael Moorcock claimed it was like "Winnie-the-Pooh posing as epic"

(125). Lastly, in the late 1990s, C. W. Sullivan III commended "Tolkien's eminently successful attempt to create a traditional narrative" (82); John Goldthwaite, after quoting a passage of a battle scene from *The Return of the King* (*RK*), stated: "Very seldom does one encounter emotion this fraudulent and writing this bad in any genre" (218). On the surface, Auden's proposal that critics either admire Tolkien or disparage him still seems applicable today.

However, critics and readers often forget that every great writer has been subject to derision or condemnation. John Galt remarked that "I have never been able to bring myself to entertain any feeling approximating to respect for the works of Chaucer; . . . his lists and catalogues of circumstances are anything but poetry" (Brewer 1: 268). Ben Jonson wished that Shakespeare "had blotted a thousand" lines, and Abraham Wright claimed that *Hamlet* is "an indifferent play, the lines but meane: and in nothing like *Othello*" (Vickers 1: 26, 29). John Davies declared that "Spencers [*sic*] confusion, and different choice of names, are things never to be forgiven" (Cummings 296). Leonard Welsted stated that if writers do not use "Skill or Delicacy" when "introducing foreign Treasures" into the English language, "the Attempt will end in nothing but an uncouth unnatural Jargon, like the Phrase and Stile of Milton, which is a second Babel, Confusion of all Languages; a Fault, that can never be enough regretted" (Shawcross 1: 244). Lady Mary Wortley Montagu assumed that *Gulliver's Travels* was some sort of insidious collaboration of Swift, Pope, and Arbuthnot and stated: "Great Eloquence have they employ'd to prove themselves Beasts" (Williams 65). Lady Bradshaigh condemned *Tristram Shandy* as "mean," "dirty," "scandelous" [sic] and "the worst that ever appear'd in print" (Howes 90).

Even the acknowledged greats of modernist literature have come under fire. Oliver St. John Gogarty succinctly offered his view of *Ulysses*: "That bloody Joyce whom I kept in my youth has written a book you can read on all the lavatory walls of Dublin" (Deming 1: 282). Wyndham Lewis, although not dismissing Virginia Woolf, considered her work and ideas to have created a "suffocating atmosphere," a kind of "tyrannical inverted orthodoxy-in-the-making" (Majumdar 337). And finally, a monumental text of the twentieth century, T. S. Eliot's *The Waste Land*, was not immune to negative and, indeed, hostile voices; Louis Untermeyer declared:

> The result [i.e. the poem]—although, as I am aware, this conclusion is completely at variance with the judgement of its frenetic admirers—is a pompous parade of erudition, a lengthy extension of the earlier disillusion, a kaleidoscopic movement in which the bright-coloured pieces fail to atone for the absence of an integrated design. (Grant 1: 151)

In short, if the mere existence of severe remarks on authors were some sort of criterion for doubting their literary worth, then *no* writer, famous or obscure, would be highly regarded.

Furthermore, the scholarship on Tolkien spans sixty years and comprises thousands of titles, and so some negative assessments of his work are not only inevitable but needlessly alarming. While critics like Edmund Wilson have influenced some studies on Tolkien, none of the condemnations has prevented either the reading of or scholarship on the author's work. I have discussed at the length the history of reception of Tolkien's works elsewhere.[1] Briefly, there has always been a steady stream of intelligent and supportive responses to Tolkien which shows no signs of abating.

Given this massive amount of positive and enthusiastic response to Tolkien, from the early reviews of *Hobbit* in 1936 to recent books by Patrick Curry, William Howard Green, Verlyn Flieger, and Joseph Pierce, the question remains why recent commentators, such as Charles Moseley, still invoke this "hostile" vs. "laudatory" paradigm.[2] Perhaps, as Auden suggested, there is critical resistance to Tolkien's *genre*. If readers have a predisposed aversion to heroic literature, imaginary realms, an elevated language, or magical creatures, then works like Tolkien's will meet with their disdain. The "modernist revolt"[3] certainly would undermine or disparage the traditional themes and forms that Tolkien employs.

Still, the author's detractors rarely recognize that the literary aspects of Tolkien's work have been prominent in Western literature from Homer to the present day. The negative views, such as those of Wilson and Roberts, might represent a majority in academic circles that is not so much against Tolkien, but against *fantasy literature*.[4] In this case, Tolkien has not been singled out for exclusion because his contemporaries in the genre, C. S. Lewis or T. H. White, or his predecessors, George MacDonald, William Morris, E. R. Eddison, and Lord Dunsany, have not received wide acceptance in literary circles. Actually, for the kind of literature that Tolkien wrote he has been esteemed above all others.

Therefore, the central issue becomes not whether Tolkien is a great writer. Many renowned critics, including C. S. Lewis, W. H. Auden, Marion Zimmer Bradley, Ursula K. Le Guin, John Gardner, Derek Brewer, and Tom Shippey, have attested to Tolkien's excellence over and over again. The key point, as Shippey has observed, is that "the literary Establishment" has excluded Tolkien from "the unstated but well-known 'canon' of academic texts" (91–2). Critics should shift their focus from the minority of "hostile" voices and direct attention to the shadowy guardians of the "canon." Although a significant number of articles, theses, dissertations, and books on Tolkien have been published by academic presses, his works are not standard or required texts in the vast majority of university English departments.

In recent times, the composition of the canon of literature has come under severe scrutiny.[5] Originally, the "canon" of texts was the body of writings in the Bible, those "officially recognized" (Frye, Baker, and Perkins 88). The canon now includes texts sanctioned by "the literary Establishment" as worthy of study in academic institutions. Many disagreements abound concerning who's in and who's out, yet Harold Bloom's lists in *The Western Canon* probably encompass most authors whom critics would regard as "canonical." (Bloom mentions Tolkien, C.S. Lewis, and Charles Williams, strangely calling the latter the "guru" [77] to the others, but none of these authors appears in Bloom's lists.) Bloom argues that despite charges of racism or sexism, the canon is a viable guide to *worthwhile* reading, though not necessarily *required* course texts (16–17). In this light, it is difficult to disagree with Bloom's selections. Still, his bias comes through as he chooses certain works and authors and leaves out others. The mere act of compiling such a list is an exclusionary process, however wide the field is marked out.

Other critics have questioned and even attacked the exclusivity of canon formation. Alastair Fowler notes that F. R. Leavis and his 'descendants' have shown a preference for "the naturalistic novel," and excluded works not in this mode (233). Fowler wishes for a recognition of neglected writers, such as Walter de la Mare (215–16, 233), but does not specify his criteria for their inclusion. The fantasy works of Morris, Lewis, or Tolkien receive no notice. Carey Kaplan and Ellen Cronan Rose take aim at the canon-wielders, and call for opposition to the "academic establishment," whose "utterances are univocal, empowering a white male elite whose differences are more apparent and real" (158). Although Kaplan and Rose appear to champion "the Common Reader" against this academic hegemony (e.g., 85), they seem to imply that various male writers of European descent should be banished as some neglected authors are included. And again, Tolkien and his direct predecessors, contemporaries, and successors are not mentioned. John Guillory in *Cultural Capital* portrays the clash over canonicity as a socioeconomic struggle. In dense, exhaustive, and (in my view) bewildering prose, Guillory charts the various movements of literary thought that have given rise to distinctions between "Canonical and Noncanonical" (e.g., 6, 82, 339). In the end, though, Guillory, like Fowler, and Kaplan and Rose, mainly raises questions (and throws darts) rather than providing a framework wherein enduring writers, such as Chaucer, Shakespeare, Dickens, and Woolf, can take their proper place in a course curriculum, while also allowing academics the freedom to include works by writers such as George MacDonald, Christina Rossetti, or Tolkien.

Harriett Hawkins is one of the few critics to grapple with the issues of "High Literature and Popular Modern Genres" in her provocatively titled *Classics and Trash*. While comic irony runs throughout her book, she might have undervalued certain works, perhaps without realizing it, by claiming that they are chiefly worthwhile for "pleasure":

> And of course the kind of things that we may, subsequently, most enjoy watching or reading or writing about in later years may well-depend on what we most vividly remember having enjoyed as children or adolescents whether watching films such as *King Kong*, or TV shows such as *Star Trek*, videos such as *Thriller*, or while reading stories such as the *Oz* books, or *Lord of the Rings* for no other purpose but pleasure. (109)

Hawkins's tone is amicable, and, to be fair, she later acknowledges that Lewis's and Tolkien's fictions show kinship with "high literature," and that readers who enjoy them often prefer the "classics" over their successors (120–21). But grouping *LR* with *King Kong* or *Thriller* reveals a lack of proportion, which if fostered, will not help Tolkien's status in the "Establishment." Works like *Star Trek* are not always trivial or superficial; I have enjoyed them and discovered artistic depths, which my elitist colleagues often have dismissed. Still, *LR* is a massive and intricate work of fiction, requiring hours and hours of close and careful reading, unlike fantasy films, TV programs, or much of children's literature.

No one need feel apologetic about Tolkien's monumental status in popular culture, which began in the mid-1960s and continues (albeit with less intensity) even today. More significantly, though, Tolkien's writings have strong, expansive, and deep roots in the literary history of Western culture. Any academic can try to block Tolkien's entry into the canon. But no enlightened reader should deny or disregard the complex and pervasive literary resonances in Tolkien's works.

The purpose of this volume of new essays on Tolkien is to recognize his stature in literary history and to examine his works afresh. There are many more fine and complex studies of Tolkien's works than has been generally acknowledged, but much of this writing is safely stored in certain libraries and inaccessible to many of Tolkien's readers. Collections of essays on Tolkien have appeared, but few are of much worth.[6] Although criticism exists on Tolkien's works in relation to medieval literature and twentieth–century fantasy, relatively few studies situate the author in a broader context. Tolkien's writings have links to every major period of English literature from Old English to Renaissance poetics to religious epic to nineteenth–century popular narrative. This collection seeks to address (and redress) the gaps in Tolkien scholarship, and especially to put Tolkien's works in their proper contexts and explore some of the springs that nurtured his vast imagination. The goals here are to enhance the literary world's sense of Tolkien's creativity and to inspire scholars to study his great contribution to literature.

The collection's essayists form an impressive and eclectic group of scholars. There are renowned medievalists, George Clark, Jonathan Evans, Geoffrey Russom, and Tom Shippey, promising critics Tanya Caroline Wood, Debbie Sly, William N. Rogers and Michael R. Underwood, and accomplished fantasy literature and Tolkien scholars Verlyn Flieger, Charles W. Nelson, Faye Ringel, David Sandner, Roger C. Schlobin, W. A. Senior and C. W. Sullivan III. Professors Flieger and Shippey deserve special notice. Their excellent articles and books have given Tolkien scholarship a strong foundation and legitimacy.

C. W. Sullivan III develops his interest in the oral nature of Tolkien's fiction, situating it within the tradition of Old Norse sagas. Sullivan avers that Tolkien's use of such ancient forms draws attention to both fantasy writers' interest in this literature and the modern critical dislike of it. Jonathan Evans examines Tolkien's dragons, whose archetypes are in the saga and epic accounts of Old English and Old Norse literature. Evans observes that Tolkien's use of the dragon motifs are both time-honored and brilliantly innovative. Geoffrey Russom explores the gold mine of Tolkien's verse. Russom proves that the author's poetry, which some of his supporters have belittled, makes subtle and intricate use of ancient metrical forms. George Clark discusses Tolkien's medieval criticism and fantasy fiction as a search for a new hero and a newly conceived heroism. Clark argues that Tolkien rewrote, replaced, and rejected the standard hero of the old Germanic world only to discover his new heroes assuming some of the character of the ancient model, which Tolkien desired in spite of himself. Roger C. Schlobin investigates the influence that *Sir Gawain and the Green Knight* may have had on Tolkien's work. Although such influence would seem logical, given Tolkien's extensive work on the medieval poem, including an edition and translation, Schlobin observes that the tone and thematic import of *Gawain*, not the specifics of the story, infused Tolkien's work. Charles W. Nelson, in the final essay that chiefly deals with medieval resonances in Tolkien's fiction, probes the way that Tolkien may have used allegorical representations of the Seven Deadly Sins, found in Chaucer, Gower, and Langland. Nelson suggests that Tolkien drew on such images when conceiving, for instance, the march of the Ents and the portrayal of Wormtongue.

In a sprightly shift of emphasis, Tanya Caroline Wood discusses the remarkable similarities between Tolkien's "On Fairy-Stories" and Sir Philip Sidney's *Defense of Poesy*. While it is going too far to call medievalist Tolkien a "Renaissance Man," Wood argues that his kinship with that period is more significant than has been generally assumed. Debbie Sly examines a related, highly relevant topic: Tolkien and Milton. Sly proposes that both writers, through their depiction of the "power of darkness," exhibit tensions between religious imperatives and artistic aesthetics. William N. Rogers II and Michael R. Underwood examine the possible connection between Tolkien's work and H. Rider Haggard's fiction. Tolkien acknowledged that he was influenced by Haggard's *She*;[7] Rogers and Underwood make a strong case that Haggard's degenerate Gagool in *King Solomon's Mines* could be a literary ancestor of Gollum.

In the final third of the collection, the essays examine Tolkien's relationship to the twentieth century. David Sandner looks at the evident connections between Tolkien and Lewis, and their perspectives on Secondary Worlds and allegory. The similarities between these two great authors and close friends have been discussed at length, yet Sandner emphasizes their profound distinctiveness as well. Verlyn Flieger tackles the difficult issue of Tolkien's presumed ecological sensitivity, noting that the author has been seized upon as a champion of eco-activism, which soared to prominence in the mid- to late-1960s at the same time as the sudden rise of Tolkien's popularity. Flieger acknowledges that Tolkien declared that he always took "the side of trees as against all their enemies"; however, she astutely observes the complications of the author's claim. Faye Ringel discusses the influence Tolkien's work on women fantasists. Ringel observes that these writers feel indebted to Tolkien, but share some ambivalence and even concern regarding his depiction of social structures and women in Middle-earth. W. A. Senior examines a central, yet understudied, aspect of Tolkien's work: the theme of loss. Senior describes the various pervading and seemingly unending instances of loss in Tolkien's writings, ranging from his personal war experiences to the decline in

Middle-earth's beauty. In this regard, Senior maintains that Tolkien surpasses and stands apart from his fantasy fiction successors. Tom Shippey anchors the collection in a strong and fitting way. Shippey examines Tolkien's images of evil, particularly the orcs, wraiths, barrow-wights, describing the way that Tolkien has borrowed and modified these monstrous figures from ancient literature. Shippey also argues that far from being escapist, self-indulgent, or irrelevant, as many more sheltered critics have claimed, Tolkien's images of evil arise out of and respond to the twentieth century's most serious issues, which modernist writers have consistently ignored.

This volume also includes a selected bibliography of Tolkien's writings and criticism of his works. Previously unknown manuscripts of Tolkien are edited and published, and a massive amount of fannish materials and scholarship appears constantly. Even the various organizations devoted to the author, such as The Tolkien Society and The Mythopoeic Society, are unable to keep up with all the new materials. Tolkien on-line list services and news groups are ways to remain up-to-date, but some of the information over the Internet is unreliable. The Tolkien "phenomenon"[8] goes on, despite the indifference of some academic and literary circles.

And so, throughout the years and into the foreseeable future, Tolkien's works continue to stand strongly on their own intrinsic merits. This collection seeks to expand the horizons of Tolkien scholarship and widen the circle of his readers, thereby making Tolkien's works part of the larger story that we all know and live.

> [A]nd you will read things out of the Red Book, and keep alive the memory of the age that is gone, so that people will remember the Great Danger and so love their beloved land all the more. And that will keep you as busy and as happy as anyone can be, as long as your part of the Story goes on.[9]

A NOTE ON CITATIONS

Since numerous editions of Tolkien's works have been published, no generally acknowledged "standard" texts exist. (Those published after 1979 have had the textual errors of the previous editions corrected.) Individual readers and critics of Tolkien have their own preferred copies, now likely in precarious shape after so many readings and personal annotations. Throughout this collection, the editors have used consistent page references and recognizable abbreviations (see below) of Tolkien's works based on the editions listed in the selected bibliography under "Primary Works."

The Hobbit – Hobbit
The Lord of the Rings – LR
The Fellowship of the Ring – FR
The Two Towers – TT

The Return of the King – RK
The Silmarillion – Silm
The Monsters and the Critics and Other Essays – Essays

NOTES

1. My article in the Tolkien issue of *Journal of the Fantastic in the Arts* summarizes briefly the major movements in Tolkien scholarship. For the main thrust of the article, I used my doctoral dissertation, "Mirror on Middle-earth: J.R.R. Tolkien and the Critical Perspectives," available from University Microfilms International (UMI).

2. In 1992, Brian Rosebury described the bulk of Tolkien criticism as "shallow and silly commentary, both hostile and laudatory" (2); in 1997, Charles Moseley echoed this view (xiii). Neither one has accurately represented the majority of Tolkien scholarship.

3. M. H. Abrams uses this term to describe the impulses of the modernist writers (109).

4. Despite a long history and virtual mountain of commentary, no generally accepted definition of "fantasy" appears available; my conception of this literary form follows Tolkien's ideas; Tolkienian "fantasy" is a story set in an imaginative realm in an ancient world, which has the clear presence of the magical or numinous coexisting rationally with the familiar and ordinary; in addition, such a work exemplifies the narrative tone and structure found in the traditional forms of myth, epic, romance, saga, and fairy tale; lastly, the story should attempt to inspire religious joy, wonder, and enchantment in the reader.

5. I am indebted to Professor William Whitlaw for the idea of looking at Tolkien's status in relation to issues of the literary canon.

6. At present the notable collection of essays on Tolkien is the *Proceedings of the J.R.R. Tolkien Centenary Conference* in 1992; Neil D. Isaacs and Rose A. Zimbardo have published two essay collections, which contain both fine and weak essays. Jared Lobdell's anthology has few bright moments. And Robert Giddings's collection, with its evident attempt to denigrate Tolkien, combines weak scholarship with strong prejudices. Verlyn Flieger and Car F. Hostetter have just recently published an important collection of essays on *The History of Middle-earth* series for Greenwood Publishing.

7. In a phone interview with Henry Resnik, Tolkien acknowledged that he was influenced by Haggard (40).

8. In 1970, Bruce A. Beatie discussed "The Tolkien Phenomenon;" his general views on the author's pervasiveness in the popular culture are still applicable today.

9. As Frodo is about to embark on a ship bound for the hidden realm of Valinor, he speaks these words of parting to Sam (*RK* 376).

WORKS CITED

Abrams, M. H. *A Glossary of Literary Terms.* 5th ed. Forth Worth: Holt, 1988.

Auden, W. H. "At the End of the Quest, Victory." *New York Times Book Review* 22 Jan. 1956: 5.

Beatie, Bruce A. "The Tolkien Phenomenon: 1954 – 1968." *Journal of Popular Culture* 3.4 (1970): 689–703.

Blissett, William. "The Despots of the Rings." *South Atlantic Quarterly* 58 (1959): 448–456.

Bloom, Harold. *The Western Canon: The Books and School of the Ages.* New York: Harcourt, 1994.

Booker, Christopher. "Bubble and Squeal." *Spectator* 17 Sept. 1977: 17.

Bradley, Marion Zimmer. "Men, Halflings and Hero-Worship." *Tolkien and the Critics: Essays on J.R.R. Tolkien's The Lord of the Rings*. Ed. Neil D. Isaacs and Rose A. Zimbardo. Notre Dame: U of Notre Dame P, 1968.

Brewer, Derek, ed. *Chaucer: The Critical Heritage*. 2 vols. London: Routledge, 1978.

Cummings, Robert M., ed. *Spenser: The Critical Heritage*. London: Routledge, 1971.

Deming, Robert H., ed. *James Joyce: The Critical Heritage*. 2 vols. London: Routledge, 1970.

Fowler, Alastair. *Kinds of Literature: An Introduction to the Theory of Genres and Modes*. Cambridge, MA: Harvard UP, 1982.

Frye, Northrop, Sheridan Baker, and George Perkins. *The Harper Handbook to Literature*. New York: Harper, 1985.

Gardner, John. "The World of Tolkien." *New York Times Book Review* 23 Oct. 1977: 1, 39–40.

Goldthwaite, John. *The Natural History of Make-Believe*. New York: Oxford UP, 1996.

Grant, Michael, ed. *T. S. Eliot: The Critical Heritage*. 2 vols. London: Routledge, 1982.

Green, Peter. "Outward Bound by Air to an Inappropriate Ending." *Daily Telegraph and Morning Post* 27 Aug. 1954: 8.

Guillory, John. *Cultural Capital: The Problem of Literary Canon Formation*. Chicago: U of Chicago P, 1993.

Hawkins, Harriet. *Classics and Trash: Traditions and Taboos in High Literature and Popular Modern Genres*. Toronto: U of Toronto P, 1990.

Howes, Alan B., ed. *Sterne: The Critical Heritage*. London: Routledge, 1974.

Hughes, Richard. "*The Lord of the Rings*." *Spectator* 1 Oct. 1954: 408–409.

Irwin, W. R. *The Game of the Impossible: A Rhetoric of Fantasy*. Urbana: U of Illinois P, 1976.

Kaplan, Carey, and Ellen Cronan Rose. *The Canon and the Common Reader*. Knoxville: U of Tennessee P, 1990.

Le Guin, Ursula K. *The Language of the Night: Essays on Fantasy and Science Fiction*. 1979. New ed. London: Women's, 1989.

Lewis, C. S. "The Gods Return to Earth." *Time and Tide* 14 Aug. 1954: 1082–1083.

Majumdar, Robin, and Allen McLaurin, eds. *Virginia Woolf: The Critical Heritage*. London: Routledge, 1975.

Manlove, C. N. *Modern Fantasy: Five Studies*. Cambridge: Cambridge UP, 1975.

Moorcock, Michael. *Wizardry and Wild Romance: A Study of Epic Fantasy*. London: Gollancz, 1987.

Moseley, Charles. *J.R.R. Tolkien*. Plymouth: Northcote, 1997.

Resnik, Henry. "An Interview with Tolkien." *Niekas* 18 (1967): 37–47.

Roberts, Mark. "Adventures in English." *Essays in Criticism* 6 (1956): 450–459.

Rosebury, Brian. *Tolkien: A Critical Assessment*. London: St. Martin's, 1992.

Shawcross, John T., ed. *Milton: The Critical Heritage*. 2 vols. London: Routledge, 1970.

Shippey, T. A. "Tolkien as Post-War Writer." *Proceedings of the J.R.R. Tolkien Centenary Conference 1992*. Ed. Patricia Reynolds and Glen GoodKnight. Milton Keynes, UK: Tolkien Society, 1995. 84–93.

Stimpson, Catharine R. *J.R.R. Tolkien*. New York: Columbia UP, 1969.

Sullivan, C.W. III. "Tolkien and the Telling of a Traditional Narrative." *Journal of the Fantastic in the Arts* 7.1 (1996): 75-82.

Timmons, Daniel. "J.R.R. Tolkien: The 'Monstrous' in the Mirror." *Journal of the Fantastic in the Arts* 9.3 (1998): 229–246.

——. "Mirror on Middle-earth: J.R.R. Tolkien and the Critical Perspectives." Diss. U of Toronto, 1998.

Vickers, Brian, ed. *Shakespeare: The Critical Heritage*. 6 vols. London: Routledge, 1974.

Williams, Kathleen. *Swift: The Critical Heritage*. London: Routledge, 1970.

Wilson, Edmund. "Oo, Those Awful Orcs." 1956. *The Bit Between My Teeth: A Literary Chronicle of 1950–1965*. New York: Farrar, 1965. 326–332.

1

Tolkien the Bard: His Tale Grew in the Telling

C.W. Sullivan III

"There is something about Tolkien's art which eludes the conventional strategies of contemporary criticism, even when these are deployed with sympathy and patience." This view from Brian Rosebury in *Tolkien: A Critical Assessment* (4) is insightful. The key words are, of course, "conventional" and "contemporary," for what Tolkien was doing, for all his contemporary popularity, was anything but writing a contemporary—or modern—novel. Given that he was not writing a modern novel, it is quite typical that conventional criticism can make little of *Hobbit* and *LR* other than reduce them to World War II allegories or mere escapist yearnings for a passing rural England (the sort of criticism continually aimed at *The Wind in the Willows,* among others). What was Tolkien doing, then? As a student of traditional narrative, I have returned to Tolkien's two most famous books from time to time and have begun an argument that I would like to continue here.[1] I believe that Tolkien committed a traditionally patterned oral narrative to paper, and that we can understand *Hobbit* and *LR* better if we look at them not through the lenses of modern critical methods but through lenses developed for the study of earlier works.[2]

Clearly, Tolkien drew his inspiration from the older literatures of the north and west of Europe and from other writers, such as (and especially, perhaps) William Morris, who made fiction based on those ancient narratives. Many critics, myself among them, have commented on the traditional Märchen plot that structures both of Tolkien's novels.[3] Other primary evidence for traditionality includes the dwarf names taken from the Elder Edda, a dragon kin to the one described in *Beowulf,* a wizard from the Merlin/Druidic tradition, a dragon slayer with the requisite magic arrow, elves and dwarves and trolls from northern European lore in general, a ring of invisibility, a band of sleeping warriors, a mirror of seeing, a throne of power, a greedy town mayor, a magical healing draught, plant seeds of exceptional fertility, a dragon's missing breastplate, and a host of other familiar motifs—and not all of them fantastic—from myth, legend and folktale.[4]

Tolkien did not "borrow" these materials from ancient prose and poetry any more than any traditional artist borrows his or her material, be it a ballad or a quilt pattern. Like traditionally recognized folk performers, Tolkien was using material that he had been conversant with, quite literally, from childhood. He may have learned much of it in more formal circumstances than a ballad singer or a quilter does, but those were the only places—that is, classrooms and books—where that material was available to him. Thus, when he came to write *Hobbit* and *LR*, it was after many years' apprenticeship in the halls of academe; and when he wrote about the dwarves, he knew their names and the pattern of their story from a lifetime of experience, just as a ballad singer knows the verses or the quilt maker knows the pattern. He made this traditional story his own by creating the hobbit, Bilbo Baggins, and by splitting the heroics, almost at the last minute, between two characters: Bilbo, who finds the answers, and Bard, of the Royal Line of Dale, who slays the dragon. The same split, this time between Frodo and Aragorn, occurs much earlier and is developed more fully in *LR*. And even that split may have been influenced by tradition.

I am not about to assert that Tolkien was a folk performer and that *Hobbit* and *LR* are folktale and legend, respectively—although Katharyn Crabbe's 1981 *J.R.R. Tolkien* does analyze them quite profitably as fairy tale and legend (the literary forms of the traditional folktale and legend). What I can provide is some evidence that Tolkien was exposed early to the dragon slayer tale, a tale that figures as a central motif in most of his later fiction, and that he was influenced by other authors, perhaps most especially William Morris, who were also attempting to write fiction patterned after older oral forms. In addition, I can offer some comments about ancient northern European literature in general and the Icelandic family sagas in particular, which will be clearly applicable to Tolkien's writing—much more applicable, in fact, than Aristotelian poetics or the theory of the properly structured novel.

Humphrey Carpenter remarks that Tolkien found that William Morris's view of literature was very like his own, and that in the prose-verse romance *The House of the Wolfings* "Morris had tried to recreate the excitement he himself had found in the pages of early English and Icelandic narratives" (70). And that is exactly what Tolkien would later do in his narratives. As T. A. Shippey suggests, "[l]ike Walter Scott or William Morris before him, [Tolkien] felt the perilous charm of the archaic world of the North, recovered from bits and scraps by generations of inquiry. He wanted to tell a story about it simply, one feels, because there were hardly any complete ones left" (54). Indeed, Tolkien himself remarked that the "prime motive [for writing *LR*] was the desire of a tale-teller to try his hand at a really long story that would hold the attention of readers, amuse them, delight them, and at times maybe excite them or deeply move them" (*FR* 11).

Shippey and Tolkien both use the word "story," and this term is yet another stumbling block to which critics have yet to pay enough attention.[5] C. S. Lewis warned us about that problem some time ago:

> Those forms of literature in which Story exists merely as a means to something else—for example, the novel of manners where the story is there for the sake of the characters, or the criticism of social conditions—have had full justice done to them; but those forms in which everything else is there for the sake of the story have been given little serious attention. (3)

Lewis points in a direction in which mythology-in-literature scholar John Vickery continues when Vickery argues that most mythology-in-literature critics would agree that "myth forms the matrix out of which literature emerges both historically and psychologically" (ix). That is, the Story came first, even though all of the uses to which it has been put and all of the critical means by which it has been interpreted have overshadowed story of late (Sullivan 18).

Furthermore, understanding the nature of traditional narrative, of story, can also put us on the road to understanding rather more complex issues in contemporary fiction: issues of story that have been overlooked in the critical rush to deconstruct the modern forest into its component postmodern trees; issues of story that have been lost in the critical study of the novel (an essentially reality-based narrative, ultimately Aristotelian in its structure and well-made according to its nineteenth-century aesthetic); issues of story that have been ignored as literature was separated into elite and popular (primarily by the New York establishment and university English departments); issues of story that have become confused as realism was championed over fantasy and then the designation "magic realism" was coined so that no one would have to admit that Borges is writing a kind of fantasy and Theroux is stealing ideas, and old ones at that, from science fiction; issues of story that have been pushed aside as literary criticism has privileged novel over narrative, privileged writer over teller, and (most recently) privileged criticism over fiction.

The inadequacy of contemporary criticism to deal with Tolkien's novels was reinforced, as I researched for this essay, by Icelandic scholar Theodore M. Andersson, who commented on the same critical situation in regard to the Icelandic family sagas.

> [T]he sagas stand outside of the ironic or intellectual tradition to which the reader of prose narrative has been accustomed since the advent of modern fiction. The saga is plane [sic] narrative with no vertical dimensions; the saga-teller does not manipulate the complicated set of mirrors used by the modern author to catch and bind together himself, his subject, and his reader. (1967, 31–32)

Andersson concludes that section of his book with a very telling comment: "In short, the saga comes very close to pure narrative" (32). In other words, what the saga is about is the story.

Andersson's study *The Icelandic Family Saga* contains a great deal that might illuminate Tolkien's art. The structure of the plots of Tolkien's novels corresponds quite nicely to the structural pattern Andersson articulates for the Icelandic family saga, with the obvious exception of the revenge element; however, the second section of his book, "The Rhetoric of the Saga," is particularly interesting. In that section, Andersson argues that the "arrangement of the material and the progress of the narrative are governed by certain principles and techniques, which may almost be formulated as saga laws and which combine to give the saga its peculiar complexion" (32–33). The rhetorical structure that Andersson advances for the saga applies to Tolkien's novels as well.[6]

The first principal Andersson advances is one of *unity*: "The saga has a brand of unity not unlike the classical injunction against the proliferation of plot in drama. . . . The story is seen only in terms of the climax. Everything that precedes the climax is conceived as preparation for it and everything that follows is conceived as a logical consequence" (33). Quite clearly the unilinear plot of *Hobbit* can be described this way, but so also can the multilinear plot of *LR*. Even after the Nine Walkers become sundered and various hobbits, men, dwarves, and elves follow several plotlines to the climax, all are headed inexorably in that direction, each following his own path. "What is unique," Andersson says of the saga, "is the deliberate and single-minded way in which the story is related to the high point and the peak of the pyramid is achieved" (35).

Andersson describes the progress of individual and sequential narrative events as *scaffolding*: "The episodes leading to the climax necessarily all tend in that direction, but they can be unrelated to each other" (35), and each episode "is an independent drama" (38). This is less true of *Hobbit*, as its plot is basically sequential, but it is certainly descriptive of the several plots in *LR* after the breakup of the Fellowship. The three main plots—Frodo and Sam, Merry and Pippin, and Aragorn, Legolas, and Gimli—are not dependent upon one another; each set of characters succeeds on its own, and the only thing the three sets of characters have in common is that they are all headed toward the same end, the narrative's climax. "Although . . . these episodes are related," Andersson concludes, "each is an independent action" (38).

Within the scaffolding structure, Andersson delineates several techniques by which the saga author "guides the action toward a conclusion." One such is *escalation*, "the technique of staggering the episodes. . . . in order of jeopardy; each succeeding adventure is more provocative or perilous than its predecessor" (38). This is certainly the case in both of Tolkien's novels. In *Hobbit*, the confrontations escalate from the almost-Cockney trolls to that most fearsome of beasts, the dragon; along the way, Bilbo develops to match the increasingly formidable challenges. In *LR,* even the secondary characters take on increasingly difficult challenges as Frodo moves from a vague fear of the Black Riders to the final confrontation with Sauron. Andersson suggests that escalation can be achieved by "an increase of danger, a multiplying of portents, a deterioration of behavior, [or] a quickening of the pace" (40).

Balancing the escalation of episodes in the saga, Andersson sees something he calls *retardation,* "a meaningful slackening of the pace" (40). This retardation "arrests the pace and leads to the anticipated climax obliquely and slowly" (42). Such breaks in the action occur in both novels. There are two major respites in *Hobbit*: the stay at the Last Homely House, a pause before heading off into the "real" wilderness, and the refuge with Beorn, a pause before beginning the last stage of the journey. There are more such respites in *LR,* but the major ones are the passage through Bombadil's enchanted wood, a stop at the Last Homely House, where the Fellowship is assembled, and the stay in Lothlórien—all three incidents in which the pace of the story is dramatically slowed and the characters are able to rest. This retardation, Andersson comments, functions "to delay the climax and concentrate interest" (42). And in Tolkien, it often serves, as does the stay in Lothlórien, to concentrate interest on the climax by showing what may be lost if Sauron triumphs.

The balance between escalation and retardation is one indication of what Andersson calls the *symmetry* of the saga. Further, he notes that the "saga authors have a fondness for the use of pairs and series in their plot structures" (43). This element of structuring is very common in traditional narratives of all kinds; for example, the number three—three sisters, three wishes, and so on—appears in a variety of legends and folktales. Tolkien's narratives are full of pairs: Bilbo and Frodo, for example, the latter enacting a plot similar to the former's adventures. The Frodo/Sam duality is set off by the Frodo/Gollum and the Gollum/Sméagol dualities, forming a triangle of dualities or series of pairs. Strider becomes Aragorn, Gandalf the Grey becomes Gandalf the White, Saruman is a small Sauron, the smaller spiders in *Hobbit* prefigure Shelob in *LR*, and so on. Even the humorous series that Andersson finds characteristic of saga symmetry (48–49) is reflected in Tolkien's books, most obviously in the arrival of the dwarves at Bilbo's hobbit-hole and later in its parallel at Beorn's home.

Andersson suggests that the "most obvious and ubiquitous rhetorical device in the sagas is *foreshadowing"* (49; my italics). Foreshadowing is certainly prevalent in both of Tolkien's novels; early in each, Gandalf sits with the main character, and, in *Hobbit*, some others, and outlines the general course of the action to follow and the challenge to be confronted. This initial foreshadowing is followed, in each work, by a more complete explication of the problem and a more detailed discussion of each quest at the Last Homely House. In addition, there are various signs, portents, maps, prophecies, and other elements that indicate, in Andersson's words, "the goal of the story" (49). By setting out the story, and prefiguring the climax, foreshadowing helps distribute "interest over the whole text and prevents the otherwise heavily stressed climax from eclipsing the rest of the story" (49).

"Just before the climax a saga frequently lapses into a fuller and denser narrative." At this point, which Andersson calls *staging,* the action slows down, details are magnified, and incidentals may be foregrounded "in order to focus the central event one last time and enhance its importance in relation to the rest of the story" (54). In *Hobbit,* the action slows down twice: once before the slaying of Smaug and once before the Battle of the Five Armies. In *LR,* there is the long and dismal trek into and through Mordor, broken up by the incident with Shelob and by Frodo's temporary capture. As the dwarves refortify the mountain, Bilbo talks about how tired he has become with the adventure; and as Frodo and Sam plod toward and through Mordor, Tolkien makes the reader feel their exhaustion. Although some of the details in the staging section of the saga—"planning of strategy, topographical details," and the like (57)—are the same in the sagas and Tolkien's novels, others are considerably different; the effect of slowing the action, however, is the same.

In addition to the major elements or motifs discussed above, Andersson finds three other techniques worth special discussion. The first of these is *shift of scene.* In the saga, the author "must shift one [party] to the other once or several times in order to balance the picture" (58). Andersson discusses the opposing parties in a saga whose clash is the climax of the work. Tolkien does shift scenes thus, but his shifts are between or among various elements aligned against a common foe—and the reader does not see the foe. In *Hobbit,* there is a late scene shift from the mountain to Laketown to find out what happened to the dragon; in *LR,* there are many scene shifts after the breakup of the Fellowship to follow the multiple plotlines that develop thereafter. Tolkien's readers get only a brief view from Smaug's perspective and a secondary view from Saruman's perspective (representing Sauron's, perhaps). Whereas the saga author uses the scene shifts to bring the two parties closer to the climax, Tolkien uses it, especially in *LR,* to bring the separated Fellowship back together and into conflict with the Enemy. In both cases, as Andersson says of the saga, the shifts of scene show the last obstacles to the climax being removed (60).

According to Andersson, the saga author does not often engage in "direct characterization," but the one time that he often does comment "on a man's physique, personality, or prowess. . . . is at the time of the hero's death" (60). Andersson calls this "recharacterization . . . associated with the hero's death . . . a *necrology"* (60; my italics). Although there is a good deal of characterization in Tolkien's novels, he uses this specific technique twice, and oddly it serves to repatriate a character whom the reader may have come to dislike. In *Hobbit,* Thorin, who had been acting in less than honorable ways, dies a hero's death and is buried with his sword; his last heroic stand is described, and we are told that Fili and Kili die with him as was their right and duty as closest kin. In *LR,* Boromir, who succumbs to the lure of the Ring and tries to take it from Frodo, also dies a hero's death defending the hobbits and receives a proper boat funeral, arrayed in his battle finery with the swords of his enemies beneath his feet. Otherwise, as the main characters survive the climactic battles and there is a great deal said about their prowess and their achievements, there is no need or opportunity for a necrology.

The final technique is one Andersson calls *posturing,* "the supreme [act of] heroism on the part of the doomed man just before he is slain" (62). Andersson uses the term "posturing" because he feels that, while the action is heroic, it is "so improbably and theatrically heroic that the term posturing is not out of place" (62). Thorin, unwilling to share the treasure, and Boromir, desirous of the Ring, begin their posturing with unreasonable demands of those who are, or should be, their allies. Both begin their redemptions with grand gestures. Thorin's last act in *Hobbit* is to lever down the wall protecting the mountain, enter the fray having resumed the title King Under the Mountain, and rally the dwarves (and anyone else who will come) to him. It is a valiant act, but in terms of the numbers arrayed against them, ultimately a futile one; Thorin dies with a pile of enemy warriors around him. Boromir, too, wages a doomed fight to protect the hobbits after he has tried to take the Ring from Frodo, and he dies full of orc arrows, both his horn and his sword broken, the hobbits Merry and Pippin carried away into captivity.

In addition to the specific rhetoric that Andersson outlines, the Icelandic sagas may have contributed to Tolkien's understanding of the structure of story in another way as well. In "Early Icelandic Imaginative Literature," Hermann Pálsson discusses the worldview of that literature.

> The literary cosmos of early Icelandic fiction divides into three primary worlds. First, there is the timeless, hypothetical world of myth, inhabited by gods and other extramundane beings. . . . Second, we have the alien, aristocratic world of heroic legend and romance, a world which is human, though it shares certain obvious features with myth: . . . Third, there is the familiar world of experience, mirroring the physical and social realities of the author's own environment. (27–28)

Certainly, Tolkien's Secondary World, Middle-earth, is a literary cosmos of just this sort.

The focus on the North not only gave Tolkien the structure, details, and rhetoric of his story but, in an interesting way, may have given him the overall tone or sense of the story. Shippey has suggested that Tolkien may have split the hero because heroes "are not acceptable any more, and tend very strongly to be treated with irony; the modern version of *Beowulf* is John Gardner's novel *Grendel* (1971). . . . [Tolkien's] response to the difficulty is Bilbo Baggins . . . a character whose initial role at least is very strongly that of mediator" (55). However, in "The Displacement of the Heroic Ideal in the Family Sagas," Andersson comments that the "outlook of this literature is not animated by selfishness or by a hectic pursuit of honor but by a search for moderation" (69) and that the "difference between the heroic ethic and the morality of the family sagas is perhaps to be explained by the supposition that heroic lays reflect the values of a warrior class while the sagas reflect the values of Icelandic society at large" (70). Thus, Tolkien's separation of the hero into the hobbit (Bilbo or Frodo) who is able to return, albeit not permanently, to the Shire after his adventure is over and the hero (Bard or Aragorn) who is able to slay the dragon and become the Lord of Dale or the High King of Middle-earth may also have come from the North. Interestingly, Tolkien himself makes a reference to the problem of heroes and heroics. Thorin says, as he lies dying at the end of *Hobbit,* "If more of us valued food and cheer and song above hoarded gold, it would be a merrier world" (271).

Thorin's comment leads directly to Patrick Curry's suggestion, in *Defending Middle Earth: Tolkien, Myth and Modernity,* regarding Tolkien's place in the postmodern world. Curry characterizes modernity as "the combination of modern science, a global capitalistic economy, and the political power of the nation-state" and argues that it has been in development since the seventeenth century. But, he continues, although there have been benefits, too many of the promises of scientific and technological progress have been broken, and people in increasing numbers are now beginning to ask hard and serious questions about the value of this progress (21–23).

> I believe Tolkien's books speak to precisely these conditions. Drawing on the power of ancient Indo-European myth, they invite the reader into a compelling and remarkably complete pre-modern world, saturated with corresponding earlier values, which therefore feels something like a lost home—and by the same token, offers hope for its recovery. (23)

Those earlier values that Tolkien celebrates are, Curry feels, exactly those "whose jeopardy we now most feel" (23); Thorin's comment about "valuing food and cheer and song above hoarded gold" urgently articulates that kind of refocusing and recovery. If Tolkien's novels are indeed postmodern by being pre–modern, as Curry suggests, then it is no wonder (and I use that term intentionally) that modern criticism cannot deal adequately with them.

The focus on the North, the Icelandic and Old English narratives, was one that was to absorb Tolkien both as a scholar and as a storyteller. His essay *"Beowulf:* The Monsters and the Critics" remains a landmark in criticism, and his edition (with E. V. Gordon) and his translation of *Sir Gawain and the Green Knight* are still the standards. In *Beowulf: The Poem and Its Tradition,* John D. Niles makes a number of analytical remarks that would be pertinent here; I will make do with just two or three. He says, referring to Tolkien's essay, that we now understand that the "marvelous in *Beowulf* is not something to be embarrassed about" (5); certainly the same should be true of the marvelous in Tolkien's narratives. Further, Niles comments, referring to the *Beowulf* poet, that such "poets rely both on memory and on *certain habitual structures of words and ideas* to recreate a song fluently without having fixed it in a single form" (33; my italics) and that what "is important is that the *Beowulf* poet not only is familiar with this type of composition, but takes it for granted" (39).

I do not maintain that what I have offered here *proves* that Tolkien was "telling" a traditional narrative on paper; but I do believe that trying to understand Tolkien in terms of the literatures and languages he studied will continue to reveal ways in which Middle-earth is related to pre–modern northern Europe. Moreover, understanding that the rhetoric of the literature that survives from that time evolved from the rhetoric of the traditional oral myth, legend, or tale should move us further in the direction of understanding that Tolkien allied himself, rhetorically, with these older bards and saga men even though the medium in which he worked was substantially different. In that medium, it remains worth emphasizing, he told a great story.

NOTES

An essay approaching this topic from another perspective was read at the 1995 International Conference on the Fantastic in the Arts and published, relatively unchanged, in the conference volume of *Journal of the Fantastic in the Arts* 7.1 (1996): 75–82 as "J.R.R. Tolkien and the Telling of a Traditional Narrative." Segments from that address and publication have been incorporated into this essay.

1. When I refer to Tolkien's two novels, I intend that to mean *Hobbit* and *LR* (often incorrectly called a trilogy); I do not believe that *Silm* is a novel in the true sense of the word but a mythology.

2. A major reason that modern criticism is unable to deal with Tolkien in particular and fantasy in general is that modern mainstream or elite fiction is future oriented and attains its validity in its originality, whereas the traditional narrative finds its validity in the past and in being a "really good" version of a story (or kind of story) that everyone knows.

3. For a brief and cogent discussion of traditional narrative and a structural outline of the Märchen plot, see Linda Dégh, "Folk Narrative."

4. Anyone who wishes a definitive reading of Tolkien's sources should consult T.A. Shippey's *The Road to Middle-earth*. Nobody does it better.

5. "There is a difference between the terms *story* and *plot* which may need some clarification. By *plot*, I assume the standard concrete definition of plot as a narrative sequence of actions and incidents. *Story*, on the other hand, is more abstract. By *story*, I mean a whole that is more than the sum of its literary handbook parts (i.e., a whole that includes the author, the text, and the reader), so that when we say, 'That was a good story,' we are speaking not only of the text but also of the experience of reading the text. The evaluation, 'That was a good story,' comes from an emotional response as well as an intellectual/analytical response to the text" (33, n. 5). See C. W. Sullivan III "Heinlein's Juveniles: Growing Up in Outer Space." *Science Fiction for Young Readers*. Ed. C. W. Sullivan III. Westport, CT: Greenwood, 1993: 21–35.

6. One of the common characteristics of traditional materials is that re-creations exhibit formula and variation. Not every ballad version of "Robin Hood" will contain the same verses as all the others; not every version of "Cinderella" has a female as its

main character. Thus, the formulaic rhetorical structure Andersson proposes for the Icelandic family sagas will be similar but not identical from saga to saga, and I believe Tolkien's rhetorical structure to be close enough to the one Andersson proposes to be considered a prime variant.

WORKS CITED

Andersson, Theodore M. "The Displacement of the Heroic Ideal in the Family Sagas."*Sagas of the Icelanders*. Ed. John Tucker. New York: Garland, 1989: 40–70.

——. *The Icelandic Family Saga*. Cambridge, MA: Harvard UP, 1967.

Carpenter, Humphrey. *J.R.R. Tolkien: A Biography*. Boston: Houghton, 1997.

Curry, Patrick. *Defending Middle-Earth: Tolkien, Myth and Modernity*. New York: St. Martin's, 1997.

Dégh, Linda. "Folk Narrative." *Folklore and Folklife*. Ed. Richard Dorson. Chicago: U of Chicago P, 1972: 53–83.

Lewis, C. S. "On Stories." *Of Other Worlds*. Ed. Walter Hooper. New York: Harcourt, 1966: 3–21.

Niles, John D. *Beowulf: The Poem and Its Traditions*. Cambridge, MA: Harvard UP, 1983.

Pálsson, Hermann. "Early Icelandic Imaginative Literature." *Sagas of the Icelanders*. Ed. John Tucker. New York: Garland, 1989. 27–39.

Rosebury, Brian. *Tolkien: A Critical Assessment*. New York: St. Martin's, 1992.

Shippey, T. A. *The Road to Middle-earth*. Boston: Houghton, 1983.

Sullivan, C. W. III. "Learning the Structure of Traditional Narrative." Guest ed. Judith Haut. *Children's Folklore Review* 15.1 (1992): 17–23.

Vickery, John B., ed. *Myth and Literature: Contemporary Theory and Practice*. Lincoln: U of Nebraska P, 1966.

2

The Dragon–Lore of Middle-earth: Tolkien and Old English and Old Norse Tradition

Jonathan Evans

Literary autobiographies often confirm our intuition that childhood experience with works of literature, sophisticated or pedestrian, encountered by chance or by design—not just *belles–lettres*—have a large part in the shaping of a literary consciousness. Unfortunately, these earliest experiences are usually inaccessible or unavailable to us; our exposure to literature broadly defined predates our consciousness of such experiences. Occasionally, however, writers may remember or re-create the origins of their own literary imaginations.[1] In the case of John Ronald Reuel Tolkien, we have been privileged to be given a glimpse into the mythical original moment of creation—a moment that over the course of most of the twentieth century would grow into an immense corpus of literary imagination represented in Tolkien's total *œuvre*. Tolkien (with C. S. Lewis, Lewis Carroll, and George MacDonald) is one of a very few writers whose works have deeply influenced the literary imaginations of millions of young readers, some of them now adults, and whose works have also won the attention of serious literary scholars. An e-mail discussion not long ago among members of the international community of Anglo-Saxon scholars revealed that close to 50 percent of them became interested in medieval literature in general and in Old English language and literature *specifically because of their early exposure to the fictional works of J.R.R. Tolkien*. A generation of readers nourished on the fantasy works of Tolkien entered the academic world beginning in the 1960s; these scholars have influenced the literary tastes of four decades of undergraduates and graduate-students. As the work of these teachers trickles down to elementary- and secondary-education courses in schools and departments of education in the universities, the stage is set for yet a third wave of influence. We may note, for example, the following appraisal of Tolkien's impact in a major textbook in the field of children's literature:

No other fantasy of our time has appealed to as broad a range of readers as has *The Hobbit* (1937); children are enthralled with it, and adults probe and discuss the inner meanings of the book and of its companion tale *The Lord of The Rings*, a complex three-volume sequel. Professor Tolkien was an eminent philologist and an authority on myth and saga, and his knowledge provided so firm a base for the mood and style of his writing that there is no need for scholarly demonstration. Middle-earth *is*. (Sutherland and Arbuthnot 231)

The textbook's proviso notwithstanding, the formation of this influential literary consciousness deserves our attention.

The Hobbit, LR, Silm, Unfinished Tales (UT), and various texts in *The History of Middle-earth (HM)* reveal rich and powerful realizations of the narrative possibilities inherent in the dragon as a motif and the dragon-slayer story as a narrative type. Tolkien was conscious and explicit about this both in his fiction writing and in his critical scholarship, and in both we can find a dependence upon medieval developments of the motif and narrative type that preserves and highlights aspects of the tradition and at the same time extends them beyond the limitations already imposed by Tolkien's medieval predecessors—going so far, in some instances, as to introduce new motifs. Further, through artful recombination of themes contributed by his most immediate literary forebears Andrew Lang and William Morris, Tolkien advances fantasy narratives of dragons and dragon slayers to a level of literary achievement which in the end would dwarf the popular, and arguably the scholarly, appeal of the writers he drew from. One might question how much more widely read are Tolkien's writings than those of either Morris or Lang—or the two combined—and propose, as an answer, that there is something in Tolkien's use of traditional medieval and nineteenth-century dragon–lore that transcends his sources.

Among the books Tolkien's mother gave him, Humphrey Carpenter states that "most of all" young Ronald

> found delight in the Fairy Books of Andrew Lang, especially the *Red Fairy Book*, for tucked away in its closing pages was the best story he had ever read. This was the tale of Sigurd who slew the dragon Fafnir: a strange and powerful tale set in the nameless North. Whenever he read it Ronald found it absorbing. "I desired dragons with a profound desire," he said long afterwards. "Of course, I in my timid body did not wish to have them in the neighborhood. But the world that contained even the imagination of Fafnir was richer and more beautiful, at whatever cost of peril." (22-23)

Carpenter is quoting from the essay "On Fairy Stories" (*Essays* 135), which reveals the manner in which Tolkien's literary tastes were formed in childhood. He generally echoes the sentiments of his friend C. S. Lewis, who in "On Juvenile Tastes" expressed displeasure at the notion that children are "a distinct *literary species*" with "childish tastes" that are by implication inferior to those of adults; "the peculiarity of child readers is that they are not peculiar," says Lewis, "[i]t is we who are peculiar" (40). The literary fashions of the adult world, Lewis thinks, do not materially affect children's predilections in reading; "bad" adult tastes in literature don't ruin them and "good" ones don't improve them, "for children read only to enjoy" (40–41). Lewis continues: "[J]uvenile taste is simply human taste, going on from age to age, silly with a universal silliness or wise with a universal wisdom, regardless of modes, movements, and literary revolutions. In ascribing something of the universal to children's automatic pleasure in reading, Lewis echoes Tolkien, who includes the universal among the ingredients of what he regarded as the most successful literature even as a child: it "awakened *desire*, satisfying it while often whetting it unbearably" (*Essays* 134).

After a general discussion of children's literary appetite for marvels, as distinguished from naïve suspension of disbelief, Tolkien says,

> I had no special childish "wish to believe." I wanted to know. Belief depended on the way in which stories were presented to me, by older people, or by the authors, or on the inherent tone and quality of the tale. But at no time can I remember that the enjoyment of a story was dependent on belief that such things could happen, or had happened, in "real life." (*Essays* 134)

Tolkien "had no desire to have either dreams or adventures like *Alice*," he says; though tales of American Indians with bows and arrows, forests, "strange languages, and glimpses of an archaic mode of life" pleased him more, stories of pirates and buried treasure, such as *Treasure Island* "left me cool" (134).[2]

> But the land of Merlin and Arthur was better than these, and best of all the nameless North of Sigurd of the Völsungs, and the prince of all dragons. Such lands were pre-eminently desirable. I never imagined that the dragon was of the same order as the horse. And that was not solely because I saw horses daily, but never even the footprint of a worm. The dragon had the trade-mark *Of Faërie* written plain upon him. . . . Fantasy, the making or glimpsing of Other-worlds, was the heart of the desire of Faërie. I desired dragons with a profound desire. (*Essays* 135)

The potency of this early encounter with Sigurd the dragon slayer must have been of particular significance. In a 1955 letter to W. H. Auden, Tolkien wrote:

> I first tried to write a story when I was about seven. It was about a dragon. I remember nothing about it except a philological fact. My mother said nothing about the dragon, but pointed out that one could not say "a green great dragon," but had to say "a great green dragon." I wondered why, and still do. The fact that I remember this is possibly significant, as I do not think I ever tried to write a story again for many years, and was taken up with language. (*Letters* 214)

By his account, Tolkien's next attempt to write a story was not until fifteen years later. In a letter written in October 1914 to Edith Bratt (later his wife) he said:

> Amongst other work I am trying to turn one of the stories—which is really a very
> great story and most tragic—into a short story somewhat on the lines of Morris'
> romances with chunks of poetry in between . . . . (*Letters* 7)

Carpenter states that the story, though never finished, "proved to be the germ" of
one of Tolkien's most moving narratives: the story of Túrin Turambar and
Glaurung the dragon from the First Age of Middle-earth (*Letters* 454). Read as
simple statements of the influences upon the beginnings of his own career as a
writer, Tolkien's reference to the sources of medieval dragon–lore—Lang and
Morris—may seem deceptive: they give no indication that behind Andrew Lang
and William Morris there lay a wealth of narrative material in the original
languages of medieval Europe upon which Tolkien would later draw to create some
of the enduring masterpieces of fantasy writing in this century. But Tolkien does
not deliberately deceive the recipients of his letters, nor does Carpenter play false
with the readers of the biography. Tolkien's letters offer rare glimpses into that
usually irretrievable moment in which a writer first embarks upon the project that
will later become his life's work. When Tolkien refers in the 1914 letter to
"Morris' romances," he no doubt means in general *The Roots of the Mountains*,
The House of the Wolfings, and *The Story of the Glittering Plain*. However, the
specific prose romance that demonstrably played a key role in shaping the subject
matter, if not the theme, of the Túrin Túrambar legend is the prose *Völsunga Saga*,
a work published in 1876 in collaboration with the Icelander Magnús Magnússon.

An investigation of the background of this chain of influences would require
considerable effort. Lang's 10-page version of the Sigurd legend is a free
condensation of Morris's 131-page prose *Völsunga Saga*, which itself is a
translation of the twelfth-century Icelandic work. The Morris/Magnússon
translation, created for a series called The Saga Library, was no mere casual
addition to the already lengthy corpus of Morris's medievalism. In a letter to
Charles Norton Eliot, Morris expressed the significance the text held for him:

> [T]he result is something which is above all art; the scene of the last interview
> between Sigurd and the despairing and terrible Brynhild touches me more than
> anything I have ever met with in literature; there is nothing wanting in it, nothing
> forgotten, nothing repeated, nothing overstrained; all tenderness is shown without
> the use of a tender word, all misery and despair without a word of raving,
> complete beauty without an ornament, and all this in two pages of moderate print.
> In short it is to the full meaning of the word inspired . (Henderson 32)

Morris in 1876 published a version in verse, "The Story of Sigurd the Volsung and
the Fall of the Nibelungs," in which he applied all his talents in what was ultimately
a failed effort to devise a poetic vocabulary for English adequate to his vision of
the importance of the saga as "the Great Story of the North" and to provide an epic
uniting English to the whole of the Germanic past.

The Lang version of the Morris adaptation of the Magnússon translation of the

Norse version of the Sigurd/Fáfnir legend thus seems to have played a fundamental role in shaping the young Tolkien's literary temperament—or perhaps we should say this in reverse: Tolkien's aesthetic and literary predilections led him to the *Völsunga Saga*, and the recurrent—sometimes central—significance of dragons, dragon–lore, and dragon slayers in the narrative cycles of his published fiction originates at this point.

Further insights into Tolkien's understanding of the narrative possibilities inherent in traditional medieval lore concerning dragons and their human opponents may be gleaned from his 1936 essay on *Beowulf*. This Old English poem, copied about 1000 A.D. and based on legendary narratives from earlier centuries, provides an apt beginning for a consideration of Tolkien's adaptation of medieval dragon–lore. *Beowulf* is the oldest epic-length heroic poem in any of the Germanic languages and contains the earliest dragon-slayer narrative in English. Moreover, in the so-called "Sigemund digression," *Beowulf* preserves the earliest extant version of the dragon/dragon-slayer legend that would flourish later in literary history in the legend of Sigurd/Siegfried and the fight with the dragon Fáfnir. The source materials from which *Beowulf* drew must have been immense indeed; *Beowulf* is part of a widespread and durable literary tradition and serves as an important repository of dragon-slayer legend and dragon–lore. As such, the poem serves also as an index of salient themes and motifs found elsewhere in medieval oral and literary tradition concerning dragons. Tolkien's usage of medieval dragon–lore drawn both directly from *Beowulf* and other medieval narratives and indirectly from the more recent writings and adaptations of Lang, Morris, and others, provides evidence of both the durability and the malleability of dragon motifs in the literary tradition within which Tolkien worked.

In *"Beowulf*: The Monsters and the Critics," Tolkien suggests that the dragon's potential as a narrative device was to a great extent unfulfilled in the surviving literature of medieval Europe: "[R]eal dragons, essential both to the machinery and the ideas of a poem or tale, are actually rare," he says, in "northern literature there are only *two* that are significant:" that is, the dragon killed by Beowulf the Geat and the dragon slain by Sigurd the Völsung (*Essays* 12). In asserting this, Tolkien sets aside dozens of dragons from the Old Norse record in order to strengthen a rhetorical point. The point can be appreciated fully only in the context of a critical debate concerning the *Beowulf* poet's aesthetic judgment—a debate Tolkien himself succeeded in redirecting—in placing the trolls and the dragon at the center of the plot of *Beowulf* and the human heroes and their tragic heroics at the outer margins. As to the agent by which Beowulf is required in the end to render up his *læne lif*, Tolkien declares

> It is an enhancement and not a detraction, in fact it is necessary, that his final foe should be not some Swedish prince, or treacherous friend, but a dragon: a thing made by imagination for just such a purpose. Nowhere does a dragon come in so precisely where he should. (*Essays* 31)

Tolkien's judgment against all the Old Norse dragons except Sigurd's and Beowulf's (echoed more recently by Kathryn Hume, who said "most . . . late medieval dragons are not much good" [8]) is an aesthetic one, but it is also literary/critical: his criterion, "essential to both the machinery and the ideas of a poem or tale," reveals a preference that he as a fantasy writer put to good use. His own invented dragons Smaug, Chrysophylax, Glaurung, Ancalagon the Black, and Scatha the Worm reveal a conception of dragons that is deeply rooted in the literary materials of his scholarly and academic pursuits. The underlying conceptions—the medieval and nineteenth–century sources—of the dragon–lore in *Hobbit*, *Silm*, and several volumes of *HM*, reflect the degree to which Tolkien borrowed and recast pre-existing material and, by contrast, the degree to which he invented some of the motifs that contribute to the ongoing popularity of Tolkien's writing.

Ancalagon the Black occupies only a small portion of the narrative machinery of *Silm*, but follows an established archetypal pattern in world religion and mythology.   However briefly described in the actual narration, the dragon Ancalagon functions as a powerful mythic figure paralleling the Miðgarðsormr —Thór's opponent at Ragnarök in the *Poetic Edda*; Typhoeus—who is hurled down to Hades by Zeus in Hesiod's *Theogony*; and Satan—who, in the form of a dragon, is cast into hell by the Archangel Michael in the *Apocalypse* of St. John the Divine:

> Before the rising of the sun Eärendil slew Ancalagon the Black, the mightiest of the dragon-host, and cast him from the sky; and he fell upon the towers of Thangorodrim, and they were broken in his ruin. (*Silm* 303)

The amount of textual space that Ancalagon occupies may be minimal, but his destruction occurs at the climax of the narrative of the War of Wrath in which the power of Morgoth, enemy of Ilúvatar, is finally broken, bringing to a dramatic and cataclysmic close the First Age of Middle-earth. The sources and development of this narrative will be examined later in greater detail.

A dragon named Scatha the Worm earns only a footnote in the histories of the Third Age[3] and thus also fails—even at the level of typography—to live up to Tolkien's criteria of narrative and thematic centrality. Nevertheless, this dragon is important to the background atmosphere of legendary history, a history of immense length and antiquity, in which *LR* excels, and serves also to indicate how well Tolkien adapted features of Anglo-Saxon culture to the background legends of the fictitious heroic society he invented.   Scatha's hoard, won by Fram, establishes the national treasury of the Rohirrim:

> "Many lords and warriors, and many fair and valiant women, are named in the songs of Rohan that still remember the North. Frumgar, they say, was the name of the chieftain who led his people to Eothéod. Of his son, Fram, they tell that he slew Scatha, the great dragon of Ered Mithrin, and the land had peace from the long-swords afterward. Fram would not yield them a penny, and sent to them instead the teeth of Scatha made into a necklace, saying: 'Jewels such as these

you will not match in your treasuries, for they are hard to come by.'" (*RK* 428).

One item within this treasure was "an ancient horn, small but cunningly wrought all of fair silver with a baldric of green; and wrights had engraven upon it swift horsemen riding in a line that wound about it from the tip to the mouth; and there were set runes of great virtue;" Éomer's sister Éowyn says, "'[t]his is an heirloom of our house. . . . It was made by the Dwarves, and came from the hoard of Scatha the Worm. Eorl the young brought it from the North'" (*RK* 310). Much as *Beowulf* depicts the bestowal of heirlooms as reward for valiant service, this horn is awarded to Meriadoc the hobbit by Éomer, Lord of the Mark, in payment for heroic service. T. A. Shippey has described the Riddermark as a hypothetical "reconstructed culture" of the Goths or of the Anglo-Saxons if they had migrated East instead of West ("Goths"; *Road*, 96–97). Tolkien's invention and placement of Scatha the Worm in the annals of this people raises the tantalizing vision of how history might read if lines 2200ff of *Beowulf* were not merely fiction but rather the retrospective product of an Old English poet's research into historical events in fourth- or fifth-century Scandinavia. Tolkien's usage of the dragon's hoard in this obscure corner of his magnificent and complex imaginative world parallels the *Beowulf* poet's employment of golden treasure in all its attributes—both positive and negative—in a society held together largely by the violent acquisition of wealth and honor and the bestowal of tribute in the form of precious objects.[4]

In short, then, the preceding overview of Tolkien's adaptation of medieval dragon–lore in Middle-earth shows that if the only dragons of critical interest are those that are central to narrative structure, it appears that Tolkien did not always practice what he preached. Despite some of his most incisive remarks to the contrary, Tolkien's achievements in narrative art seem sometimes to have exceeded the acuity of his critical judgments.

For those of his works in which dragons really do play a central role, both narratively and thematically, there is no question about the centrality and the allusiveness of Tolkien's development of traditional dragon–lore. The death of Smaug, even in a children's story, is a masterpiece of dramatic narrative in which the dragon is central (*Hobbit* 236–7); the superb story of Túrin Túrambar and the slaying of Glaurung achieves a tragic effect worthy of the best dragon-slayer episodes in Germanic tradition ("Narn i Hîn Húrin," *UT* 57–162; "Of Túrin Túrambar," *Silm* 238–73).

In Tolkien's Middle-earth the dragon–lore of our own Middle Ages is analyzed into its elementary components, rationalized and reconstituted, and then reassembled to fit the larger thematic purposes of Tolkien's grand narrative design. Tolkien treated the disjointed inferences and disparate motifs found in medieval literature as if they were the *disjecta membra* of a once–unified whole—that is, as if there really were a coherent underlying medieval conception of the dragon from which all scattered references drew information. This is in fact a fiction; but it is an example of what Shippey has described as the reconstruction of a hypothetical, original *Zusammenhang* of "asterisk reality" that characterizes Tolkien's vision and method. It is analogous to, and for Tolkien part and parcel of, comparative historical linguistic reconstruction of the lost words and the lost grammar of lost, or largely lost, languages and thus lost worlds (Shippey, *Road* 15–18, 48, 59). The dragon–lore embedded in the medieval literature of the external world (our world) is *not* coherent: it springs from sources as diverse as medieval European geography, ancient Semitic and Hellenistic cosmology and cosmogony, Roman mythology and popular legend, Latin hagiography, and Germanic legend and folklore.

Tolkien had plenty of medieval dragon motifs from which to choose, though he did not use all of them, and he invented some. Inger M. Boberg's *Motif-Index of Early-Icelandic Literature* classifies Old Icelandic dragon motifs according to five main categories: Origin, Form, Habitat, Habits, and Deeds, with two additional categories for dragons "as power of good" and the narrative episode of the "fight with a dragon." Boberg does not break this category down into contrastive constituents, but she does provide ample examples of Norse texts in which the motifs she cites are manifest. In his *Studien zur Germanischen Sagengeschichte* volume of 1910, Friedrich Panzer's study of *Beowulf* as an analogue of the "Bear's-Son" folktale type classifies dragon slayers according to two principles: regarding the *motive* for the fight, Panzer follows Danish folklorist Axel Olrik in labeling the hero who fights a dragon to win its hoarded treasure as the "Sigurd" type, and the hero who does so to rescue a people or save a nation as the "Thor" type. On the other hand, if classified according to the *outcome* of the fight, Panzer identifies a third main narrative type consisting of the dragon fight to free a captive female—a maiden or a princess—derived ultimately from the Perseus/Andromeda legend and labeled the "St. George" type (Olrik 310–11). Unless we include the "maidens" of the town of Dale said to be consumed by Smaug, Tolkien leaves the St. George motive completely alone, making plentiful use of the Sigurd and Thor types both singly and—as in *Beowulf*—in combination. From the five categories of dragon motif—Origin, Form, Habitat, Habits, Deeds—he borrowed freely, though selectively, while again, he sometimes invented his own. Tolkien ignores the motifs of the dragon transformed from a human (as in the *Völsunga saga* and other Norse sources)[5] or from a worm (as in *Ragnars saga Lóðbrokar*) and makes up his own history of dragon origins. The dragon's various medieval forms as modified or hybrid serpents, eagles, horses, and so on, do not appear in Tolkien either, with a notable exception of some dragons as hybrids of animals and machines. Dragons' colors vary in medieval literature, and Tolkien takes note: Glaurung is golden, and Smaug is red-gold.

Tolkien's dragons at first seem to lack fire-breathing ability, only to acquire it later under Morgoth's malevolent design, as described in *The Book of Lost Tales, Part II (BLT2)*.

> Many are the dragons that Melko has loosed upon the world and some are more mighty than others. Now the least mighty—yet were they very great beside the Men of those days—are cold as is the nature of snakes and serpents, and some of

them a many having wings go with the uttermost noise and speed; but the mightier are hot and very heavy and slow-going, and some belch flame, and fire flickereth beneath their scales, and the lust and greed and cunning evil of these is the greatest of all creatures: and such was the Foalókë whose burning there set all the places of his habitation in waste and desolation. (96-97).

Christopher Tolkien comments:

> At the end of *The Silmarillion* (p. 252) Morgoth "loosed upon his foes the last desperate assault that he had prepared, and out of the pits of Angband there issued the winged dragons, that had not before been seen." The suggestion is that winged dragons were a refinement of Morgoth's original design (embodied in Glaurung, Father of Dragons who went upon his belly). According to the *Tale of Turambar* (pp. 96–97), on the other hand, among Melko's many dragons some were smaller, cold like snakes and of these many were flying creatures; while others, the mightier, were hot and heavy, fire-dragons, and these were unwinged. As already noted (p. 125) there is no suggestion in the tale that Glorund was the first of his kind. (*BLT2* 142–43)

None of the special habitats identified for Old Norse dragons seem to be used in Middle-earth. Again, the earlier dragons in the First Age lack the capability of flight, and are so endowed only at the climax of the Wars of Beleriand when Ancalagon is launched. Not one of the dragons of Middle-earth appears as powers of Good; not one guards a bridge to the other world or flies to its nest with a human being. Only Smaug eats the horses of Thorin Oakenshield's company and presumably would not shy away from oxen. No dragons are fought to free a princess, man, or lion.

The central motif for medieval Germanic dragon–lore seems to be the characteristic association between the dragon and hoarded treasure; this motif perhaps more than any other informs the conception that Tolkien adopted and adapted most extensively in his fiction. Much has already been written in Old English and Old Norse critical scholarship about the motif of the dragon on the hoard. The conception lies close to the heart of the dragon episodes in *Beowulf* and the *Völsunga Saga*, the principal sources to which Tolkien's imagination returned again and again from childhood on. It is extant in lesser-known medieval prose texts—Norse sagas, mainly, but also others—too numerous to list here, and it is deeply embedded in the poetic diction of Scandinavian skáldic verse dating from much earlier than the classic prose sagas (Hungerland) or the manuscript of *Beowulf*, and in Icelandic *rímur*—ballads—dating somewhat later (Þórólfsson). Tolkien's poem "Iumonna Gold Galdre Bewunden," later "The Hoard," provides keys for a reading of Smaug and other dragons both in medieval literature and in Middle-earth: as Shippey suggests, this seems to represent an allusive expansion of the underlying insight that the curse on the dragon's hoard in *Beowulf* and, by extension, in *Hobbit*, might well be "*avarice itself*" (*Road* 67). The thematic possibilities for tragic narrative are held in suspension in the story of a "bourgeois burglar," but they are developed to a much greater degree in the story of Túrin Túrambar from *Silm* and *UT*, which Christopher Tolkien said "is in some respects the most tangled and complex of all the narrative elements in the story of the First Age" (*UT* 6).

The first book through which Tolkien reached, and still reaches, a widespread, popular audience is, of course, *Hobbit*. While the book was written ostensibly for children, it contains many asides to an adult audience, not all of them equally deftly handled; it also exhibits a fascinating preoccupation with proverbs, maxims, or traditional sayings, suggesting a rich background of folkloric wisdom concerning dragons and their behavior. The first chapter of *Hobbit* is filled with allusions—some vague, some specific—to the idea that dragons were popularly believed in by hobbits and other personal beings in Middle-earth: the idea that there was a body of folklore concerning dragons that everyone could be counted upon to know and, when necessary, to use.

The device is effective since the reader, it seems, is supposed to share in what is presented as proverbial, gnomic, and thus universally held wisdom concerning dragons in Middle-earth; thus, by implication, the reader is drawn almost imperceptibly into the imaginary world in which the action of *Hobbit* takes place. Gandalf, for example, describes Bilbo as "fierce as a dragon in a pinch." No doubt the absolute quality is meant initially to apply to the dragon, and the qualifier as a description of Bilbo; the comment could be paraphrased, "in a pinch, Bilbo is as fierce as a dragon." However, the narrator then provides a context that suggests a bit of dragon–lore: "If you have ever seen a dragon in a pinch, you will realize that this was only poetical exaggeration applied to any hobbit" (27). From this chapter we learn that dragons breed and grow: Thorin refers to the Withered Heath as "'where the great dragons bred'" (29), and Gandalf says of the five-foot high entrance to the dragon's lair, "'Smaug could not creep into a hole that size, not even when he was a young dragon'" (30). This statement, together with the detail that Smaug has devoured many men and horses of Dale, also suggests the monster's large proportions.

Dragons' universal love of treasures provides the folkloric background to Smaug's particular expression of it, which is central to *Hobbit* as the narrative device driving the plot forward from beginning to end. The motif is articulated again and again as central to *draconitas*, "dragonness," and, through Tolkien's awareness of it in medieval Scandinavian material, it is linked further to folkloric representations of dwarves as smiths. Smaug's prehistory is as follows. Among the dragons in the North in the days of Thorin's grandfather Thror, Smaug, "a most specially greedy, strong and wicked worm," settled on Thror's mountain with a spout of flame and destroyed both dwarves and men—"the usual unhappy story . . . only too common in those days—and took the dwarves' wealth. "He has piled it all up in a great heap far inside, and sleeps on it for a bed," says Thorin, representing this as typical of dragons' behavior:

Dragons steal gold and jewels, you know, from men and elves and dwarves, wherever they can find them; and they guard their plunder as long as they live (which is practically for ever, unless they are killed), and never enjoy a brass ring of it. (32)

The "you know" is no mere aside, but draws the reader in. Here we also learn dragons are extremely long-lived. Further, the commentary on *draconitas* describes dragons' greed in terms both of bad economics and bad craftsmanship: they cannot distinguish good workmanship from bad, do not know the market value of their wealth, nor does their greed produce enjoyment. Interestingly, too, "they can't make a thing for themselves, not even mend a little loose scale of their armour," says Thorin Oakenshield (32). This feature of dragons' armor as the forged product of artistic craftsmanship reappears in an early draft of *Silm* as some of the dragons loosed by Morgoth on Gondolin appear to be mechanical devices of cunningly wrought interlocked rings of metal with fire in their bellies.

In *Hobbit* and in all Tolkien's writings, the principal feature distinguishing dragons is their watchful love of treasure, the word "dragon" itself deriving from Greek *drakon*, a noun based on the Indo-European root **derk-* (cp. Gk. *derkomai*), "to see." Though most ancient world mythologies include a monstrous serpent, usually in the role as nemesis of the gods or human heroes, the Greek innovation, which passed into Latin, and thence to the Germanic world in the early Middle Ages, made the monstrous *drakon* the serpent "who watches," a function seen in the story of Jason and the Golden Fleece as well as the epigrams of Martial and the fables of Phaedrus and Hyginus (Evans 34–38). Frequently in Tolkien's writing, as also in ancient and medieval legends and folklore concerning them, dragons' keen eyesight is fundamental to their role as the guardians of treasure. When their treasures are threatened, their ferocious greed provokes them to violent deeds, which then requires warriors and heroes to battle and slay them.

It is widely recognized that Tolkien drew the main outlines of the plot of the episode of the dragon's rampages from the plot of the final third of *Beowulf.* Just as in *Beowulf*, the dragon's onslaught is provoked by the theft of a cup from the dragon's proverbial hoard of golden treasure. Also, the dragon wakes to discover the theft and flies out of its lair in a paroxysm of fiery rage, burning the dwellings of people living nearby; further, the dragon in *Hobbit* is slain by a human hero—that is, a man—rather than by a dwarf, an elf, or a hobbit (the other principal races in Middle-earth). And lastly, the person who steals the cup is not the hero who slays the dragon. In *Beowulf*, the theft is perpetrated by an unknown person—a servant, slave, or thief—who, also as the thirteenth man in the expedition, eager to regain favor from his master for some unknown crime or violation, breaks into the dragon's lair seeking a gift with which to purchase his pardon.[6]

In chapter 12, which mostly has to do with Smaug, there are many more references to an assumed body of dragon–lore in Middle-earth. It is not only assumed: when Smaug tries to tempt Bilbo into stepping closer (presumably to kill and eat him), the narrator says, "Bilbo was not quite so unlearned in dragon–lore as all that" (212) and Bilbo keeps his distance; the narrator comments, however, that Bilbo "had never heard about dragons' sense of smell" and that it "is also an awkward fact that they can keep half an eye open watching while they sleep, if they are suspicious" (211). When Bilbo and Smaug converse, Bilbo cleverly keeps his name and identity a secret. Again, assumptions about dragons come into play:

> This of course is the way to talk to dragons, if you don't want to reveal your proper name (which is wise), and don't want to infuriate them by a flat refusal (which is also very wise). No dragon can resist the fascination of riddling talk and of wasting time trying to understand it. (213)

Similarly, Bilbo's growing suspicions that the dwarves have led him into this danger deliberately are attributed to the proverbial "effect that dragon-talk has on the inexperienced." Later, Balin the dwarf comforts Bilbo: "It cannot be helped, and it is difficult not to slip in talking to a dragon, or so I have always heard" (218).

But the most important bit of dragon–lore referred to in this story is the proverbial weak spot dragons are known to have in a certain point of their underbelly. Bilbo mentions this casually in conversation with the dwarves: "'Every worm has his weak spot, as my father used to say'" (211), says Bilbo, certain that his father knew it not by experience but by precept: he learned it through folklore, not through direct encounters with dragons. Still, Bilbo's direct encounter with Smaug proves the folklore true. After Smaug has rolled over to reveal his weak spot, he spouts huge bales of flame at Bilbo, who barely escapes up the tunnel alive. The scene concludes with one more reference to proverbial dragon–lore, this time in a new saying coined by Bilbo himself: "'Never laugh at live dragons, Bilbo you fool!' he said to himself, and it became a favourite saying of his later, and passed into a proverb" (216). Tolkien has described the actual moment of creation of a new saying about dragons. Clearly, Tolkien's professional knowledge of gnomic verse in Old English and Old Norse, combined with his knowledge of dragon–lore derived from poetry and prose in these and other languages, provided him with the raw material needed to invent dragon-lore for his imaginary world of Middle-earth. Tolkien's imaginative creation of the fictional origins and early pseudo-history of dragons is not to be found in his well-known works, the books with which popular audiences are most familiar, but rather in the previously unpublished narratives that Christopher Tolkien organized after his father's death and edited, sometimes extensively, to produce the posthumous summary of the legendarium in *Silm*, published as volumes 1–5 and 10–12 of *HM*. In these volumes there are layers of composition, from the first adumbration of the Túrin legend in 1914 to the final stages of tinkering in the months preceding Tolkien's death in 1973, reveal successive developments of the legend hinted at from the beginning.

The edited version of *Silm* published in 1977 includes only two named dragons—Glaurung and Ancalagon—which are "essential to both the machinery and the ideas" of the tale. Glaurung is significant as the apparent progenitor of his monstrous race, and the winged dragon Ancalagon is significant as the zenith of the further evolutionary development of the race and as the physical agent of the destruction of Thangorodrim, Morgoth's fortress. The origins of dragons as an offensive device against the Noldor in the Wars of Beleriand are to be found in the first appearance of Glaurung, who is released from Angband by night as the "first of Urulóki, the fire-drakes of the North" some 200 years after Dagor Aglareb, the third battle between the Noldor and Melkor. There, he appears "young and scarce half-grown," and as a result is repulsed by the Noldorin elf Fingon (138). Glaurung appears later in the vanguard of Melkor's army at the Dagor Bragollach, the Battle of Sudden Flame, as "Glaurung the golden, father of dragons, in his full might" (181), and in the Battle of Unnumbered Tears he is wounded, though not slain, by Azaghâl, the Lord of the Naugrim in Belegost, and flees the battlefield wounded. In his final appearance in the Túrin story, Glaurung is slain; here the universal motif of dragons' lust for treasure and the singular motif of the dragon as a speaking, rational, brute beast taken from the Sigurd material are combined with the tragic circumstances of Túrin's life, impetuousness, and unwitting incest.

At this juncture in the structure of *Silm* there remain two narrative passages in which dragons are involved. The first is the account of the Fall of Gondolin; the second is that of the War of Wrath at the conclusion of *Silm* in which the Valar destroy Melkor's realm and thrust him through the Door of Night into the Void, expelling him from Arda forever. In the first instance, Glaurung's brood have grown to be "many and terrible" in a scene of cataclysmic destruction that in *Silm* is as moving as it is spare in its detail:

> At last, in the year when Eärendil was seven years old, Morgoth was ready, and he loosed upon Gondolin his Balrogs, and his Orcs, and his wolves; and with them came dragons of the brood of Glaurung, and they were become now many and terrible. . . . Of the deeds of desperate valour there done, by the chieftains of the noble houses and their warriors, and not least by Tuor, much is told in *The Fall of Gondolin*. . . . The fume of the burning, and the steam of the fair fountains of Gondolin withering in the flame of the dragons of the north, fell upon the vale of Tumladen in mournful mists. (292–93)

One of the great ironies of this passage is the fact that although many other narratives were extended and expanded over the decades, the Fall of Gondolin, one of the earliest stories conceived, never progressed beyond the version composed for *The Book of Lost Tales* in 1917 and was in fact contracted, not expanded, in its final version edited by Christopher Tolkien for *Silm*. The 1917 text is considerably longer than *Silm*'s two sparse paragraphs and comprises some ten pages of detailed narration. Some ingenious invention is found here. At the behest of the traitor Meglin, Morgoth/Melkor devises hybrid animal-mechanical dragons for the assault upon the elves' realm:

> Then on a time Melko assembled all his most cunning smiths and sorcerers, and of iron and flame they wrought a host of monsters such as have only at that time

been seen and shall not again be till the Great End. Some were all of iron so cunningly linked that they might flow like slow rivers of metal or coil themselves around and above all obstacles before them, and these were filled in their innermost depths with the grimmest of the Orcs with scimitars and spears; others of bronze and copper were given hearts and spirits of blazing fire, and they blasted all that stood before them with the terror of their snorting or trampled whatso escaped the ardour of their breath; yet others were creatures of pure flame that writhed like ropes of molten metal, and they brought to ruin whatever fabric they came nigh, and iron and stone melted before them and became as water, and upon them rode the Balrogs in hundreds; and these were the most dire of all those monsters which Melko devised against Gondolin. (*BLT2* 170)

The account of the battle and fall of the city that follows describes a veritable paroxysm of chaos sustained for many pages at the peak of climactic excitement, a series of scenes depicting coiling and lashing dragons accompanied by hordes of Balrogs, rivers of flame, and geysers of smoke and steam—all of this canceled later in favor of the high and distant mythic rhetoric characteristic of the rest of *Silm*. A taste of the earlier, more elaborate version can be gathered from the following:

Then the Balrogs continued to shoot darts of fire and flaming arrows like small snakes into the sky, and these fell upon the roofs and gardens of Gondolin till all the trees were scorched, and the flowers and grass burned up, and the whiteness of those walls and colonnades was blackened and seared: yet a worse matter was it that a company of those demons climbed upon the coils of the serpents of iron and thence loosed unceasingly from their bows and slings till a fire began to burn in the city to the back of the main army of the defenders. (*BLT2* 178)

This narrative, which continues at some length, mentions "serpents of bronze . . . with great feet for trampling" that climb over the serpents of iron, opening a breach in the walls of Gondolin "where through the Balrogs might ride upon the dragons of flame" (180). Here we learn something concerning the nature of Melko's flaming dragons, whose fires must be replenished periodically "from the wells of fire that Melko had made in the fastness of his own land" (180). Tuor, beaten down by Gothmog, the "Lord of Balrogs" and son of Melko (183), is saved by Ecthelion, who then is cast into the fountain and, weighed down by his own armor, drowns (184). Recovering his strength, Tuor, with the help of others, entraps one of the Fire-drakes "and forced him into the very waters of the fountain that he perished therein," turning its pools to steam and drying up its spring. As the Square of the Fountain is "filled with mists of scalding heat and blinding fogs," a remnant of Gondolin's inhabitants escape through hidden tunnels before the onslaught of "the hugest of drakes" that "came on and glared in the fog" (184).
The climax of this extensive battle comes as a dragon coils around the steps of the palace at the base of the king's tower and, spouting flame, "lashed and rowed with his tail" until the tower itself

leapt into a flame and in a stab of fire . . . fell, for the dragons crushed the base of it and all who stood there. Great was the clangour of that terrible fall, and therein passed Turgon King of the Gondothlim, and for that hour the victory was to Melko. (187)

Finally, in Morgoth's last throw in the War of Wrath, a still further development appears: winged dragons.

> Morgoth quailed, and he dared not to come forth himself. But he loosed upon his foes the last desperate assault that he had prepared, and out of the pits of Angband there issued the winged dragons, that had not before been seen; and so sudden and ruinous was the onset of that dreadful fleet that the host of the Valar was driven back, for the coming of the dragons was with great thunder, and lightning, and a tempest of fire. (*Silm* 303)

The text proceeds quickly to the death of Ancalagon the Black, "mightiest of the dragon-host," and the destruction of Thangorodrim wherein "well-nigh all the dragons were destroyed" (303). Thus ends the First Age. An earlier draft of this passage from the *Quenta Silmarillion* written in 1930, and published in *The Shaping of Middle-earth*, says "all the dragons were destroyed save two alone; and they fled into the East" (160).[7] They must have been male and female: the 1930 text goes on to say for "a while his Orcs and Dragons breeding again in dark places troubled and affrighted the world, as in far places they do yet." (164). The text of the *Akallabêth* carries this thread further into the Second Age, when "Men dwelt in darkness and were troubled by many evil things that Morgoth had devised in the days of his dominion," among them "demons, and dragons, and misshapen beasts" (*Silm* 312). A passage evocative of the passage of time and the slow unfolding of history describes the transition to the Third Age:

> Many things of beauty and wonder remained on earth in that time, and many things also of evil and dread: Orcs there were and trolls and dragons and fell beasts, and strange creatures old and wise in the woods whose names are forgotten; Dwarves still laboured in the hills and wrought with patient craft works of metal and stone that none now can rival. But the Dominion of Men was preparing and all things were changing, until at last the Dark Lord arose in Mirkwood again. (360)

The passage hints at the transition from the history of Middle-earth to the earliest ancient period of our own history, and the stage is set for the classic Third-Age narratives of *Hobbit* and the Appendix to *LR* in which winged, fire-breathing, treasure-hoarding dragons such as Smaug and Scatha appear as a rarity, a holdover from earlier epochs much as in our world the dragons of the Geats and the Völsungs appear in Old English and Old Norse "as rare as they are dire," says Tolkien, to trouble men.

Tolkien imaginatively and selectively has developed medieval dragon motifs for his reconstructions of the "asterisk-history" of these diverse elements in such a way as to present something like a "natural history" of dragons from their first emergence in what is called the First Age of Middle-earth, through several stages of physiognomic elaboration involving the intensification of their aggressive features and capabilities, to their waning and near extinction at the end of the First Age and their reemergence in the Third Age of Middle-earth. Tolkien thus prepares the way for a Fourth Age—in Middle-earth the age in which the race of Men dominates—in which dragons survive only as a memory. To the extent that Middle-earth's Fourth Age is analogous to the ancient epoch of our own world (as Tolkien himself explicitly noted), then Tolkien's fictionalized history of dragons is meant to connect seamlessly with the legendary dragons in medieval literature, where they appear as facts about an earlier time in a world now accessible only through the imagination in epic, elegy, legend, and folklore.

NOTES

An earlier version of this essay is published in the *Journal of the Fantastic in the Arts* 9:3 (1998), pp. 175–191.

1. For example, in a 1955 letter to a friend, Flannery O'Connor commented: "The only good things I read when I was a child were the Greek and Roman myths which I got out of a set of a child's encyclopedia called The Book of Knowledge. The rest of what I read was Slop with a capital S. The Slop period was followed by the Edgar Allan Poe period which lasted for years and consisted chiefly in a volume called The Humerous [sic] Tales of EAPoe." O'Connor goes on to recall details from the Poe collection with obvious parallels in her own stories, concluding "I didn't really start to read until I went to Graduate School and then I began to read and write at the same time." After a long list of authors she was influenced by, O'Connor states "But always the largest thing that looms up is The Humerous [sic] Tales of Edgar Allan Poe" (950–51).

2. Though elsewhere it is recorded that Lewis's and Tolkien's literary tastes overlapped to a great degree, they were not identical. Lewis lists *Treasure Island* among the "list of books which . . . have been generally liked by the young," including himself (39).

3. See Appendix A, Section II, "The House of Eorl" in *RK* (426–37). The author cites, as his source of these Annals, copies of the Red Book of Westmarch "written in Gondor, probably at the request of the great-grandson of Peregrin, and completed in S.R. 1592 (F.A. 172)," (*FR* 35).

4. See, for example, Ernst Leisi, "Gold und Manneswert in *Beowulf*," *Anglia* 71 (1952–53), pp. 259–273; M. D. Cherniss, "The Progress of the Hoard in *Beowulf*," *Philological Quarterly* 47 (1968), pp. 473–86; Stanley Greenfield, "Gifstol and Gold Hoard in *Beowulf*," in *Old English Studies in Honor of John C. Pope*, ed. Robert B. Burlin and Edward B. Irving Jr. (Toronto: U of Toronto P, 1974), pp. 107–117; J. C. McGalliard, "Poet's Comment in *Beowulf*," *Studies in Philology* 75 (1978), pp. 243–270; Paul Beekman Taylor, "The Traditional Language of Treasure in *Beowulf*," *JEGP* 85 (1986), pp. 191–205.

5. See Joyce Tally Lionarons's recent discussion of the "monstrous double" inherent in the dragon myth, whereby the human hero not only mirrors or is mirrored by his monstrous opponent, but in a reversal of actantial narratological functions (Claude Brémond) actually *is transformed into* the image of his opponent. See also Einar Haugen, who discusses the figure of Fáfnir as a transgression of categorical dichotomy between *human* and *monster* in Old Norse mythology.

6. See Theodore M. Andersson, "The Thief in Beowulf" (*Speculum* 29 [1984], 493–508) for arguments concerning the thief's identity and the Germanic background as evidenced in Scandinavian law and popular consciousness. Andersson argues the emendation of the defective l. 2223b to *þ(egn) nathwylces* ("a slave of someone"), which, some have proposed, obscures the subtle dynamics of the passage; Andersson's reading of the background suggests instead *þ(eof)* or *þ(eow)* ("thief" or "servant") is more appropriate.

7. In *RK*, Appendix A, "Durin's Folk," it states: "Thráin I, Náin's son, came to Erebor, the Lonely Mountain, near the eastern eaves of Mirkwood, and there he began new works, and became King under the Mountain. In Erebor he found the great jewel, the Arkenstone, Heart of the Mountain. But Thorin I his son removed and went into the far North to the Grey Mountains, where most of Durin's folk were now gathering; for those mountains were rich and little explored. But there were dragons in the wastes beyond; and after many years they became strong again and multiplied, and they made war on the Dwarves, and plundered their works. At last Dáin I, together with Frór his second son, was slain at the doors of his hall by a great cold-drake. . . . So the rumour of the wealth of Erebor spread abroad and reached the ears of the dragons, and at last Smaug the golden, greatest of the dragons of his day, arose and without warning came against King Thrór and descended on the Mountain in flames. It was not long before all that realm was destroyed, and the town of Dale near by was ruined and deserted; but Smaug entered into the Great Hall and lay there upon a bed of gold" (439–440). In Appendix B, "The Tale of Years: The Third Age," these annals preserve the history of the reemergence of dragons:

2570	Baldor son of Brego enters the Forbidden Door and is lost. About this time Dragons reappear in the far North and begin to afflict the Dwarves.
. . .	
2589	Dáin I slain by a Dragon.
. . .	
2770	Smaug the Dragon descends on Erebor. Dale destroyed. Thrór escapes with Thráin II and Thorin II.
. . .	
2941	. . . Bard of Esgaroth slays Smaug . . . (*RK* 462–64).

WORKS CITED

Andersson, Theodore M. "The Thief in *Beowulf*." *Speculum* 29 (1984): 493–508.

Boberg, Inger Margrethe. *Motif-Index of Early-Icelandic Literature*. Copenhagen: Munksgaard, 1968.

Carpenter, Humphrey. *Tolkien: The Authorized Biography*. Boston: Houghton, 1977.

Cherniss, M. D. "The Progress of the Hoard in *Beowulf*." *Philological Quarterly* 47 (1968): 473–86.

Greenfield, Stanley. "Gifstol and Gold Hoard in *Beowulf*." *Old English Studies in Honor of John C. Pope*. Ed. Robert B. Burlin and Edward B. Irving, Jr. Toronto: U of Toronto P, 1974. 107–117.

Evans, Jonathan D. "The Dragon." *Mythical and Fabulous Creatures: A Source Book and Research Guide*. Ed. Malcolm L. South. New York: Greenwood, 1987. 27–58.

——. "Medieval Dragon–lore in Middle-earth." *Journal of the Fantastic in the Arts* 9.3 (1998): 175–191.

Haugen, Einar. "The Mythological Structures of the Ancient Scandinavians: Some Thoughts on Reading Dumézil." *To Honor Roman Jakobson: Essays on the Occasion of his Seventieth Birthday.* The Hague: Mouton, 1967. 855–68.

Henderson, Philip, ed. *The Letters of William Morris to his Family and Friends.* London: Longmans, 1950.

Hume, Kathryn. "From Saga to Romance: The Use of Monsters in Old Norse Literature." *Studies in Philology* 77 (1980): 1–25.

Hungerland, Heinz. "Zeugnisse zur Vǫlsungen- und Niflungensage aus der skaldendichtung (8–16 jh.)." *Arkiv for Nordisk Filologi* 20 (1904): 1–142.

Leisi, Ernst. "Gold und Manneswert in Beowulf." *Anglia* 71 (1952–53): 259–273.

Lewis, C. S. "On Juvenile Tastes." In *Of Other Worlds: Essays and Stories.* Ed. Walter Hooper. New York: Harcourt, 1966. 39–41.

Lionarons, Joyce Tally. "*Beowulf:* Myth and Monsters." *English Studies* 77 (1996): 1–14.

McGalliard, J. C. "Poet's Comment in *Beowulf.*" *Studies in Philology* 75 (1978): 243–270.

O'Connor, Flannery. *Flannery O'Connor: Collected Works.* Ed. Sally Fitzgerald. New York: Library of America, 1988.

Olrik, Axel. *Danmarks Heltedigtning.* København: Thiele, 1903.

Panzer, Friedrich. *Studien zur Germanischen Sagengeschichte I, Beowulf.* Munich: Beck, 1910.

Shippey, Thomas A. "Goths and Huns: The Rediscovery of the Northern Cultures in the Nineteenth Century." *The Medieval Legacy: A Symposium.* Ed. Andreas Haarder, Iørn Piø, Reinhold Schröder, and Preben Meulengracht Sørensen. Proceedings of the Sixth International Symposium, Center for the Study of Vernacular Literature in the Middle Ages, Odense University. Odense: Odense UP, 1981. 51–70.

——. *The Road to Middle-earth.* Boston: Houghton, 1982.

Sutherland, Zena, and May Hill Arbuthnot. *Children and Books.* 7th ed. Glennview, IL: Scott, Foresman, 1986.

Taylor, Paul Beekman. "The Traditional Language of Treasure in *Beowulf.*" *JEGP* 85 (1986): 191–205.

Þórólfsson, Björn K. *Rímur fyrir 1600.* Safn fræðafjelagsins um Island og Islendinga, 9. København: Møller, 1934.

3

J.R.R. Tolkien and the True Hero

George Clark

TOLKIEN: THE HEROES AND THE CRITIC

Many readers of Tolkien's fantasy fictions are unaware that the author of *Hobbit* and *LR* also wrote seminal studies of *Beowulf*, the most important surviving work of Anglo-Saxon or Old English literature, and of *The Battle of Maldon* (*Maldon*), often regarded as the purest surviving expression in (Old) English of the heroic ethos of the old Germanic world. Those critical studies are "*Beowulf*: The Monsters and the Critics" ("Monsters") and "The Homecoming of Beorhtnoth Beorhthelm's Son" ("Homecoming") and in them, as in his fictions, Tolkien conducted his own quest.

Tolkien sought a true hero motivated by a heroic ideal consistent with his own religious and moral ideals, but he could not rid himself of his desire for the glorious heroes of old. In *Hobbit* he shares the search for the new hero with the wizard Gandalf, an alter ego, and they find Bilbo Baggins of Bag End. On their first encounter, Gandalf announces that he is looking for someone "to share in an adventure" and that takers are hard to find (12). Bilbo Baggins insists he has no interest in an adventure, but before the two of them part, Gandalf has promised it to the hobbit (14). In response to World War II, Tolkien renewed his and Gandalf's search, now an urgent quest for a moral meaning in a world of horrors. *LR* realizes in its fantasy narrative the experience of a world engaged in a terrible war (Timmons 115–18). The hero and the heroism Tolkien sought were meant to justify the ways of a hidden God to a world that had felt the power of evil.

One might wonder how Tolkien, a devout Catholic, could justify spending his most productive years writing a very long book that does not explicitly bear witness to his Christian faith. *LR* embodies a Christian worldview in a narrative with no explicitly Christian references. Tolkien followed the strategy, as he saw it, of the *Beowulf* poet and the authors of some of the Old Icelandic sagas. The saga authors, when telling the story of persons who lived before the conversion of Iceland, generally avoid anachronistic references to Christianity but sometimes attribute a kind of natural monotheism to favored heroes like Askel in *The Saga of the People of Reykjadal* (Hreinsson 4, ch. 7). The *Beowulf* poet makes his nobler characters explicitly monotheistic, but includes no explicitly Christian references and makes only one undoubted and two possible references to the Old Testament. The *Beowulf* poet whom Tolkien imagined was a learned Christian who re-created a heroic world and story in an implicitly Christian universe governed by a God whose existence and nature the poem's wiser characters intuit without the benefit of revelation. Tolkien's *Beowulf* poet was a version of himself, and his authorial persona in creating *LR* was a version of that *Beowulf* poet. Following his creative predecessor, Tolkien set *LR* in what can be seen as a time before the Incarnation, possibly even in the time of the patriarchs, yet the wiser characters in *LR*, as in *Beowulf* and some of the sagas, are aware of the presence of a force they cannot name.

Tolkien knew and loved the literature that preserved the heroic ethos of the old Germanic world, but he could not accept the heroic vision of man's fate or the traditional heroes represented in those literatures. His fantasy fiction rewrites heroic literature and the hero; so do his critical studies. "Monsters" and "Homecoming" ultimately separate *Beowulf* and *Maldon* from the heroic tradition and make those works critiques of heroic society, its values and heroes. Early in the text of "Monsters," Beowulf almost becomes the new hero—"something more than a standard hero is before us, a man faced with a foe more evil than any human enemy is before us" *(Essays* 17), but this contrast between Beowulf and the "standard hero" gives way to a comparison of Beowulf with the "standard" pagan warrior-hero later in the essay and appendices. The heroic world prized prowess, courage, and material success. More darkly, at least to some modern imaginations, avenging wrongs to members of one's in-group (by blood or association) had a positive value. In "Monsters" and "Homecoming," Tolkien leaves that motive for heroic action out of his analysis of texts which mention the duty of revenge explicitly and often. Nor do these essays take explicit note of the motive of material gain. In the Icelandic sagas, a heroic venture is frequently said to be conducted *til fjár ok frægðar* ("for wealth and fame"); Beowulf returns from Denmark with magnificent gifts from Hrothgar as well as fame and good report.

Tolkien's critical essays do, however, treat, and with increasing asperity, the heroic desire for fame. In the heroic age, on the literary evidence at least, a fierce competition for honor coexisted within group solidarity and an ideal of mutual loyalty between leaders and followers. The Anglo-Saxon adjective *hold* ("loyal") could describe the relationship of the leader to the follower, or the follower to the leader ("loyalty up, loyalty down"). Gifts strengthened loyalty up, and gift exchange cemented the loyalties of competitive and warlike men. The competitive pursuit of wealth and fame put the hero in harm's way; the heroic oath kept him on his dangerous course. The oath, vow, or promise bound the hero to a future course of dangerous action and was not a boast or exaggerated statement about past deeds.

Oaths frequently admitted the possibility of failure, and death, in the attempt to keep the promise. The heroic world of early Northern Europe, in the pagan and in the early Christian era, was a "shame culture" in which a man's essential worth was defined by his reputation, his honor among his peers, the judgment passed on him by those qualified to judge (Jones 96–158).

Ideas of fate and luck were a prominent part of the heroic worldview. Heroic literature frequently implies that fate (or Fate) rules the hero's destiny, but that decisive role is sometimes ascribed to luck, which seems more erratic, capable of leaving the hero, for example, in the lurch on what may seem contingent considerations. Material success may depend upon luck or fate, but fame often blesses those doomed to die, or perhaps especially favors them. This fatalism might be characterized as "pagan," but it survived into the Christian era. Pierre Maury, the shepherd a reader might call the hero of Ladurie's *Montaillou*, resolved to follow his fate and live as he had always done rather than attempt to evade the inquisition that eventually claimed him (131–32). In the same spirit, Gunnar, the great hero of *Njal's Saga*, refused to go into temporary exile, which would have saved him from what he saw as his fate (Hreinsson 3, ch. 75). And fate or Fate rules in larger matters than the life and death of individual mortals: the gods themselves are doomed. At least in the Old Norse survivals of Germanic paganism, the gods themselves must die in battle against the forces of darkness. But wealth was mortal, too; fame was the spur and the hero's hope of immortality. Man's fate, the gods' fate, the world's fate was defeat and death. Sigurður Nordal wrote that near the end of the pagan era in Iceland "the old pessimism, the fear of an evil, hidden fate, the conviction that all would perish" still "hung over the minds of men" (120). Much as Tolkien loved the literature of the old heroic world, its faith and his were incompatible.[1]

READING AND WRITING THE HERO

Tolkien's readings mentally erased large portions of *Beowulf* and *Maldon*, but those erasures freed the space for his own writing. In "Monsters," Tolkien virtually erased Beowulf, a character too close to "the actual heathen *hæleð* [hero]" (27) or "standard hero" (17) for comfort, but in *Hobbit*, Tolkien attempted to rewrite the hero. In "Homecoming," Tolkien found the meaning of *Maldon* in his interpretation of two lines that he took as the author's moralization of his story, chastising the "standard hero" of that poem. The wise doctrine "Never trust the teller, trust the tale," had no influence on Tolkien's reading of *Maldon,* which indeed erased most of the story. For all Tolkien's skill at telling a story, his studies of *Maldon* and *Beowulf* read the texts as lyrics rather than narratives. In "Monsters," he describes *Beowulf* as "*static*" in structure and declares the poem is "not meant to advance" *(Essays* 28).

As *Hobbit* opens, the wizard Gandalf claims he has sought already for "a mighty Warrior, even a Hero" (31) but reports that "warriors are busy fighting one another in distant lands, and in this neighborhood heroes are scarce, or simply not to be found" (31). The quest for the dragon's treasure in times when warriors occupy themselves elsewhere and no heroes are here now depends on finding a new hero, an unpromising youth, or a timid fellow who will, in the pinch, prove to have the courage and strength required. Such heroes abound in folklore. Even Beowulf, one brief reference in the poem indicates, was once regarded as "slack" (Klaeber line 2087). When Gandalf assembles the dwarves at Bilbo's comfortable hobbit hole, Thorin grandly asserts that they will soon begin a journey from which some or all may not return. Bilbo shrieks and collapses, calling out "'struck by lightning, struck by lightning'" (25). Gandalf smooths over this contretemps: "Excitable little fellow . . . Gets funny queer fits, but he is one of the best, one of the best—fierce as a dragon in a pinch" (25).

Bilbo recovers in the parlor, creeps to the door, and hears Gloin scoffing at his alleged ferocity: "As soon as I clapped eyes on the little fellow bobbing and puffing on the mat, I had my doubts. He looks more like a grocer than a burglar" (28). Bilbo responds to the challenge: "He suddenly felt he would go without bed and breakfast to be thought fierce. As for *little fellow bobbing on the mat* it almost made him *really* fierce" (28). Bilbo opens the door and accepts the challenge in the pursuit of what Beowulf or his poet would call *lof* and *dom*, praise and good report. Gandalf preemptorily announces: "I have chosen Mr Baggins and that ought to be enough for all of you. If I say he is a Burglar, a Burglar he is, or will be when the time comes. There is a lot more in him than you guess and a deal more than he has any idea of himself" (29). The next morning, despite some qualms, Bilbo reaffirms his commitment to the adventure when he accepts the letter setting out the terms of his adventure: "Terms: cash on delivery, up to and not exceeding one fourteenth of total profits (if any), all traveling expenses guaranteed in any event, funeral expenses to be defrayed by us or our representatives, if occasion arises and the matter is not otherwise arranged for" (38).

Accepting the letter, like making a formal vow, binds Bilbo to a venture that may cost him his life. His initial motives, to be thought fierce and to collect one-fourteenth of the profits arising from plundering a dragon's hoard, comically re-create the heroic ethos. Bilbo Baggins, like a hero of old, sets out *til fjár ok frægðar*, for wealth and fame, his commitment to the adventure sealed by a contract as binding as a heroic oath confirmed with a drink of the bright mead. Besides the wizard Gandalf, Bilbo's partners in the adventure are twelve dwarves who hope to gain the dragon's treasure, and perhaps fame as well, but who also seek revenge on Smaug for the deaths of companions, kinsmen, and a late lord. The usual motives for heroic action are all present and accounted for: wealth, fame, revenge, an oath or vow, loyalty, and leadership impel these small heroes on to confront a dragon.

Naturally enough, the successful outcome of the adventure depends on Bilbo's physical and moral courage and on his moral choices, including a decision to give up his share of the treasure. Bilbo does not shoot the dragon Smaug or lead the victors in the battle of the five armies. The great exploits belong to more than life-sized figures: Bard the archer and Beorn who takes the form of a great bear to turn the tide of battle. But at the crucial moments, Bilbo's actions secure the success of the good cause, and he receives the praise and good report of true judges: "The Elvenking looked at Bilbo with new wonder: 'Bilbo Baggins!' ... You are more worthy to wear the armour of elf-princes than many that have looked more comely in it'" (256); and "an old man, wrapped in a dark cloak [Gandalf in disguise], rose from a tent door where he was sitting and came towards them. 'Well done! Mr Baggins!' he said clapping Bilbo on the back. 'There is always more about you than anyone expects'" (257). In earning these praises, Bilbo has acted with physical courage, altruism, and loyalty to his comrades even as he attempts to stave off the war Thorin's desire for the dragon's whole hoard has made likely. Bilbo Baggins has grown thinner, stronger, braver in the long march from the comfortable Shire to the Lonely Mountain; danger makes a new hobbit of him, or rather, brings out the latent quality Gandalf had perceived in Bilbo long before.

In *Hobbit* and in Bilbo Baggins, Tolkien creates a new heroism and a new hero. The new hero is summoned to his dangerous mission by a nearly supernatural person who will brook no denial. In contrast, Beowulf, on hearing of Grendel's raids, abruptly orders a ship fitted out and, according to Tolkien, sets off to win *lof* and *dom* with his physical strength or *mægen (Essays* 27). Beowulf, however, attributes his desire to visit the Danes to the Danish king's need of men (lines 199b–201); Hrothgar surmises that God has sent Beowulf to defend the Danes against Grendel (lines 38lb–84a) and acknowledges that he will be obligated to reward Beowulf (lines 384b–85). An altruistic impulse to defend those under attack could easily be seen in Beowulf's actions. Similarly Beowulf's fight with the dragon has been taken as an instance of altruistic self-sacrifice (Klaeber 1–1i), but that reading is ignored in "Monsters" and rejected in "Homecoming" (17–18). Beowulf's physical strength borders on the superhuman, but Bilbo, the new hero, has no such prowess. He has a sense of honor, moral and physical courage, and the resolve to die, if need be, in the good cause.

Tolkien clearly wished to find an alternative hero in the text of *Beowulf*, hence Beowulf's surprisingly small part in "Monsters" and Tolkien's pointed comparison of Hrothgar, the King of the Danes, with Beowulf. Tolkien writes that the poet "turned naturally when delineating the great King of Heorot to the Old Testament. In the *folces hyrde* [shepherd of the people] of the Danes we have much of the shepherd patriarchs and kings of Israel, servants of the one God," whereas "the traditional matter in English, not to mention the living survival of the heroic code and temper among the noble households of ancient England, enabled him [the *Beowulf* poet] to draw differently and in some respects much closer to the actual heathen *hæleþ* [hero, warrior], the character of Beowulf, especially as a young knight who used his great gift of *mægen* [strength] to earn *dom* and *lof* [good report, fame] among men and posterity" *(Essays* 27). In Appendix B to "Monsters," Tolkien is still more negative about the poem's hero, noting that unlike Hrothgar, Beowulf "refers sparingly to God, except as the arbiter of critical events. ... We have in Beowulf's language little differentiation of God and Fate" (40) and that as he lay dying, Beowulf thought "only of his barrow and memorial among men, of his childlessness, and of Wiglaf the sole survivor of his kindred" (39). But Beowulf, dying dragon-poisoned and in pain, assures Wiglaf that the treasures he has won will (presumably as rewards for warriors) serve his people's need (lines 2799–801a).

Despite Tolkien's admiration of the hapless King of the Danes, Hrothgar merits only one brief reference in part 2. No amount of critical goodwill can make a hero of Hrothgar. In "Monsters," the *Beowulf* poet himself nearly becomes a rival hero. Tolkien characterizes the poet as a Christian learned in the traditions and poetry of the pagan era, who expressed his Christian conception of the war between good and evil in the poem without allegory and without explicitly Christian language (13–14, 17, 23–7, 33). This description of the *Beowulf* poet and his work reads like Tolkien's idea of himself as a scholar—a Christian contemplating the nobility, the hopelessness, the beauty, and the tragedy of the pagan and heroic world depicted in *Beowulf* and the literature of ancient Scandinavia. And, of course, his idea of the *Beowulf* poet's intention and means seems to reflect Tolkien's intention and means as author of *LR*.[2] In 1936 ("Monsters") and 1937 (*Hobbit*) Tolkien questioned entrenched critical opinion that the old literary texts, especially *Beowulf*, idealized an ancient heroism. In his scholarship and his fiction, Tolkien almost constructed a new hero and new heroism, but the old model and the "standard hero" were visible in the new heroism and in Bilbo Baggins, nor could Beowulf be utterly banished from his poem.

Tolkien's *LR* and "Homecoming" (1953 and 1954) rejected traditional heroism still more decisively, but Tolkien's love for the idea of heroes, men of prowess and courage fighting a desperate battle for the right against seemingly overpowering odds, makes one strand of the story told in *LR*. In the other strand of that epic, the heroic struggle is internal and spiritual. The heroic strand of *LR* resembles Raphael's history of the war in heaven, an extended metaphor for the spiritual reality of the conflict Milton's Adam (and Eve) would not have understood. The spiritual strand in *LR* is the story of the Ring-bearers' progress to Mount Doom and the only fire that can unmake the Ring of power. If that quest succeeds, victory over Sauron and his immense force is assured otherwise all is lost. Aragorn, the great leader of the heroic strand, and his followers, like the gods and heroes of Old Norse mythology, are prepared to fight to the death against "the monsters and the outer darkness" ("Monsters" 25) even if there is no hope of victory. The large heroes of *LR* do not aspire *til fjár ok frægðar*; no desire for *lof* and *dom* motivates them. Their duty to the good cause calls them and they cannot, will not, refuse. The war pits the good against absolute evil, but the good appear, almost metaphorically, in the shapes and forms of the heroic age. The outcome of this vast struggle, however, depends completely upon the success or failure of two small figures, Sam and Frodo.

Tolkien's desire for heroes drove him to give the spiritual strand of the story its own heroic metaphor, heroic valor, violent heroic action, and a hero who feels the longing for *lof* and *dom* that guided Beowulf's life. The wisest members of the Council of Elrond, Gandalf and Elrond himself, mistook or misidentified the hero of their story. The successor to the place of the true hero, briefly occupied by Beowulf, then by Bilbo Baggins, is not Frodo Baggins, Bilbo's designated heir and Gandalf's choice for Ring-bearer, the chosen one for whom, according to Elrond, the task was "appointed" (*FR* 354). The unexpected hero, much like the unpromising youth of folktales or a future saga hero lazing by the fire and called a fool until called to great actions by great needs, proves to be Samwise Gamgee. The Council of Elrond recapitulates the earlier private conference on the Ring between Frodo and Gandalf, designates Frodo as the Ring-bearer, foreshadows the narrative shape of Sam and Frodo's story, and directs the audiences' attention to the moral meanings of the spiritual strand of his trilogy. The foreshadowing does not fully match the action to come and, moreover, the instructions for reading the story's moral meaning are not in complete harmony with the story itself.

Contradictions between the substance of the Council of Elrond and subsequent revelations in Lorien and the story of Sam and Frodo demonstrate Tolkien's difficulty in creating the new hero and heroism he longed for over the opposition of his passion for those unsatisfactory, earthly "standard" heroes of old. At the Council, Elrond announces, "We must send the Ring to the Fire" (*FR* 349), just as Gandalf had said much earlier to Frodo, who agreed he wanted the Ring destroyed, but protested "I am not made for perilous quests. . . . Why was I chosen?" (91). That protest, "why me?" implies acceptance of the quest, which Frodo repeats on the way to Rivendell and confirms there. There Frodo formally accepts, under some external inspiration, the task of taking the Ring to Mount Doom, "wondered to hear his own words, as if some other will was using his small voice," and undertakes the quest though he does not "'know the way'"; Elrond responds, "I think that this task is appointed for you, Frodo; and that if you do not find a way, no one will. This is the hour of the Shire-folk, when they arise from their quiet fields to shake the towers and counsels of the Great" (354). Shortly thereafter Elrond advises that the Ring must set out shortly but "those who go with it must not count on their errand being aided by war or force" (359). The conflict, we must suppose, will be entirely spiritual. The Lady Galadriel, wisest of the wise, later confirms that impression when she warns the company, "your Quest stands on the edge of a knife. Stray but a little and it will fail, to the ruin of all" (*FR* 463).

Tolkien's readings of *Maldon* and *Beowulf* erased those texts' references to the institution of the heroic vow and his fiction explicitly disapproves of such vows. Yet a heroic vow is part of Sam's emergence as hero. An ancient story reported in *RK* runs that one Baldor son of Brego rashly vowed to enter the "Paths of the Dead" and was never seen again (79). Before the Fellowship of the Ring leaves Rivendell, Elrond tells Frodo's companions, "You may tarry, or come back, or turn aside. . . . no oath or bond is laid on you to go further than you will." Gimli protests that those who leave when the going is tough are faithless, but Elrond counsels against oaths, in sharp opposition to the traditions of the heroic world; Gimli objects again, declaring that "sworn word may strengthen quaking heart," but Elrond counters, "[o]r break it" (*FR* 366). But Sam has already sworn an oath or a heroic vow, and his faithful performance of his oath is crucial to the story of the Ring. Before the hobbits leave the Shire, Frodo warns Sam of the likelihood that neither of them will come back from the quest (which Frodo implicitly accepts even before the Council of Elrond), and Sam replies "[i]f you don't come back, sir, then I shan't, that's certain" (123). Sam's immediate answer makes, in fact, a heroic oath or vow identical in substance to the vow that Offa made to Byrhtnoth before both died at Maldon.

When Sam and Frodo reach the land of Mordor, Sam rather than Frodo finds the way, leads and sometimes carries his master on the way, and gives Frodo most of their food and nearly all of their water. In his rescue of Frodo from the orcs, Sam is, briefly, the Ring-bearer; to escape detection he puts it on and overhears an orc report, "there's a large warrior loose, Elf most likely, with an elf-sword anyway" (*TT* 438). Metaphorically Sam becomes a large elf-warrior and relishes the identification. And though neither large nor an elf, Sam proves a warrior at need. Early in *LR*, Sam composes some comic verses about the stone troll (left over from *Hobbit*) and Frodo predicts that Sam will become "a wizard—or a warrior" (*FR* 277). Sam wounds and routs the monstrous Shelob with Sting the elf-sword (*TT* 424–26), and disarms (de-arms) an orc with it (*RK* 221), and on these violent and warlike actions, despite Elrond, the success of the mission depends. When Sam realizes the orcs have found what he supposes is Frodo's corpse, he abandons his plan to carry the Ring to Mount Doom by himself. Loyalty to Frodo is his first duty. As he rushes to battle the orcs and avenge his beloved master, he states: "'How many can I kill before they get me? They'll see the flame of the sword, as soon as I draw it, and they'll get me sooner or later. I wonder if any song will ever mention it: how Samwise fell in the High Pass and made a wall of bodies round his master" (*TT* 433). To die valiantly and be remembered in a song is to win *lof* and *dom*. Sam unconsciously models his intended course of action on the heroic deaths of the heroes remembered in the song or poem *Maldon*. Among them was Offa who fell and "lay, as befits a thegn, near his lord" (line 294) precisely as Sam proposes to do. To avenge Frodo, Sam leaves the larger war out of consideration, and in that he follows the faithful heroes of *Maldon*, who say nothing about the war between Æthelred II and the Vikings but speak of their duty to avenge Byrhtnoth and of their intention to avoid the shame of failing in that obligation.

The Ring of power or the Great Ring or the One Ring in *LR* is merely magical in *Hobbit*. Some of the contradictions in the myth of the Ring arise from the necessity to account for the transformation of a ring of invisibility into the Ring. T. A. Shippey has ingeniously compared the Ring's power over its possessors to the action of an addictive drug (1992, 122–27), but the contradictions seem not to be defeated so easily. Gandalf (*FR* 72, 91), Elrond (350) and Galadriel (474–75) indicate that if a person of power gains the Ring and uses it to defeat Sauron, it will in time turn the possessor into another Sauron, but if a person without power attempts to use the Ring, it will betray the possessor to Sauron. To defeat the power of evil embodied in Sauron requires a "Ring-bearer" willing to destroy it and forgo the power and glory a personal victory over Sauron would entail.

In the event, this seems not to happen. On the way to Mount Doom, Frodo can hardly support the burden of the Ring; he is exhausted by the inward struggle, and completely dependent on Sam for his progress. At the Crack of Doom, the fissure down to the only fires that can destroy the Ring, Frodo recovers his strength and turns into a powerful figure as he loses the battle with the Ring and yields to its temptation. Sam sees Frodo standing "black against the glare, tense, erect, but still as if he had been turned to stone" and cries 'Master!'"; Frodo speaks "with a clear voice, indeed with a voice clearer and more powerful than Sam had ever heard him use, and it rose above the throb and turmoil of Mount Doom, ringing in the roof and walls. 'I have come,' he said. 'But I choose not to do what I came to do. I will not do this deed. The Ring is mine!' And suddenly he set it on his finger" (*RK* 268–69). Frodo has failed the test and strayed more than a little, but the result is victory over Sauron after all. Providentially, Gollum bowls Sam over, bites off Frodo's ring finger, and dancing with joy at regaining his "precious," falls into the Crack of Doom. Sauron's great army collapses, and the victory of the age is achieved (270).

This hardly seems the spiritual victory we expected; the destruction of the Ring apparently depends on the providential intervention of Gollum, who intends to reclaim it for himself, and the surefooted Slinker's fortunate fall. The prescient Gandalf, on hearing of Gollum's escape from the elves, muses "he may yet play a part that neither he nor Sauron have foreseen" (*FR* 335), one of the many hints in the trilogy that an unseen but benevolent providence guides the Ring-bearers and the forces of right despite their errors and imperfections. But if Gollum's unwilling part is crucial, the triumph of the good seems undeserved, spiritual defeat is reversed by a *deus ex machina*. Galadriel's warning that if the company of the Ring-bearer should "[s]tray but a little" (*FR* 463), all would be lost, like some of Elrond's pronouncements, seems to miss the mark. In fact, the spiritual victory over the Ring's seductive power is Sam's and has been adumbrated first by Bilbo's resignation of the Ring—the first possessor ever to give it up according to Gandalf (*FR* 75)—and then by Galadriel's refusal of the Ring. In Lórien, Frodo offers the Ring to Galadriel, who has indeed contemplated possessing the Ring and using it. In that conference, she reveals herself as she would be at first if she accepted Frodo's offer of the Ring, then shrinks into "a slender elf-woman" and announces, "I pass the test . . . . I will diminish and go into the West and remain Galadriel" (*FR* 475).

Sam is Samwise, not Samuel as one might expect, and despite its meaning, the full name becomes an honorific in *LR*. The prefix *sam-* in Anglo-Saxon means "half," hence Samwise is "half-wise." One might think "half-witted," but The Old Norse wisdom poem *Hávamál* (*Sayings of the High One*), as Tolkien knew very well, advises that one should be "[a]veragely wise . . . never too wise" (Larrington, stanza 55). Tolkien characterizes Sam as dim before the beginning of the quest, but once it has begun, Sam is wise enough to see things as they are and himself as he is, wise to recognize the Ring's temptation and reject it. The change from Sam as dim, to Sam who sees as through a glass darkly, comes in his first meeting with elves, the people of his dreams and longings. As the hobbits set out from the Shire they meet a company of elves. Sam talks with some of the elves and absorbs their counsel and seemingly receives a portion of their wisdom. Sam sleeps while Frodo talks with the leader of the elves, but the next morning, Frodo is astonished to hear a changed Sam saying "after last night I feel different. I seem to see ahead, in a kind of way. I know we are going to take a very long road into darkness; but I know I can't turn back" (*FR* 124).

In Mordor, convinced that Frodo is dead, Sam passes the test under harder conditions than Galadriel's. As Ring-bearer, Sam feels

> that he had from now on only two choices: to forebear the Ring, though it would torment him; or to claim it, and challenge the Power that sat in its dark hold beyond the valley of shadows. Already the Ring tempted him, gnawing at his will and reason. Wild fantasies arose in his mind; and he saw Samwise the Strong, Hero of the Age, striding with a flaming sword across the darkened land, and armies flocking to his call as he marched to the overthrow of Barad-dûr. And then all the clouds rolled away, and the white sun shone, and at his command the vale of Gorgoroth became a garden of flowers and trees and brought forth fruit. He had only to put on the Ring and claim it for his own, and all this could be. (*RK* 210)

Sam's "love of his master" and personal wisdom, "his plain hobbit-sense" assures him "he was not large enough to bear such a burden, even if such visions were not a mere cheat to betray him" (*RK* 210). Sam, like Galadriel, freely chose, despite the temptation to claim and use the Ring, to remain himself. In contrast, Frodo at Mount Doom indeed puts on the Ring and claims it as his own, whereas Sam had taken it off before and surrendered it to Frodo (*RK* 224). The spiritual victory is Sam's, his teacher in achieving it, Galadriel. Sam's free choice not to use the Ring, and indeed to will its destruction, is crucial to the great victory, but so is the hidden, benevolent fate or providence that rescues Frodo from his folly by the seemingly improbable instrument of Gollum and then trips Gollum up by the heels at the edge of the abyss (*RK* 270).

In *LR* a benevolent providence supplants that "evil, hidden fate" Nordal saw darkening the heroic literature of the north. Hobbits, dwarves, humans, and, naturally, the evil or corrupted seem unaware of this hidden force in their world, but the supernaturally wise and good, Tom Bombadil, the leading elves, and Gandalf, share an awareness that some divinity or force shapes the course of events when hobbits, dwarves, and others encounter difficulties their own strengths cannot overcome. Gandalf repeatedly implies the operation of a benevolent purpose in the course of events as when he asserts "'There was more than one power at work, Frodo. . . . [T]here was something else at work, beyond any design of the Ring-maker. . . . Bilbo was *meant* to find the Ring, and *not* by its maker. In which case you also were *meant* to have it" (*FR* 84). Frodo does not agree this is an encouraging thought, but admits he does not understand Gandalf. In that first meeting between Frodo and the elves' leader, Gildor, tells Frodo "[i]n this meeting there may be more than chance" (*FR* 121), and one consequence of the meeting is the change in Sam's vision and determination on which the success of the quest ultimately depends. Shortly thereafter, Old Man Willow threatens to end the quest prematurely, but Tom Bombadil providentially intervenes and subsequently assures the hobbits that "chance brought me then, if chance you call it," (*FR* 173–74) and obviously the hobbits should not. Elrond makes that point clear at his Council to which those present have been "called . . . though I have not called you to me. . . You are come and are here met, in this very nick of time, by chance it may seem. Yet it is not so" (*FR* 317).

THE SUBORDINATE HERO

Literary scholarship and creative writing merge in Tolkien's "Homecoming," which combines a play suited for reading rather than performance, and a critical essay "Ofermod" ("overmastering pride" in Tolkien's gloss). The play or closet drama and essay ostensibly make two ways of reading the poem *Maldon*, a minor masterpiece of Anglo-Saxon or Old English literature, but the whole can be seen as a revision of "Monsters" and an intensification of Tolkien's rejection of the heroic ethos. In "Homecoming," a young poet and an old farmer experienced in battle search among the slain for the body of Byrhtnoth (Tolkien's spelling of the name—Beorhtnoth—corrects the Anglo-Saxon poem), the commander of an English force defeated near the town of Maldon. Their darkling search through the battlefield and conversation re-create, from the perspective of the morning after, Tolkien's idea of the Anglo-Saxon poem and its meaning—or, indeed, its moral. The young poet idealizes war and battle, the old farmer deflates some of those illusions, but essentially both agree that the battle at Maldon was lost because Byrhtnoth allowed a Viking force to cross a narrow causeway from their island encampment to a pitched battle on even terms with the English. The old farmer's judgment is unequivocal: "[O]ur lord was at fault / . . . He let them cross the causeway, so keen was he / to give minstrels matter for mighty songs" (10). In short, the desire for the *lof* and *dom* that heroic songs confer and preserve led Byrhtnoth to a wrong decision, one fatal to himself and his faithful followers. In Tolkien's view Byrhtnoth treated "a desperate battle" as "a sporting match, to the ruin of his purpose and duty" (15).

Tolkien asserts that Byrhtnoth was "chivalrous rather than strictly heroic" (15), that is, he sought honor for his valor rather than exercising his valor only and strictly in the service of his duty. Tolkien traces Byrhtnoth's fatal flaw to "a defect of character" ("pride" evidently) but a character "not only formed by nature, but moulded also by 'aristocratic tradition,' enshrined in tales and verse of poets now lost save for echoes" (15). Byrhtnoth's fault or tragic flaw, in Tolkien's reading, is both individual and social; in social terms, the hero's world and its poetry has taught him to seek *lof* and *dom*. That teaching has taken firm hold of Byrhtnoth because of his pride, his innate desire for praise and good report. In the event, as Tolkien saw it, Byrhtnoth erred in making a decision that promised to enhance his personal glory rather than subordinating the quest for honor to duty of defending the land against the Vikings. The young poet who shares the battlefield search for Byrhtnoth's body in "Homecoming" is, like Byrhtnoth, under the spell of the poetic tradition that conferred *lof* and *dom*, and a kind of immortality upon its heroes. In his commentary, however, Tolkien blames Byrhtnoth for "chivalry," a desire for "honour and glory" (*lof* and *dom*) which leads the flawed hero to act "beyond the bleak heroic necessity" (14–17). Though "Homecoming" comments directly on the meaning of *Maldon*, both parts of the work, the verse drama and the following critical essay, refer explicitly to *Beowulf*.

Having made his case for Byrhtnoth's tragic flaw—"chivalry" or an excessive desire for *lof* and *dom*—Tolkien applies his argument to *Beowulf*, which is, I believe, the real point of the work. In Tolkien's view, young Beowulf acts recklessly, chivalrously in the Grendel adventure, but he risks only his own life when he undertakes the mission and made his fight with Grendel a "'sporting' fight" between an unarmed man and an unarmed monster (14). In his old age and as king of the Geats, Beowulf's chivalry impels him to fight the ravaging dragon single-handedly and only the help of a subordinate saves the hero from a defeat that would have left the dragon "at large" (14–15). Even so, Beowulf is killed by the dragon's poison, and "the people lose their king disastrously" (15). In short, Beowulf ventures battle against the dragon, as he should not do (but he should also not leave the dragon "at large"). Beowulf's excess, Tolkien implies, was Byrhtnoth's: their desire for honor conflicted with the heroes' duty to their followers. Thus Tolkien, having written in 1936 that the last word in *Beowulf*, "*lofgeornost*," represented the "summit of the praise for the dead hero" (*Essays* 36), found in 1953 that the word struck "an ominous note" and compared its disapproving force to the "severely" critical meaning of "ofermod" in *Maldon*.

In "Homecoming," Tolkien rejects the heroic desire for *lof* and *dom* and the old heroes so strongly that even Samwise, who wonders if his last heroic stand will be remembered in a song, might seem liable to censure. But Samwise, seven times major of the Shire and celebrated in many songs, remains the true hero because he acts as a loyal subordinate serving his master, like the true heroes of *Maldon* who died to avenge their lord even though (in Tolkien's view) Byrhtnoth had blundered. To Sam's chagrin, he and not Frodo takes the hero's place of honor in the Shire. Frodo assures Sam's father that his son is "one of the most famous people in all the lands and they are making songs about his deeds from here to the Sea and beyond the great river" (*RK* 357). We may trust those imagined singers of tales for the true hero of the age, Samwise Gamgee.

NOTES

1. Most of the elements of the heroic code (uncodified and subject to varying interpretations) are illustrated in *Maldon* and *Beowulf* and are discussed in this paper, but the curious reader might consult Alain Renoir's classic article for the heroic oath and the demand for revenge. Chapters 26–37 of the *Jomsvikinga saga* (Blake) tell a story of heroic

oaths leading to danger, death, and some oath-breaking. The idea of fate dominates the "Greenlandic Lay of Atli" (Dronke 1, 77–98), and the idea of "luck" seems equally important in *Viga-Glums saga* (Hreinsson 2, ch. 6, 25) where the hero's fortunes depend on possessing his grandfather's gifts, which eventually he has to give up. As noted earlier, "The Sayings of the High One" (Larrington) make clear that fame is the one permanent value in a passing world; the first section of *Beowulf* asserts that the pursuit of fame is the precondition of success in all societies (lines 24–25), in the first part of the poem Hrothgar assures Beowulf that his victory over the Grendel-kin has won him worldwide fame (lines 1703–5): the poem's final lines assert that of all kings, Beowulf was the most eager to win fame.

2. T. A. Shippey argues ("Tolkien" 16) that Tolkien believed he was saying in "Homecoming" what the poet of *Maldon* meant to say—which modern critics had missed.

WORKS CITED

Blake, Norman F., ed. and trans. *The Saga of the Jómsvikings*. London: Thomas and Nelson and Sons, 1962.

Dronke, Ursula. *The Poetic Edda: Heroic Poems*. Oxford: Clarendon, 1969.

Hreinsson, Viðar et al. eds. *The Complete Sagas of the Icelanders*. 5 vols. Reykjavik: Leifur Eiriksson, 1997.

Jones, George Fenwick. *The Ethos of the Song of Roland*. Baltimore: Johns Hopkins P, 1963.

Klaeber, Fr., ed. *Beowulf*. 3rd ed. with 1st and 2nd supplements. Boston: D. C. Heath, 1950.

Ladurie, Emmanuel Le Roy. *Montaillou: The Promised Land of Error*. Trans. Barbara Bray. New York: Vintage, 1979.

Larrington, Carolyne, trans. The Poetic Edda. Oxford and New York: Oxford UP, 1996.

Nordal, Sigurður. "Three Essays on the Völuspá." Trans. B. S. Benedikz and J. S. McConnell. *Saga Book of the Viking Society* 18 (1970–71). 79–135.

Renoir, Alain. "The Heroic Oath in *Beowulf*, the *Chanson de Roland* and the *Nibelungenlied*." *Studies in Old English Literature in Honour of Arthur G. Brodeur*. Ed. Stanley B. Greenfield. Eugene, OR: U of Oregon P, 1963. 237-66.

Shippey, T. A. "Tolkien and 'The Homecoming of Beorhtnoth.'" *Leaves from the Tree: J.R.R. Tolkien's Shorter Fiction*. London: Tolkien Society, 1991. 5-16

——. *The Road to Middle Earth*. 2nd ed. Hammersmith: Grafton, 1992.

Timmons, Daniel. "Mirror on Middle-earth: J.R.R. Tolkien and the Critical Perspectives." Diss. University of Toronto, 1998.

4

Tolkien's Versecraft in *The Hobbit* and *The Lord of the Rings*

Geoffrey Russom

J.R.R. Tolkien incorporates a considerable body of verse into his fantasy narratives, but none in iambic pentameter, the characteristic form of English poetry from Chaucer to the Romantics. Instead, Tolkien offers a varied assortment of archaic and folkloric meters, sometimes realized with unusual strictness, sometimes with unusual freedom. These metrical preferences may express the yearning for a vanished past that permeates Tolkien's writing, yet they also register dissatisfaction with the predominance of a single form in the English literary canon. The wide-ranging metrical experiments of the nineteenth and twentieth centuries make it clear that confinement to one form becomes intolerably stifling to poets. Lack of metrical variety also interferes with natural development of appreciation. An exclusive meter will eventually be felt as an arbitrary set of more or less clerical requirements with no artistic value. Experience with a variety of forms makes it much easier to apprehend the dynamic relationships that give good music. Composer Donald Swann regards Tolkien as particularly successful in communicating this kind of appeal through the "lilt and movement" of his poetic language.[1] Here I offer an explicit account of "lilt and movement."

Linguists have frequently turned to poetry for insight into universal characteristics of human language. An important by-product of this research has been the discovery of principles that apply to poetic composition generally rather than to a single form. The first principle needed for analysis of Tolkien's diverse meters was discovered by Roman Jakobson:

> I. Units of metrical form (metrical positions, feet, verses) are projected from units of natural language (syllables, words, phrases, clauses, sentences).[2]

By principle I, a metrical unit is rather like a shadow puppet projected from human hands. The shadow is somewhat simplified, retaining some features of the hands (their shape as viewed from one angle), but not others (three-dimensional form, color). Similarly, a metrical position projected from a syllable will retain features relevant to syllables generally, such as presence or absence of stress, but not the features of particular vowels or consonants. At a higher level of poetic form, metrical positions can be incorporated into feet with the syllabic pattern of a word or small phrase. English words like *reMAIN* and small phrases like *the MAN*, with stress on the second syllable, will project into a foot with a weak-strong contour, traditionally known as an *iamb*.[3] A foot pattern traditionally called a *trochee*, with a strong-weak contour, will be projected from words like *SERpent* and small phrases like *STOP it!* In the notation used below, an iamb is represented as /WS/ and a trochee as /SW/, where *S* represents a strong position, *W* represents a weak position, and the slash represents a foot boundary. Less familiar kinds of feet can be projected from other words and phrases. At a still higher level of poetic form, the verse is projected from a large phrase, clause, or sentence and is flanked by boundaries of its own (notated with a double slash below). Verse patterns may incorporate a specified number of feet. Once learned, a verse pattern takes on a life of its own in the mind, existing independently of the actual words that *fill* or *occupy* it in a particular case. Since the pattern is composed of simplified speech units, we can align it with the poet's verses during reading or recitation and determine at once whether the verses fill the pattern properly.

Tolkien's poems illustrate metrical principles with clarity because he finds ways to incorporate direct realization of verse patterns. Consider the following rhymed couplet:

(1) // we GO, / we GO, / we GO / to WAR,//
     // to HEW / the STONE / and BREAK / the DOOR//
                                    (*TT* 106)

The two verses in the couplet are examples of a four-foot pattern //WS/WS/WS/WS//, traditionally called *iambic tetrameter*. In these realizations of the pattern, each S position is occupied by a stressed noun like *STONE* or a stressed main verb like *HEW*. Each W position is occupied by an unstressed grammatical word such as a pronoun (*we*), preposition (*to*), or definite article (*the*). Each foot is occupied by a small, tightly bound phrase, and each verse is occupied by a clause.[4] In such cases there is a very close correspondence between the abstract verse pattern and the poetic language that fills it. The only simpler way to realize the pattern would be a verse like // reJOICE, / reJOICE, / reJOICE, / reJOICE!//, with each foot filled by an even more tightly bound unit: a single word. In a personal statement by a contemporary poet, verses like those of (1) would probably seem *too* simple. Within the context of Tolkien's fantasy narrative, however, such verses can be assigned to an appropriate character, in this case Treebeard, represented as slow, direct, natural, and deliberate in contrast to his enemy Saruman, whose most emphasized character traits are impatience, deceptiveness, and false sophistication.

Treebeard does not always express himself with such metrical directness. In one of his more complex couplets, the first foot boundary does not coincide with a word boundary:

(2) to I- / senGARD / with DOOM / we COME!
        with DOOM / we COME, / with DOOM / we COME![5]
                                        (*TT* 106)

I refer to complexities of this kind as *boundary mismatches:* mismatches between boundaries of natural-language units and boundaries of metrical units.[6] In iambic tetrameters assigned to Treebeard, Tolkien firmly restricts the number of boundary mismatches. In addition, he situates these mismatches according to a universal principle of closure:

II. Correspondence between the poet's language and abstract metrical form should normally be closest at the ends of metrical domains (verses, couplets, stanzas, whole poems.)[7]

In example (2), the boundary mismatch is situated at the beginning of the first verse of the couplet, in strict conformity with principle II.

Mismatches are employed more freely in verses assigned to other characters. Here are some examples from iambic tetrameter poems of normal rather than extreme strictness:

(3) there MA- / ny a GLEAM- / ing GOLD- / en HOARD
                                        (*Hobbit* 24)

(4) beNEATH/ the ROOF / there is / a BED
                        (*FR* 112)

(5) BUCKler / and CORS- / let, AXE / and SWORD
                        (*FR* 412)

Example (3) has multiple boundary mismatches. Its second foot also contains an instance of *elision*, a traditional option allowing one metrical position to be occupied by adjacent vowels. In this instance a single W position is occupied by the unstressed vocalic *y* of *many* and the following unstressed *a*. Adjacent vowels are shortened in pronunciation and tend to coalesce, so elision is grounded in linguistic reality.[8] English poets also elide vowels that are separated by a single weakly pronounced consonant such as *l, m, n, r, w,* or *v.* Instances from the same poem include *over* (stanza one, line one), *flowering* (stanza four, line two), and *towers* (stanza eight, line four). Spellings like *o 'er* and *tow 'rs* are sometimes used by early editors of English verse to indicate that elision has taken place. Verse (4) above contains an example of what I call *stress mismatch.* In this case, the S position of the third foot is filled by unstressed *is,* which would provide a better match for a W position.[9] Placement of a weak syllable on a strong position, traditionally known as *pyrrhic substitution*, occurs freely in canonical English poems and seems to interfere very little with perception of verse form. Double stress mismatch to the WS foot pattern, with a strong syllable on the weak position and vice versa, is more carefully controlled, appearing most often in the first foot of the verse after a phrase boundary, as in (5). At the speed of recitation or reading, it seems we cannot perceive stress very well unless there is a preceding unstressed syllable in the same phrase for comparison (Halle and Keyser 168–75). Since the phrase-initial stress of *buckler* is muffled, it is not unacceptably prominent on a W position, though it does add to metrical complexity there. The sense of a metrical norm is maintained despite mismatches like those in (3) and (5) because Tolkien adheres to a third universal principle:

> III. Restrict the number and variety of mismatches appropriately within a given metrical domain.

In verse (3), with its multiple boundary mismatches, there are no stress mismatches. In verses (4) and (5), the feet that contain stress mismatches have no boundary mismatches. The definition of "appropriately" is left open in principle III. Finding the appropriate degree of strictness for a given poem is an advanced problem of versecraft requiring detailed consideration of the audience and the occasion.[10]

Complex verses such as the following show that Tolkien understood the linguistic basis for traditional mismatches.

> (6) WEST of / the MOON, / EAST of / the SUN
> (*RK* 375)

> (7) and STONES / CRACK in / the FROS- / ty NIGHT
> (*FR* 356)

> (8) in a / FAR LAND / beYOND / the SEA[11]
> (*FR* 114)

Tolkien must have realized that trochaic inversion in the first foot involves muffled stress after a phrase boundary because he sometimes inverts after a phrase boundary internal to the verse, as in (6), where the relevant boundary is punctuated with a comma. Verses like (6) are rarer than those like (5) because the principle of closure imposes stricter constraints on mismatch toward the end of the verse. The second foot of (7) contains a less familiar type of inversion. Stress on monosyllabic words like *crack* is apparently somewhat muffled because there is no unstressed syllable for comparison within the word and no immediately preceding unstressed syllable within the phrase (Kiparsky 191; Youmans 188–90). In the second foot of example (8), both words are stressed monosyllables, but the prominence pattern of *far land* would be weak-strong in many dialects of English, with *land* receiving phrase-final stress.[12] There are no word-boundary mismatches in the feet that contain these unusual stress mismatches. When reciting Tolkien's poems, incidentally, we must render even the most extreme mismatches straightforwardly rather than trying to regularize them through artificial pronunciation. Tolkien's lilt and movement are created through controlled departure from the norm followed by return, a dynamic process equivalent to musical tension and release.[13]

Iambic meters traditionally allow for *headless* verses with the first weak position unfilled. In a work song of the forest elves, all twenty-six iambic tetrameters are headless. Kiparsky observes that headless tetrameters allow the poet to shift back and forth between iambic and trochaic movement for rhythmical variety (226). Consider this excerpt from the work song in which the empty positions are represented with a parenthesized *W*:

(9) (W) PAST / the RU- / shes, PAST / the REEDS,
     (W) PAST / the MAR- / sh's WA- / ving WEEDS,
     (W) through / the MIST / that RI- / seth WHITE
     (W) UP / from MERE / and POOL / at NIGHT!
                               (*Hobbit* 177)

Since trochaic meters can be *tailless*, with the final W position empty, placement of word boundaries in the second line above might suggest scansion as trochaic tetrameter (PAST the / MARsh's / Waving / WEEDS (W)). The meter of the poem as a whole is clearly indicated, however, by its last line, which has well-marked iambic rhythm ((W) BACK / to LANDS / you ONCE / did KNOW). Here and in other cases the principle of closure provides an important aid to scansion.

Iambic tetrameter is used in English romances during the later Middle Ages and in song settings throughout the modern English period. Some hymn books refer to this popular form as *long meter*. A form with similar range of uses has iambic tetrameter in odd-numbered lines and iambic trimeter (//WS/WS/WS//) in even-numbered lines. This is sometimes called *common meter*.[14] The opening lines of a song by Bilbo illustrate the essential features of common meter along with some traditional mismatches:

(10) i SIT / beSIDE / the FIRE / and THINK
      of ALL / that I / have SEEN,
      of MEA- / dow-FLOWERS / and BU- / tterFLIES
      in SU- / mmers that / have BEEN;
                           (*FR* 363)

Verses two and four have an unstressed syllable on an S position in the second foot (pyrrhic substitution). Verses three and four have boundary mismatches at the hyphenation points. In verse three the word *flowers* occupies a single S position by elision. Though often unstressed, the form *been* matches the final S position of verse four because it has acquired the special stress assigned to phrase-final words in English.[15]

Several poems in long meter and common meter permit expansion of a W position to include two syllables, which creates a homely or folkloric effect:

(11) (W) CHIP / the GLA- / sses and CRACK / the PLATES!
       (W) BLUNT / the KNIVES / and BEND / the FORKS!
                                                    (*Hobbit* 23)

In the first verse above, the W position of the third foot contains two unstressed syllables that cannot be elided. The corresponding W in the following verse contains only one syllable, indicating that expansion is optional. Tolkien never expands a W position to include more than two syllables. In the poem from which (11) is excerpted, S positions of the first ten verses are always filled by stressed syllables that provide clear markers for the right edge of the foot. Verse fourteen, which ends the poem, is surprisingly complex by comparison:

(12) So, CARE- / fully! CARE- / fully with / the PLATES!
                                                    (*Hobbit* 23)

By now we have been exposed to enough straightforward expressions of this pattern to deal with the boundary mismatches in (12) and to intuit that *-fully* takes up all the available space in the expanded W position of the third foot, so that unstressed *with* must occupy the S position of an expanded pyrrhic (all this happens in an instant without conscious thought, of course).[16] The verse remains complex, but a restful closure would be inappropriate, since we are still wondering whether Bilbo's crockery can withstand the dish-washing practices of his guests.

In prophetic verse uttered by the Lady Galadriel, an expanded W position sometimes contains a stressed syllable:

(13) (W) NEAR / is the HOUR / when the LOST / should COME *FORTH*, /
       (W) and / the GREY *COM-* / pany RIDE / from the NORTH.
       but DARK / is the PATH / aPPOINT- / ed for THEE:
       the DEAD / WATCH the *ROAD* / that LEADS / to the SEA.
                                                    (*TT* 130)

Her *come, grey,* and *watch* have a stress that is significant but weaker than the stress of the word on the following S position (italicized). The effect is grave and folkloric, as of traditional wisdom, but not at all homely, in contrast to (11). By assigning this form to a character with dignity and power, Tolkien challenges the familiar assumption that it is inherently childish or comic.[17]

In some of Tolkien's poems, a W position internal to the verse may have no syllabic content, like the external W position of a headless or tailless verse. One four-line work song makes frequent use of these empty positions:

(14) (W) ROLL - / (W) ROLL - / (W) ROLL - / (W) ROLL,
       (W) ROLL- / ROLL-*RO-* / lling DOWN / the HOLE!

> (W) HEAVE / (W) HO! / (W) SPLASH / (W) PLUMP!
> (W) DOWN / they GO, / (W) DOWN / they BUMP!
> > (*Hobbit* 176)

In the first verse of (14), as printed in *Hobbit*, the sites of internal W positions to be filled with pauses are marked with prominent dashes similar to musical rest notations. Assignment of overt syllables to all internal W positions of the following verse makes the intended metrical pattern clear. In verse two, I assume that the second instance of *roll* has relatively weak stress.[18] Tolkien uses empty internal positions most often for boisterous, grim, or violent effects,[19] but this type of mismatch can also provide dramatic pauses in a poem of opposite mood:

(15) (W) SIGH / no MORE *PINE*, / till the WIND / of the MORN!
      (W) FALL / (W) MOON! / (W) DARK / be the LAND!
      (W) HUSH! / (W) HUSH! / (W) OAK, / ASH and *THORN*!
      (W) HUSHED / be all WA- / ter, till DAWN / is at HAND!
> > (*Hobbit* 279)

In this concluding passage from a lullaby of the elves, realization of the W position is quite varied. Such a position may be filled minimally, by a pause, or maximally, by two weak syllables of which one may bear significant stress, as in Galadriel's prophecy. The lullaby obeys strict rules of its own, however. Its verse-initial W positions are sometimes filled with a single unstressed syllable, but *never* contain two syllables. When its verse-internal W positions are filled with syllabic material, on the other hand, they *always* contain two syllables. The result is an extreme yet controlled variation ranging from short verses such as the middle two in (15) to much longer verses such as the following:

(16) the WIND'S / in the TREE- / TOP, the *WIND'S* / in the HEA(ther).
> > (*Hobbit* 279)

Here the extrametrical syllable after the last stress, a traditional option in all iambic meters, extends the verse to maximum length.[20]

In a particularly intricate poem, Tolkien uses a form that might be analyzed as iambic tetrameter or as iambic trimeter with two extrametrical syllables at the end of the verse. The more complex scansion is suggested by some peculiar rhymes. Consider the opening of the poem:

(17) eÄ- / rendil / was a MA(riner)
      that TA- / rried in / arVER(nien);
      he BUILT / a BOAT / of *TIM*(ber FELLED)
      in NIM- / brethil / to JOUR(ney in);
> > (*FR* 306)

The rhymes of (17) have approximate matching in three syllables rather than canonical matching in one or two. At the end of the fourth verse, *journey in* provides a multiword match for verse-final *-vernien*. Long words and phrases internal to the even-numbered verses match long words and phrases at the ends of the odd-numbered verses, with *tarried in* echoing *mariner* and *Nimbrethil* echoing *timber felled*. The scheme is realized consistently throughout the poem. In canonical iambic poetry, the first stressed vowel of the rhyme is placed on the last S position of the verse and any following syllables are extrametrical, as in (16) above. Since the line-final rhymes of (17) begin on the third S position, we may perceive them as trimeters. If we set aside the evidence of rhyme, on the other hand, many lines in the poem scan most naturally as iambic tetrameter. Out of context, we would surely scan the third line of (17) in this way (he BUILT / a BOAT / of TIM- / ber FELLED). It is hard to rule out the alternative scansion as iambic tetrameter with end-rhyme placed early and frequent stress mismatch on the last S position. This analysis has complexities of its own, of course. By undoing the usual relations between rhyme and meter, Tolkien encourages us to look more deeply into both.[21]

Shorter forms employed by Tolkien include examples with two feet (dimeters) and three feet (trimeters). A special form of iambic trimeter appears in thematically related poems about exiled kings:

> (18) his HALLS / shall E- / cho GOL(den)
>   to SONGS / of YORE / re-SUNG
>   (*Hobbit* 190)

> (19) reNEWED / shall be BLADE / that was BRO(ken),
>   the CROWN- / less aGAIN / shall be KING.
>   (*FR* 230)

Odd-numbered verses always end with an extrametrical syllable in these poems. In the eight-line poem about Aragorn represented by (19), the verse-initial W position is expanded only once, but all internal W positions are expanded.[22] This looks like a variation on the metrical theme of the poem about the dwarf king, which realizes internal W positions more simply, as in excerpt (18).

Initial and internal W positions are distinguished systematically in comic dimeters improvised by the elves for their guests:

> (20) to FLY / would be FO(lly),
>   to STAY / would be JO(lly)
>   (*Hobbit* 56)

Of the 26 dimeter verses in the poem, 25 have a single overt syllable on the first W position and two syllables on the internal W position. In 24 of 26 dimeters, there is an extrametrical unstressed syllable verse-finally. The last two dimeters end in monosyllables, providing closure through more direct realization of the abstract verse pattern in this respect.[23]

The verse patterns of English rhymed poetry are constructed by repetition of a single foot pattern. In Old English alliterative poetry, a foot can be projected from any word pattern, and the only constant feature at the level of the verse is the number of feet (two). Some poetic catalogues recited by Treebeard (*TT* 79, 239) employ a strict form of Old English meter that marks them as ancient lore. Below are simple, two-word examples of Old English *verse types* employed by Tolkien for this kind of poetry:

(21) SERpent / COLdest
           (*TT* 79)

(22) the / *LA U*ghing-FOLK
           (*TT* 239)

(23) the / *ELF*-CHILdren
           (*TT* 78)

(24) BEAR / *BEE*-HUNter
           (*TT* 78)

(25) *HALF*-GROWN / HObbits [Pippin's suggestion]
           (*TT* 79)

Example (21) consists of two words with a trochaic pattern, the most common pattern for Old English words. The verse type represented by this example is the most frequently employed by Old English poets and is generally regarded as simplest or normative. Verse (22) consists of an unstressed grammatical word and a compound word with alternating stress. Verse (23) is similar except that the compound has adjacent stresses. The heavy verse (24) consists of a stressed monosyllable followed by a compound. Verse (25) is also heavy, with a compound followed by a stressed trochaic word. The first stressed syllables in the compounds are italicized to show that they are more prominent than the second stressed syllables. Here and elsewhere Tolkien uses hyphens to emphasize two-word structure visually.

Old English verses occur in couplets linked by alliteration, usually printed as long lines. The long line below has alliteration on words beginning with H:

(26) HOUND is / HUNgry, // HARE is / FEARful
           (*TT* 78)

Each verse in this couplet is a variant of the type represented by (21), with a word group substituting for a trochaic word in the first foot. In Treebeard's strict usage, verses with more than two words are usually of this type, which as noted above is the simplest. The simplicity of the basic pattern seems to offset the complexity introduced by the substitution. Due to changes in the structure of the language, it has become quite difficult to compose modern English poetry in alliterative meter of this strictness. Treebeard's poetic catalogue is a tour de force requiring somewhat archaic syntax. In idiomatic modern English, example (26) would be something such as "The hound is hungry, and the hare is fearful."

When Tolkien assigns alliterative poetry to other characters, the form is handled more freely:

> (27) (from) DARK / *DUN*-Harrow // in the / DIM MORning
>   (with) THANE and / CAPtain // RODE / THENgel's SON
> (RK 87)

The parenthesized prepositions would not appear in strict realizations of the verse types to which they have been added here, and the *Beowulf* poet would have found it relatively easy to avoid such words because their meanings were often expressed by grammatical endings in Old English. In the line-final verses, the phrases *dim morning* and *Thengel's son* have been substituted for compounds like *elf-children* and *laughing-folk*. Verses with this kind of complexity are acceptable in *Beowulf*, though Treebeard seems to prefer the simpler realizations with compounds. Tolkien's alliterative lines generally have the traditional patterning, with single alliteration in the line-final verse and single or double alliteration in the line-initial verse. Alliteration ordinarily falls on the first stressed word of the verse in *Beowulf*, but need not do so when that word is a tensed verb, which has a significant but relatively weak stress in Old English. Non-alliterating *rode*, a verb in the past tense, has no adverse effect on the meter of the second line in (27).[24]

Tolkien uses the pattern of (21) primarily for alliterative verse, but trochaic feet appear in other kinds of poems as well. Consider first the opening lines of a fourteen-line riddle:

> (28) aLIVE / without BREATH;
>   as COLD / as DEATH;
>   NEver / THIRsting, // Ever / DRINking;
>   CLAD in / MAil, // NEver / CLINking,
> (TT 282)

Here the first two verses look like iambic dimeters with optional expansion of an internal W position. Then we encounter seven trochaic words in four dimeters printed as long lines. The change is so extreme that it causes a shift into trochaic meter, as opposed to trochaic movement within iambic meter. Scansion of these long lines as iambic would require an implausibly large number of mismatches relative to the size of the domain, contrary to Jakobson's principle III. Dimeters in the following four lines, though more complex, are most naturally analyzed as trochaic. After line eight we return to monosyllabic rhyme, with iambic meter firmly reestablished by line ten (so SLEEK, / so FAIR). The metrical shifts are communicated effectively to the audience because contrasting meter is introduced in a simple form and repeated for emphasis.[25]

In the unusual poem of six long lines (*TT* 23), Tolkien seems to switch from trochaic feet to iambic feet at the fifth metrical position. Line one establishes the pattern:

(29) GONdor! / GONdor, // beTWEEN / the MOUN- / tains and / the SEA!

The first two words of the line create a strong initial impression of trochaic meter, but the next four feet scan most plausibly as iambic. Though extremely complex, this pattern is sufficiently well marked to allow for an extrametrical syllable verse-initially, as in line five:

(30) (O) GONdor, / GONdor! // shall MEN / beHOLD / the SIL- / ver TREE

The option allowing for an extrametrical syllable at the beginning of a trochaic verse is the mirror image of the option in iambic meters, which have extrametrical syllables verse-finally, as we have seen. When I recite (30), the exclamatory *O* does not seem to interfere with trochaic realization of the first two feet even though the next two feet have markedly rising rhythm. Since there is always a major phrase boundary after the fourth metrical position of this long line pattern, it splits easily into a trochaic dimeter and an iambic tetrameter. Here as elsewhere what gets printed as a line may be determined by visual priorities.

A short riddle recited by Gollum seems to have empty verse-final W positions in alternate lines:

(31) VOICEless it / CRIES, (W)
       WINGless / FLUtters,
       TOOTHless / BITES, (W)
       MOUTHless / MUtters.
                    (*Hobbit* 79)

The frequency of trochaic words in this riddle indicates that verses one and three are tailless trochaic dimeters rather than headless iambic dimeters.[26] Verse one illustrates expansion of a W position in a trochaic foot. Scansion of (31) as iambic would be much less plausible, with four empty W positions rather than two and extrametrical syllables at the ends of even-numbered verses.

The meter assigned to Tom Bombadil allows for a great deal of rhythmical freedom. It is arranged as long lines of two verses, perhaps in order to have each printed line end with a rhyming word. The basic line pattern seems to consist of a tailless trochaic tetrameter followed by a trochaic trimeter. An excerpt from *Good King Wenceslas,* which realizes this pattern rather strictly, can serve as a yardstick for Tolkien's practice:

(32) BRIGHTly /SHONE the /MOON that / NIGHT, (W)
      THOUGH the / FROST was / CRUel

Bombadil's freer realization of the pattern often employs empty W positions verse-internally to create a boisterous effect:

(33) OLD (W) / TOM (W) / BOMba- / DIL (W)
      is a / MErry / FEllow
                                    (*FR* 171)

It is actually quite difficult to find verse-pairs in Bombadil's songs comparable to (32), with all positions filled except the verse-final (W) of the tetrameter. These do appear occasionally, however:

(34) SLENder / as the / WIllow- / WAND, (W)
      CLEARer / than the / WAter
                                    (*FR* 165)

Bombadil's trimeter verses usually close with a trochaic word, as above. The tetrameter verses often close with a three-syllable word like *Bombadil* or *willow-wand*. Since the last syllable of such a word normally has less prominent stress than the first, there is often a special kind of falling rhythm at the end of the tetrameters. In both trimeters and tetrameters, the first syllable of the verse is usually stressed, establishing a falling rhythm for Bombadil's verse generally. Trochaic feet are filled by trochaic words more frequently than in *Good King Wenceslas*. Tolkien takes special pains to ensure that his complex form is perceived as trochaic by readers most accustomed to iambic meter. Although details of rhythmical patterning are subject to extreme variation in this form, striking local regularities can be found, as in the following verse-pairs:

(35) LIGHT (W) / on the / BUdding / LEAF, (W)
      DEW (W) / on the / FEAther,
      WIND (W) / on the / Open / HILL, (W)
      BELLS (W) / on the / HEAther,
                                    (*FR* 169)

There are frequent mismatches to the abstract metrical pattern in (35), but the adjacent verse-pairs match each other perfectly in rhythm, syntactic structure, and placement of word boundaries.

When matching constraints are so relaxed that there is no perceptible regularity of form, rhythmic and syntactic parallels can become the most conspicuous features of Tolkien's versecraft:

(36) WHERE is the HELM and the HAUberk,
      and the BRIGHT HAIR FLOWing? //

> WHERE is the HAND on the *HARP*STRING,
> and the RED FIRE GLOWing? //
> WHERE is the SPRING and the HARvest
> and the TALL CORN GROWing?
>
> (*TT* 137)

The verses of this poem are printed as eight long lines in which the only constant feature seems to be a trochaic rhyming word at line end. Many of the other verses are quite unlike those above. Alliteration is frequent but not placed according to rule. I do not represent foot structure because I am not sure any is intended. What cannot be ignored is the near-identity of word rhythm and syntax in the adjacent verse-pairs of (36). The unexpected emergence of poetic structure from natural speech rhythm creates a special kind of folkloric effect here.[27]

Principle I allows small-scale metrical units to be projected from syllables and words, but it is also possible to construct a meter in which the verse is projected directly from a clause or whole sentence, with no metrical positions or feet. This kind of verse regularizes the inherent properties of clauses: meaning and syntactic structure. Once again we can turn to Treebeard, who exhibits this form. Consider the opening of an eighteen-line elegy:

> (37) In the willow-meads of Tasarinan I walked in the Spring.
> Ah! the sight and the smell of the Spring in Nan-tasarion!
> And I said that was good.
> I wandered in Summer in the elm-woods of Ossiriand.
> Ah! the light and the music in the Summer by the Seven Rivers of Ossir!
> And I thought that was best.
>
> (*TT* 84)

Excerpt (37) falls into two parallel sets of three verses each. The main assertion of the sentence in verse one, *I walked*, is paralleled by *I wandered* in verse four. Both verses are filled out by prepositional phrases of time and place, with *in the Spring* paralleled by *in Summer* and *in the willow-meads of Tasarinan* paralleled by *in the elm-woods of Ossiriand.* Verses one and four would be assigned the same underlying syntactic structure by a linguist, with the word order of verse one derived by optional movement of a prepositional phrase to sentence-initial position. Verses two and five are parallel exclamations. The visual element common to *the sight* and *the light* is supported by rhyme. Other senses are engaged by *the smell* and its parallel *the music.* Time and place are specified by parallel prepositional phrases with varied prepositions (*of the Spring: in the Summer: in Nan-Tasarion: by the Seven Rivers of Ossir*). The order of phrases is identical in these lines, with no optional movement. Lines three and six have strictly identical word order, with *said: thought* and *good: best* providing parallels of meaning. The parallels are supported in these particular lines by identity of syllable count and stress patterning, much as in (36). Many parallels of syntax and meaning in (37) are maintained in the following three-line units of the poem devoted to Autumn and

Winter. The identity of stress and syllable count in lines three and six is not maintained, however, showing that it is not an essential feature of this form.[28] The eagle's song of triumph (*RK* 292) adapts the form more freely in a style resembling English translations of the Old Testament psalms, which make conspicuous use of syntactic and semantic parallelism.[29]

Academic metrists can most often be found at work on rule systems that define a particular form with rigorous precision, distinguishing strings of words that the poet would accept as metrical from strings of similar length that the poet would reject. Decades of such efforts have led to the realization that a meter is not an isolated set of arbitrary requirements but one application among many of universal principles intimately bound up with the human language faculty. The diversity of forms used by Tolkien registers intuitive awareness of this recent finding, and his poems provide the perfect opportunity to illustrate its consequences for appreciation. If every meter applies a manageable set of principles, readers of poetry will benefit most from learning the principles rather than any particular application of them. Through persistent alternation of forms in his writing, Tolkien discourages us from focusing too myopically on any single form. His use of unassuming poet-characters allows for direct realization of basic patterns at regular intervals, highlighting principles that will be found to apply even in the most ambitious verse. As a result, Tolkien's readers find themselves well prepared to explore the world of poetry at large, from the earliest beginnings to the most recent experiments.

NOTES

1. Tolkien and Swann, *Road* (v). Readers interested in Elvish poetry should consult Tolkien's scansions in pp. 57–68 of this work.

2. For detailed application of this principle, see Jakobson, "Mácha's Verse."

3. Here and below I represent stressed syllables with capital letters, suppressing other capitals. In such representations, consonants are capitalized only if they would be pronounced in the same syllable with the stressed vowel, and hyphenation is phonetic.

4. Failure of a verse boundary to coincide with the boundary of a large phrase, clause, or sentence is traditionally called *enjambment*. Conspicuous examples can be found in the fourth stanza of a poem recited by the dwarves (*Hobbit* 24–25), where adjacent verses end in the middle of verb phrases, between verb and direct object (On silver necklaces they strung // The flowering stars, on crowns they hung // The dragon-fire).

5. I have used the format of example (2) for clarity, though other couplets in this meter (including example 1) are printed as long lines. The format of (2) is also used for some of the long-line couplets discussed below. From here on I will often omit the notation for verse boundaries (//) to minimize visual clutter.

6. For detailed discussion of mismatch at foot boundaries, see Kiparsky, "Rhythmic Structure." The term *bracketing mismatch* used in that article presupposes an audience of linguists.

7. On the importance of this principle in otherwise diverse poetic traditions, see Hayes, "Grid-based Theory" (373).

8. People who listen to Noah Adams on public radio can hear him pronounce his name as something like "No Adams," unifying the word-final vowel of *Noah* with the word-initial vowel of *Adams*. The *h* of *Noah* is of course silent.

9. Here I adapt Kiparsky's more general term *labeling mismatch* for analysis of stress-based meters in particular.

10. On combinations of stress and boundary mismatches avoided by canonical English poets, see Kiparsky (201–11).

11. The stress in the second syllable of *beyond* has uncertain metrical significance. Stress is often disregarded in prepositions even when they have two syllables, and similarly for common monosyllabic adverbs like *there* in example (3), which I represent as unstressed. The adverbs and long prepositions of highest frequency are the least likely to bear significant stress.

12. Kiparsky (191) finds that phrases consisting of two stressed monosyllables are usually placed within the same /WS/ foot by canonical English poets, as in (8), though verses like (7) are also acceptable. The special complexity of the mismatch in (7) may highlight the verb that causes it, adding a kind of expressive force.

13. For discussion of the musical dynamic, see Lerdahl and Jackendoff (179–88).

14. Thanks are due to poet Keith Waldrop for calling my attention to these useful terms.

15. See Halle and Keyser (23–24, 26). In the trochaic phrase *STOP it!*, the closely bound grammatical word following the verb has been transformed into something like a grammatical ending (encliticized), thus becoming ineligible for the stress on phrase-final words.

16. As with rules of ordinary speech, application of metrical rules is normally unconscious. For detailed discussion with evidence from illiterate bards, see Jakobson, "vowel alliteration."

17. The verse patterns most favored by Tolkien were already treated with contempt by Chaucer, notably in *Sir Thopas*. Many of these patterns were used with great skill by an anonymous contemporary of Chaucer's in *Sir Gawain and the Green Knight*, a poem edited by Tolkien. Distinguished practitioners of common meter include Emily Dickinson.

18. On the "rhythm rule" that assigns alternating prominence to three or more adjacent stressed syllables, see Kiparsky (218–20). His comparable example is *good old man*, where *old* has the weakest stress.

19. For additional examples see *Hobbit* (67–68, 80 [first riddle, last line], 82, 107–8, *FR* (193 [second line]).

20. Extrametrical syllables are parenthesized to show that they do not occupy metrical positions, being literally "outside the meter." See Kiparsky (234). Additional poems in long meter can be found in *Hobbit* (80 [second riddle], 107 [first orc song], 126–7, 247, 281); *FR* (58, 107, 112–13, 114, 128, 142, 148, 156, 249, 411–12, 466-67); *TT* (145, 183, 425); *RK* (323). A variant in *FR* (257–59) has an unstressed syllable on the last S position of every fourth line, with the rhyme beginning on the third S. Additional poems in common meter can be found in *Hobbit* (156); *FR* (441–42); *RK* (220). The form is printed as long lines in *FR* (484); *TT* (95–96, 104-5). Complex variants with expanded and empty W positions appear in *TT* (17–18 [printed as long lines], 253). The mother-goose variant in *FR* (215–16) incorporates an extra tetrameter at regular intervals.

21. A similar form is used for the immediately following poem in Elvish (*FR* 311) Tolkien identifies this as iambic tetrameter in *Road* (63). The horrible spell in the language of Sauron, which comes shortly afterwards (*FR* 332–33), has similar rhythm in its closing line.

22. Another instance of this form with closely related content (*FR* 322) realizes W positions in the same way.

23. And LI- / sten and HARK // till the END / of the DARK. The unique unbroken sequence of three expanded Ws in this couplet seems to produce a kind of acceleration toward closure. The last three stanzas end with an ultrashort verse (HA! HA!), presumably a one-foot monometer of the form /WS/, and the last two repetitions of this minimal refrain are preceded by other monometers that link their stanzas through something like medieval "tail rhyme" (in JUNE ... to our TUNE). More dimeters can be found in *Hobbit* (277–78); *TT* (281–82, 316).

24. More poems in Old English meter can be found in *TT* (149); *RK* (58–59, 132, 140, 141, 147, 308). A line of alliterative verse in Entish (*TT* 83) adheres to the basic principles of the form. For systematic discussion of alliterative versecraft, see Russom, *Old English Meter*.

25. Early Celtic poets made systematic use of repetition to support pattern switching. For detailed discussion see Travis, *Celtic Versecraft* (1–14). Tolkien also shifts to trochaic rhythm for all dimeters in a comic poem consisting mostly of longer iambic lines (*FR* 276–77). Regular placement of dimeters within stanzas supports the pattern switching in this case.

26. The relative frequency of trochaic words also prompts the reader to insert pauses that create trochaic feet in the elegy for Snowmane in *RK* (141).

27. Other poems with relaxed matching accompanied by parallelism can be found in *Hobbit* (79); *FR* (77); *RK* (167 [called doggerel by an obtuse character], 180, 283).

28. Compare line nine, "It was more than my desire"; line twelve, "My voice went up and sang in the sky." Since the rhythmical effects in excerpt (37) are incidental rather than structural, I have not capitalized its stressed syllables.

29. An obvious Biblical echo occurs at the conclusion of Tolkien's third stanza: *and he shall dwell among you // all the days of your life*. Compare this with the conclusion of the Twenty-third Psalm, for example.

WORKS CITED

Halle, Morris, and Samuel Jay Keyser. *English Stress: Its Form, Its Growth, and Its Role in Verse*. New York: Harper, 1971.

Hayes, Bruce. "A Grid-based Theory of English Meter." *Linguistic Inquiry* 14 (1983): 357–93.

Jakobson, Roman. "Toward a Description of Mácha's Verse." *Selected Writings*, vol. 5. The Hague: Mouton, 1979: 433-85.

——. "On the so-called vowel alliteration in Germanic verse." *Selected Writings*, vol. 5. The Hague: Mouton, 1979: 189–97.

Kiparsky, Paul. "The Rhythmic Structure of English Verse." *Linguistic Inquiry* 8 (1977): 189–247.

Lerdahl, Fred, and Ray Jackendoff. *A Generative Theory of Tonal Music*. Cambridge, MA: MIT P, 1983.

Russom, Geoffrey. *Old English Meter and Linguistic Theory*. Cambridge, Eng.: Cambridge UP, 1987.

Tolkien, J.R.R., and Donald Swann. *The Road Goes Ever On: A Song Cycle*. Boston: Houghton, 1967.

Travis, James. *Early Celtic Versecraft*. Ithaca, NY: Cornell UP, 1973.

Youmans, Gilbert. "Reconsidering Chaucer's Prosody." *English Historical Metrics.*
     Ed. C. B. McCully and J. J. Anderson. Cambridge, Eng.: Cambridge UP, 1996:
     185–209.

5

The Monsters Are Talismans and Transgressions: Tolkien and *Sir Gawain and the Green Knight*

Roger C. Schlobin

Any attempt at a source study of J.R.R. Tolkien's *Hobbit* and *LR*, especially with *Sir Gawain and the Green Knight* (*Gawain*), is dangerous. An extraordinarily well-read scholar, Tolkien brought a large hoard of reading and knowledge to any task, be it fiction or nonfiction. In some source studies, paths of transmission are difficult to identify; in Tolkien's case, they are far too easy. This is especially true when attempting to use such often slippery elements as character, setting, and device, which can be fraught with uncertainty. T. A. Shippey's extraordinary work with philology, in *The Road to Middle-earth* and elsewhere, provides far greater precision. Nonetheless, there are tempting literary possibilities for the origins of Tolkien's fantasy epic in *Gawain*, but without an effort as dedicated as John Livingston Lowes's *The Road to Xanadu: A Study into the Ways of the Imagination* (1927); it may be that Tolkien is too eclectic to be pinned to any specific inspirations although, perhaps, not quite as impossible as C. S. Lewis indicated: "No one ever influenced Tolkien—you might as well try to influence a bandersnatch" (Carpenter 201).

Yet even with the possibility of misadventure so immediate, *Gawain* is a very alluring prospect for a source if, ultimately, from only a moral or philosophical perspective. This proposition is made even more daunting than just Tolkien's erudition could make it because he never mentioned any specific influences and there is very little that is original to *Gawain* (cf. Brewer). As with most great literature, it is not what the romance does but how it does it. Thus, Tolkien could have just as easily found a generic element of the romance not specifically in it but in any one of a number of its sources and analogues. Still, John M. Fyler speculates that the romance "was much on Tolkien's mind when he was writing the trilogy" (120–22), and his observation draws merit from Tolkien's long involvement with it. He first encountered *Gawain* at King Edward's School, probably when he was about fifteen or sixteen (Carpenter 35), and it remained a lifelong preoccupation and a focus for much of his scholarly activity. Christopher Tolkien, Miriam Youngerman Miller, and Shippey summarize Tolkien's formal activity with *Gawain*: his first edition in 1925, his W. P. Ker lecture in 1953 (reprinted in *Essays*), and his verse translation in 1975 (*Essays* 1–2; Miller 345; Shippey, "Tolkien" 213–14). He struggled with his translation and reported in September of 1963 that he hoped it would go to press soon (*Letters* 333), but by November of 1965, he was still trying to finish the apparatus, especially the introduction (*Letters* 364). Tolkien had one other excursion into explicitly Arthurian fiction, his unfinished poem *The Fall of Arthur*. He abandoned it sometime in the mid-1930's despite enthusiastic reactions by E. V. Gordon and R.W. Chambers (Carpenter 168) and his own 1955 indication that he still hoped to finish it (*Letters* 219).[1]

Exactly how tempting sources can be, as well as how hazardous, is illustrated by Miller's odd observation that Smaug is an obvious allusion to the dragon in *Beowulf* (346). Certainly, both episodes include a thief, a ravaging dragon and its hoard, and a dragon slayer. Unfortunately, these similarities are far too superficial to be convincing. On one hand, in *Beowulf*, the protagonist is abandoned by his thanes and aided only by Wiglaf. Together, the heroic two directly attack the dragon, and it is slain through their prowess. Beowulf dies to save his people (not "needlessly" as Jane Chance has suggested [152]). Wiglaf survives as a promise that the Anglo-Saxon cycle of woe to joy to woe may, one day, turn to joy again. On the other hand, in *Hobbit*, Smaug has considerably more personality than Beowulf's dragon, as well as a history (31–34); he is a sentient, conversational creature (212–16), not just a beast. Bilbo, the company's designated "burglar" (31), and the Anglo-Saxon thief do randomly steal a valuable object, but Bilbo steals a second time and his prize, the Arkenstone of Thrain, is specific, not random, and is pivotal later in the narrative (257). Furthermore, Tolkien's characters do not advance on the dragon as Beowulf and Wiglaf do. Bilbo and company fear destruction, and they rely on stealth rather than confrontation. Smaug is not even slain by Bilbo or any of his company but by Bard, Captain of Esgaroth, whose black arrow finds the one missing scale in the dragon's armor (237). Tolkien's source for Smaug could have been any number of childhood dragon tales, heard long before his formal education began. For example, he was fascinated with Andrew Lang's *Red Fairy Book*, especially the tale of Fáfnir and Sigurðr (Carpenter 22–23). Also, he could just as easily have discovered or constructed the ubiquitous combination of the dragon, hoard, thief, and battle in the *Poetic Edda* and other Northern European epics (Garmonsway and Simpson 333-9), the Roman tale of Regulus and the Carthaginian serpent (264-241 B.C.E.), the Assyro-Babylonian Marduk and Tiamat-as-dragon, or even the Chinese treasure dragon fu-ts'ang lung (Shuker 89). In short, the hoard-coveting dragon versus the hero is no more distinctive to *Beowulf* as a source than its mead hall and *wyrd* are.[2]

Miller, drawing extensively on Tolkien's "On Fairy-Stories" (in *Essays* 109–61) also suggests parallels between the settings of *Gawain* and *LR*. However, to postulate secondary or tertiary worlds in medieval romance (348) and to suggest that medieval romance could be considered fantasy (350) neglect the period's immanent cosmology (cf. Huizinga, esp. 220–33). Little occurred that was not "meaning filled," so much so that authors resorted to dream visions to suspend emphatically the supernaturally saturated everyday. Certainly, in 1400, Gawain's excursions into wonder would be questioned only by the most skeptical or empirical. This, of course, would not prevent the creative Tolkien from seeing it as fantasy, although the scholarly Tolkien would have been shocked at such conclusions. In fact, his exposures to secondary worlds are by no means restricted to a modern reading of *Gawain*, and by "On Fairy-Stories'" first presentation (1939), Tolkien was already forty-seven years old and the beneficiary of a large reading experience, some of which contained alternate worlds. For example, he was well aware of the works of William Morris, George MacDonald, and his friends C. S. Lewis and Charles Williams (Carpenter 69–70, 242, 150) although he had varying affections for the first two and very little for Lewis's *Chronicles of Narnia* (Carpenter 201).[3]

Characters have also presented alluring possibilities to scholars. John M. Fyler draws a parallel between Frodo's and Gawain's "passive endurance" (121), and Miller suggests one between Tom Bombadil and the Green Knight/Bertilak. Certainly, both Frodo's and Gawain's commitment to their quests demonstrate their comparable endurance. However, Gawain is hardly passive. His aggressiveness is demonstrated by his willingness to stop Arthur from accepting the Green Knight's challenge, his energetic response to Bertilak's wife on the second day, and his prompt readiness for combat after he has been nicked by the Green Knight's axe. No, Gawain is forceful in his dedication, not passive. Passivity seems to be the wrong description for Frodo as well. Hobbits are resilient. Like the archetypal fool (Schlobin, "Survival" 124), Hobbits consistently bounce back; they are indomitable. For example, three hobbits, lest Sméagol/Gollum's origins be forgotten (*FR* 82–83), arrive at the Crack of Doom. Furthermore, there "is a seed of courage hidden (often deeply, it is true) in the heart of the fattest and most timid hobbit, waiting for some final and desperate danger to make it grow" (*FR* 192). Samwise is probably a better illustration of this resiliency than Frodo since he is not infected by the Ring and is more of a "pure hobbit." After the Ring's destruction and Frodo's acceptance of "the end of all things," it is Samwise who says, "But after coming all that way I don't want to give up yet. It's not like me, somehow, if you understand" (*RK* 275).

Miller's suggested parallel between the Green Knight and Tom Bombadil also seems flawed. Both, as Miller suggests, have lovely wives, are physically similar when Bertilak is in human form (353–54), and are lords of small domains. These do not seem to be the compelling parallels that constitute a source relationship. Miller cites John Gardner's observation, in *The Complete Works of the Gawain Poet* (1965), that the Green Knight is a symbolic representation of the forces of nature just as Tom Bombadil is the controller of nature in his domain and sees them both as "nature figures" (354–55), which some Medieval scholars have identified as a vegetation numen, although the Green Knight is a generative figure only in appearance – an icon without substance. However, Bertilak is only associated with the vegetation god, and thus like Bombadil, when he is temporarily the Green Knight, not when he's himself. More pertinently, Bombadil is very much his own person whereas Bertilak is Morgan le Faye's pawn in either guise. Bombadil is not "morally neutral," as Miller asserts (355). Tom knows "about evil things and good things, things friendly and things unfriendly, cruel things and kind things" (*FR* 178). He is certainly morally active and benevolent enough to sing Merry and Pippin free from Old Man Willow, deliver the hobbits from the Old Forest, and save them from the Barrow-wight and arm them (*FR* 166, 194–98). Gandalf and Elrond explain that the Ring has no power over him, a fact foreshadowed by its not making him invisible, and that it is of utterly no interest to him. He would be a "most unsafe guardian" (*FR* 348) since he would just forget the Ring or throw it away. He is known to the elves as "oldest and fatherless," a creature from a cosmos that precedes them all, and while he could not defy Sauron, he would probably be the last to fall (*FR* 179–81, 347–78). Thus, while Tom is not simply "morally neutral" and is enormously powerful in his realm, he is just not part of the game of the Ring. He's an anachronism and not one of the strategic pieces that even the ancient Ents are or that Morgan makes Bertilak and his wife. As such, Bombadil anticipates Merlin's later lack of effectiveness due to his better-left-undisturbed magic in C. S. Lewis's *That Hideous Strength* (1945).[4]

Among the more intriguing parallels between the *LR* and *Gawain* is their absentee villains. Sauron is not visible, and Morgan le Faye appears only briefly. While Sauron exists in person in a number of *The History of Middle-earth* volumes—most notably in "Beren and Luthien" in *Silm* —in *Hobbit* and *LR*, he exists only as a disembodied presence, described nominalistically rather than incarnately. Both work their mayhem through pawns and, like most of fantasy's villains, are the creative nemeses of conservative good (cf. Schlobin, "In Search" passim). Morgan serves as the scapegoat by absolving Bertilak and his lady from the responsibility for their acts (Benson 35), thus allowing the two knights to part as friends after the nick at the Green Chapel. Bertilak's and his lady's equivalents in *LR* are the Ringwraiths and the Mouth of Sauron as well as, perhaps, the Ring itself. However, Tolkien never recognizes Morgan as the romance's puppeteer. He insists that Bertilak's abode and the place of temptation is "a real chivalrous castle, no mirage of enchantment or abode of fays, where the laws of courtesy, hospitality, and morality run" (*Essays* 82). Also, Tolkien believes that "we learn in the end that the lord and lady were conniving" (*Essays* 82). This is very odd since he certainly knew of Morgan, as his note in the first edition of *Gawain* indicates (Tolkien and Gordon 130), but he attributes no significance to her in his discussions of the romance, and mentions her directly only in regard to the Green Knight's confidence in her and indirectly in asserting that even "*faierie*" is "ultimately under God" (*Essays* 103). It is hard to imagine that he did not know of Lucy Allen Paton's 1903 study of Morgan's hatred of Arthur and its pervasiveness in medieval literature (13–24) or of Morton W. Bloomfield's and Albert B. Friedman's later confirmations of this animosity. It was so apparent to medieval audiences that Morgan is eliminated from the later *The Grene Knight*, a debased version of *Gawain* (Tolkien and Gordon xx), and replaced with the neutral Agostes to shift *Grene Knight*'s focus to *camaraderie* rather than antagonism (Schlobin, "*The Turke*" 112). Perhaps Tolkien ignores Morgan because he chose to focus on Gawain's confession and absolution (Shippey, "Tolkien" 217) or on what he perceives as the work's didacticism (*Essays* 73), which requires free will. Of course, another possibility is Tolkien's general disinterest in female characters in *LR* and elsewhere; he does, for example, also omit Grendel's mother from "The Monsters and the Critics." The wonderfully willful and assertive Éowyn is the only significant, multidimensional woman amid numerous male ones. The Lady Galadriel is important, but she is idealized beyond humanity and singular. Hobbit wives appear, most notably Rosie; Entwives have disappeared and Goldberry entertains, but they are homely rather than critical presences. Given Tolkien's inability to see Morgan, it is unlikely that as an absentee villain, she had any influence on the creation of Sauron on any basis other than the most subliminal.

Another tempting connection is the works' heroes. Miller suggests that both *Gawain* and *LR* are heroic quests that they can be analyzed within Joseph Campbell's monomyth, and that Frodo is a hero (346–47). Both share the departure and the arduous tasks, although Gawain's are more amorous than difficult until he must kneel in the Green Chapel. However, Frodo does not make the cyclic return, the departure and return, that Gawain does, and if anyone completes the monomyth, it would be Samwise. Rather, Frodo pauses in the Shire, largely watching others scour it, before he departs with the rest of the marvelous characters for Valinor (*RK* 378). Tolkien explained this to his son, Christopher, prior to writing it:

> The Book will prob. end up with Sam. Frodo will naturally become too ennobled and rarified by the achievement of the great Quest, and will pass West with all the great figures; but S[amwise] will settle down to the Shire and gardens and inns. C[harles] Williams who is reading it all says the great thing is that its *centre* is not in strife and war and heroism (though they are understood and depicted) but in freedom, peace, ordinary life and good liking. (*Letters* 105).

Like Gawain, Frodo is bound by the same *geas* that compels Gawain and all the virtuous and inescapable promises that even affect Gollum (*TT* 369) and ultimately extend to Samwise (*TT* 429). However, on one hand, Gawain's motivations are honor (or the avoidance of shame) and his fear for Arthur's safety, while, on the other hand, Frodo's is love (*RK* 225; *Letters* 327). Although honor would be too lofty a virtue for hobbits to discuss or claim, Frodo always tries to avoid being "'faithless'" (*TT* 373), and he believes that sacred promises are such in Middle-earth that "all but the wickedest feared to break them" (*FR* 31). Even the dead, the Men of the Mountains, are ultimately drawn to honor theirs (*RK* 59, 69–70). Gandalf, also, makes his own specific commitment quite clear: "' [T]he rule of no land is mine. . . . But all worthy things that are in peril as the world now stands, those are my care'" (*RK* 29).

Of course, like Gawain, Frodo "fails his ultimate test" (Miller 360; Tolkien, *Letters* 251) but for very different reasons. Gawain's fall is because of selfish reasons, although Tolkien either resisted or rejected this interpretation. Gawain is nicked because he takes the green girdle in the false hope that it will save his life, a transgression he takes far more seriously than Arthur's court, which is overjoyed just to see him alive again. Gawain's failure is individual and moral; Frodo's is not. Frodo, too, believes the Ring will be to his advantage if he keeps it, but this isn't really personal or selfish because he never masters the Ring. Ever it drags at him as he suffers under the glare of Sauron's "Eye" (*TT* 296), a dread and a despite later echoed so virulently in Stephen R. Donaldson's *Thomas Covenant* series. The Ring is Sauron's "creature"; like a familiar, it is saturated with his transferred power and belongs only to him just as he belongs to it. Under the Ring's spell, Frodo mistakenly believes he can claim it as his own and rejects his task (*RK* 269). As Tolkien explained, "I do not think Frodo was a *moral* failure. At the last moment the pressure of the Ring would reach its maximum—impossible, I should have said, for any one to resist, certainly after long possession, months of increasing torment, and when starved and exhausted" (*Letters* 326). Later, he adds, "If you [Miss J. Burn] re-read all the passages dealing with Frodo and the Ring, I think you will see that not only was it *quite impossible* for him to surrender the Ring, in act or will, especially at its point of maximum power [the Crack of Doom], but that this failure was adumbrated from far back" (*Letters* 251; also, see no. 246). Also, neither Gawain nor Frodo was strong enough. As Tolkien observes:

> Frodo had become a considerable person, but of a special kind: in spiritual enlargement rather than in increase of physical or mental power; his will was much stronger than it had been, but so far it had been exercised in resisting not using the ring and with the object of destroying it. He needed time, much time, before he could control the Ring or (which in this case is the same) before it could control him; before his will and arrogance could grow to a stature in which he could dominate other major hostile wills. (*Letters* 329)

Boromir of Gondor may be closer to the more traditional failed hero, like Gawain, just as Aragorn is to the noble hero. Miller indicates that Boromir fails in "his own trial of temptation by the Ring" (359). His early attempt to convince Gandalf of the Ring's efficacy as a weapon of their (or his) own foreshadows his later attempt to take it from Frodo (*FR* 350, 479–80, 516–18; *TT* 289). His madness passes, but he does a far greater penance than Gawain for his transgression (*TT* 12; *RK* 99). However, Boromir is difficult to recognize in this capacity because, despite all tales of his earlier prowess, he lacks Gawain's and Aragorn's general nobility or sensitivity to the noble. He even doubts the Lady Galadriel, for which Aragorn chastises him (*FR* 465). In this, he perhaps serves as the archetypal naysayer just as Unferth does in *Beowulf*. In short, Aragorn is more like Gawain in his chivalry and protectiveness whereas Boromir does have something of Gawain in him in his valiant, yet doomed protection of Merry and Pippin. Ultimately, it is important to note that Frodo, in *"The story of the Nine-fingered Frodo and the Ring of Doom"* (*RK* 275), is the Ring-bearer, not the Ring-destroyer (that position falls to the ill-fated Gollum). Frodo is not the traditional hero. In *LR*, traditional heroes, in the Campbell monomyth mode, are relegated to being the diversion. Gandalf's, Aragorn's, and the rest of the Fellowship's final task is only to draw and misdirect the Eye of Sauron in futile assault (*RK* 187) while Frodo and Sam do the most significant work.

Moreover, the talismans in the two works are also potent, yet for opposing reasons. The green girdle is a placebo but has power because of Bertilak's wife's persuasiveness and because Gawain so desperately wants it to be real. Tolkien's Ring, however, is real with powers and desires of its own, so much so that it functions as a character. Gandalf warns of Sauron's device's self-determination, "'A Ring of Power looks after itself, Frodo. *It* may slip off treacherously, but its keeper never abandons it'" (*FR* 83). The wizard further relates that Bilbo became "'*Thin and stretched* . . . [a] sign that the ring was getting control'" (*FR* 73). Tolkien reiterates this immense and corrupting power a number of times: "the power of Evil in the world is *not* finally resistible by incarnate creatures, however 'good'" (*Letters* 252). "It is possible for the good, even the saintly, to be subjected to a power of evil which is too great for them to overcome—in themselves" (*Letters* 252–53). Frodo becomes the Ring's puppet just as Bertilak and his lady are Morgan's. Gawain, in contrast, might initially be motivated by chivalry, a faith he wholly embraced, and later blemished by inappropriate self-preservation, but in either case, his negative motivations come from within. Frodo's come from without. In the end, it may be that there is no source relationship, that *Gawain* does not have a functional set of similarities with *Hobbit* and *LR*. Yet it might also be that the parallels are philosophical and moral, rather than direct and specific.

As is typical in fantasy's and medieval romance's extreme moral orders, Tolkien is quick to condemn the evil and forgive the good. He might appear to be very patient with Saruman, Gollum, and the cannibalistic Wormtongue, despite their foulness, but they have important functions at the end of the epic that justify their survival, and they perish before closure. For the good, there is a strong sympathy toward error and mercy in Tolkien's idiosyncratic interpretation of the medieval poem and his epic. In his analysis of *Gawain*, unlike many other scholars, he concentrates on Gawain's confession and absolution (*Essays* 87–88), not on his fault. This is a very forgiving stance. For him, the poem is didactic, not only for the audience, but for Gawain as well (73). As he explained, "We have seen a gentle courtly knight learn by bitter experience the perils of Courtesy" (99). This emphasis on correction and education, through experience, seems to extend into *LR* as well, especially in a very telltale passage in which Gandalf instructs Pippin after the hobbit was drawn to gaze into the Palantir that Wormtongue threw from Orthanc:

"You knew you were behaving wrongly and foolishly; and you told yourself so, though you did not listen. I did not tell you all this before, because it is only by musing on all that has happened that I have at last understood, even as we ride together. But if I had spoken sooner, it would not have lessened your desire, or made it easier to resist. On the contrary! No, the burned hand teaches best. After that advice about fire goes to the heart." (*TT* 255)

However, there are far greater lessons and penalties in *Hobbit* and *LR* than burned hands and nicked necks, lessons that benefit others at the sufferers' expense. These fall initially to Bilbo and ultimately to Frodo as he suffers far greater hardships than Gawain's three days and personal humiliation. In fact, Frodo's ordeal and fall makes the knight's appear domestic. Tolkien goes out of his way to stress Frodo's martyrdom: "There exists the possibility of being placed in positions beyond one's power. In which case (as I believe) salvation from ruin will depend on something apparently unconnected: the general sanctity (and humility and mercy) of the sacrificial person" (*Letters* 252). It is within this context that

> Frodo undertook his quest out of love—to save the world he knew from disaster at his own expense, if he could; and also in complete humility, acknowledging that he was wholly inadequate to the task. His real contract was only to do what he could, to try to find a way, and to go as far on the road as his strength of mind and body allowed. He did that. I do not myself see that the breaking of his mind and will under demonic pressure after torment was any more a *moral* failure than the breaking of his body would have been—say, by being strangled by Gollum, or crushed by a falling rock. (*Letters* 327)

Throughout his *Letters*, Tolkien stresses the inevitability of Frodo's (and, by analogy, Gawain's?) fall to greater and stronger forces and the necessity for the Fellowship and friends to accomplish an effective self-sacrifice:

> It is possible for the good, even the saintly, to be subjected to a power of evil which is too great for them to overcome—in themselves. In this case the cause (not the 'hero') was triumphant, because by the exercise of pity, mercy, and forgiveness of injury, a situation was produced in which all was redressed and disaster averted. (*Letters* 252–53)

This necessity for generous and unfailing support to overcome evil, when it cannot be done individually, is stressed throughout *LR*. It may be Boromir's death; the Elves' *lembas*, which, along with Samwise, are all that sustain Frodo (*RK* 256); the heroes' diversion at the Gates of Mordor; the eagles' rescues; the Ents' purposeful agitation; Tom Bomdadil's sanctuary and rescues; Éowyn's and Merry's courage at the Battle of Pelennor Fields; Shadowfax's bearing of Gandalf; Ghân-buri-Ghân's guidance to Gondor. The list seems endless. It is within this context that Gollum's survival is justified, not only because of his role at the Crack of Doom, but for what Frodo's kindness gains for him amid a much larger context:

> Frodo had done what he could and spent himself completely (as an instrument of Providence) and produced a situation in which the object of his quest could be achieved. His humility (with which he began) and his sufferings were justly rewarded by the highest honour; and his exercise of patience and mercy towards Gollum gained him Mercy; his failure was redressed. (*Letters* 326)

Thus, within the violence of the epic form and within his interpretation of *Gawain*, Tolkien chooses the kindlier virtues—forgiveness, mercy, pity, learning, nobility, humility, friendship, loyalty—much as the *Gawain* poet does. Frodo and Gawain are both lauded for their accomplishments. This does not mean that arduous prices are not paid in *LR*: Denethor falls to despair, Théoden to the Lord of the Nazgûl; Gandalf falls with the Balrog and will survive only until his task is done (*TT* 106); and Bilbo and Frodo will never again be the carefree creatures they once were, which is why they are granted entry into Valinor with the Elves while the rest of the hobbits remain behind. The Ring almost consumes Frodo and Bilbo, leaving their flesh frail, if long-lived, but their spirits glowing. This is because Tolkien did create an immanent world in Middle-earth just as the *Gawain* poet reflected his. Nothing is without meaning; higher goals and powers must be served. Individual sacrifices are costly, but they are for the greatest good as the world is left safe. Thus, while it is probably almost certain that nothing can be directly proved regarding the influence of *Gawain*, Tolkien's epic does share an intrinsic commitment to responsible virtue, which may be the result of the discovery of a great medieval poet by an impressionable teenager.

NOTES

I am indebted to Richard West of the University of Wisconsin Libraries for his intelligence, support, and proofreading of significant portions and references in this essay. Also, Daniel Timmons has been a welcome source of materials that have saved me significant amounts of time and energy. Douglas A. Anderson graciously and effectively proofread and commented.

1. Reportedly, some of Tolkien's poetry is currently being edited, but there is no estimated publication date.

2. *Beowulf* was likely a source for "Turambar and the Foalókë" (cf. *BLT2* 105–12, *Silm* 266–73) and for *Hobbit*, and Fáfnir may have been the source for Smaug. See Jonathan Evans's essay in this collection for an excellent discussion of Tolkien's sources for his dragons.

3. Tolkien evaluated Lewis's *The Lion, the Witch and the Wardrobe* by saying to Roger Lancelyn Green, "It really won't do! I mean to say: 'Nymphs and Their Ways, The Love-Life of a Faun!'" And later, he remarked, "It is sad that 'Narnia' and all that parts of C.S.L.'s work should remain outside the range of my sympathy, as much of my work was outside his" (Carpenter 201). For an extended discussion of Tolkien's reaction to Lewis's Narnia, see Joe R. Christopher's "J.R.R. Tolkien: Narnian Exile." *Mythlore* No. 55 (Autumn 1988): 37-45; No. 56 (Winter 1988): 17–23. For his relationship with Charles Williams, see John D. Rateliff's "'And Something Yet Remains to Be Said': Tolkien and Williams." *Mythlore* No. 45 (Spring 1986): 48–54.

4. The chronological relationship between Tolkien's Bombadil and Lewis's Merlin is difficult to ascertain. Tolkien obviously created his character (1934) before Lewis did his, and Tolkien had completed the first twelve chapters of *The Fellowship of The Ring* by early 1939. Lewis would have heard these, then, before he began writing *That Hideous Strength* in 1942.

WORKS CITED

Benson, Larry D. *Art and Tradition in Sir Gawain and the Green Knight*. New Brunswick: Rutgers UP, 1965.

Bloomfield, Morton W. "*Sir Gawain and the Green Knight*: An Appraisal." *Critical Studies of Sir Gawain and the Green Knight*. Ed. Donald R. Howard and Christian Zacher. Notre Dame and London: U of Notre Dame P, 1968. 24–55.

Brewer, Elisabeth. *From Cuchulainn to Gawain: Sources and Analogues of Sir Gawain and the Green Knight*. Cambridge, UK: Brewer, 1973.

Carpenter, Humphrey. *Tolkien: A Biography*. Boston: Houghton Mifflin, 1977.

Chance, Jane. "Tolkien and His Sources." *Approaches to Teaching Sir Gawain and the Green Knight*. Ed. Miriam Youngerman Miller and Jane Chance. New York: MLA, 1986. 151-55.

Friedman, Albert B. "Morgan le Fay in *Sir Gawain and the Green Knight*." *Speculum* 35 (1960): 260–74. Rpt. *Sir Gawain and Pearl: Critical Essays*. Ed. Robert J. Blanch. Bloomington and London: Indiana UP, 1966. 135–58.

Fyler, John M. "Freshman Composition: Epic and Romance."*Approaches to Teaching Sir Gawain and the Green Knight*. Ed. Miriam Youngerman Miller and Jane Chance. New York: MLA, 1986. 120–22.

Garmonsway, G. N., and Jacqueline Simpson. *Beowulf and Its Analogues*. New York: Dutton, 1971.

Huizinga, Johan. *The Autumn of the Middle Ages*. 1921. Trans. Rodney J. Payton and Ulrich Mammitzsch. Chicago: U of Chicago P, 1996.

Loomis, Laura Hibbard. "*Gawain and the Green Knight*." *Critical Studies of Sir Gawain and the Green Knight*. Ed. Donald R. Howard and Christian Zacher. Notre Dame and London: U of Notre Dame P, 1968. 3–23.

Manning, Stephen. "A Psychological Interpretation of *Sir Gawain and the Green Knight*." *Critical Studies of Sir Gawain and the Green Knight*. Ed. Donald R. Howard and Christian Zacher. Notre Dame and London: U of Notre Dame P, 1968. 279–94.

Miller, Miriam Youngerman. "'Of sum mayn meruayle, Þat he myṣt Ìt trawe': *The Lord of the Rings and Sir Gawain and the Green Knight* [sic]." *Studies in Medievalism* 3.3 (Winter 1991): 345–65.

Paton, Lucy Allen. *Studies in the Fairy Mythology of Arthurian Romance*. 2nd ed. 1903. New York: Burt Franklin, 1970.

Schlobin, Roger C. "In Search of Creative Solitude in Modern Fantasy: An Essay on the Fascination with Evil." *Journal of the Fantastic in the Arts* Summer 1990: 5–13.

——. "The Survival of the Fool in Modern Heroic Fantasy." *Aspects of Fantasy: Essays from the Second International Conference on the Fantastic in Literature andFilm*. Ed. William Coyle. Westport, CT, and London: Greenwood, 1986. 123–30.

——. "*The Turke and Gowin, The Marriage of Sir Gawaine*, and *The Grene Knight*: Three Editions with Introductions." Diss. Ohio State University, 1971. *DA* 32 (1971–72): 6391A.

Shippey, T.A. *The Road to Middle-earth*. London: Unwin, 1982. Rev. enl. ed. London:

HarperCollins, 1993.

——. "Tolkien and the *Gawain*-Poet." *Mythlore* 80 (1995): 213–19. *Proceedings of the J.R.R. Tolkien Centenary Conference 1992*. Ed. Patricia Reynolds and Glen GoodKnight.

Shuker, Karl. *Dragons: A Natural History*. New York: Simon, 1995.

6

The Sins of Middle-earth: Tolkien's Use of Medieval Allegory

Charles W. Nelson

During the Council of Elrond, the elven lord declares that "nothing is evil in the beginning. Even Sauron was not so" (*FR* 350). This statement reflects Tolkien's version of creation in which Erú intended that everything should be good. Yet even early in *Hobbit*, evil obviously exists in Middle-earth—and not only in Dol Guldur—as first the trolls and then the goblins demonstrate their wickedness all too clearly. After the almost fatal adventure on Caradhras in *FR*, Aragorn remarks that "there are many evil and unfriendly things in the world . . . that are not in league with Sauron, but with purposes of their own" (378). Among these are Shelob, the Balrog, and the "nameless things" gnawing at the roots of the world that Gandalf observes during his pursuit of the Balrog under Moria (*TT* 128). All these instances remind us of the extent to which evil has permeated Middle-earth.

Another kind of evil in Tolkien's world poses an even greater threat to the good characters: the wickedness within members of the various races of Middle-earth. Sméagol, Boromir, Saruman, and Denethor are all examples. None of them were villainous at first, but their moral failures endangered the Fellowship and its mission. Indeed, almost every character in the story could turn to evil. In a series of related scenes, every major figure is tempted by the power of the Ring and resists or fails. Gandalf explains that the power in the Ring works on the major flaw of all characters and by this means attempts to turn them to evil (*FR* 91).

Thus in the adventures of his main characters, Tolkien shows the origins of evil through the faults of individuals; moreover his work as a whole may embody a moral philosophy. Tolkien suggests this aim in his letter to Milton Waldman:

> Myth and fairy-story must, as all art, reflect and contain in solution elements of moral and religious truth (or error), but not explicit, not in the known form of the primary 'real' world. (*Letters* 144)

In one sense, then, *LR* may be a morality tale in which Tolkien's entertaining adventures teach serious moral lessons. He has declared this purpose of his writing:

> [T]he encouragement of good morals in this real world by the ancient device of exemplifying them in unfamiliar embodiments that may tend to bring them home. (*Letters* 194)

But how does Tolkien go about this? Ever since the publication of *LR* there has been much discussion of his use of multiple races and peoples in his sub-creation of Middle-earth. Many critics such as Paul Kocher in *Master of Middle-earth*, Randel Helms in *Tolkien's World*, Robert Reilly in "Tolkien and the Fairy Story," and Richard Purtill in *J.R.R. Tolkien: Myth, Morality and Religion* have examined these characters in detail and theorized about their roles in the trilogy. Purtill even begins to examine the traditional Seven Deadly Sins as exhibited by the peoples of Tolkien's world, but soon leaves off (76). Given his understanding of the Middle Ages, it would seem plausible that Tolkien may have used his various peoples in a similar way to medieval writers—as the personified figures of the principle vices in the Christian code known as the Seven Deadly Sins: Greed, Pride, Envy, Sloth, Gluttony, Lechery, and Anger. With her emphasis on repentance and goodness, the medieval Church naturally provided a parallel list of the Saintly Virtues, which were the remedies for these sins: Generosity, Humility, Meekness, Zeal, Abstinence, Chastity, and Patience. These lists are of ancient origin and appear first in the writings of the desert monks and anchorites early in the Christian era; these traits were referred to as the faults that most disturb the monastic life (Bloomfield 23).

These figures of sin were most popular and best known during the Middle Ages, when they were used more than any other allegorical depiction to graphically portray the effects of these most ancient of vices (Robertson 118). Chaucer's the "Parson's Tale" is just one example of a detailed and graphic treatise on these sins and their attendant vices. Well into the twentieth century, the official catechism of the Catholic Church (in which faith Tolkien was raised and lived) still used these traditional figures showing the results of sin to impress their seriousness on the young (*Baltimore* 48). What could be more natural than for Tolkien to adapt this venerable device to his own purposes as part of the moral teaching that he acknowledges his work has? He clearly uses this device and points his readers in the right direction through his insistence on the greed displayed by the dwarves and the way in which it shaped their characters. From this starting point, the identification of his races and their characteristic sins clearly show themselves.

Here we will consider the mortal Men and the shapes of the old men assumed by the Maiar who came to Middle-earth in the guise of wizards as one race, and the Orcs, Hobbits, Ents, and Elves as the others. Their characteristic sins as Tolkien describes them are: Dwarves-Greed, Men-Pride, Elves-Envy, Ents-Sloth, Hobbits-Gluttony, Wormtongue-Lechery, and Orcs-Anger. Among the medieval writers who describe and depict the Seven Deadly Sins, William Langland in his *Piers the Plowman* (ca. 1385), John Gower in his *Confessio Amantis* (1390), and Geoffrey

Chaucer in his "Pardoner's Tale" (ca. 1395) give the fullest portrayal of each sin individually and include the sub-vices attendant to the major transgressions. These works will be our guides in this examination.

Since Tolkien clearly depicts the dwarves as representations of Greed, it is appropriate to begin with this Deadly Sin, especially because in the framework of Tolkien's own world, possessiveness is one of the worst of transgressions; this is starkly evident in Sauron's overwhelming desire to own all of Middle-earth and its peoples, in Saruman's desperate attempt to control all the lands around Orthanc, and in Gollum's insane attachment to the One Ring. Interestingly, Chaucer's Pardoner repeats this sentiment in the tag line to his sermon, "*Radix malorum est cupiditas*—Greed is the source of all evil" (*Tales* 336); Chaucer also depicts a scene of friends murdering another friend for possession of the gold, just as Smeagol murders Deagol for the same reason. Gower, as well, reminds us that in the beginning, Adam and Eve lived happily in the garden; there was no strife for worldly goods because all things were held in common and no one wanted what he did not have. Soon, however, avarice appeared with all the other wrongs associated with it as Adam and Eve argued even about which parts of the garden each owned (Gower 179). And Langland makes the figure representing this sin a gross caricature:

> And then came Covetousness; no words can describe him, he looked so hungry and hollow, such a crafty old codger! He had beetling brows and thick, puffy lips, and his eyes were as bleary as a blind old hag's. His baggy cheeks sagged down below his chin, flapping about like a leather wallet, and trembling with old age. (66)

This portrayal could be compared to the condition of Thrain when Gandalf finds him "witless and wandering" in the dungeons of Dol Goldur (*Hobbit* 35). It does not take long for this sin to appear in *Hobbit*; at Bilbo's unexpected party, he perceives through the dwarves' songs their "love of beautiful things made by hand and by cunning . . . the desire of the hearts of the dwarves" (25). Much later, Thorin will not admit his real mission to the elf king for fear of having to share the treasure of Smaug with someone else. When the company finally gets into the Lonely Mountain, the dwarves' fascination with and delight in the gold and jewels goes on far longer than Bilbo's, whose thoughts naturally turn to the more practical considerations of food and drink.

In *LR*, we learn that the greed of the dwarves specifically for mithril (whose worth was ten times that of gold and later beyond price since it was so scarce) brought about their own destruction and downfall: "[T]hey delved too greedily and too deep, and disturbed that from which they fled, Durin's Bane [the Balrog]" (*FR* 413). As mentioned above, Gower also describes the attendant vices that come along with the Seven Deadly Sins. First, with Greed comes Covetousness, which Thorin displays when he talks and dreams of the Arkenstone and his plans for possessing it again. It even leads him to agree to some of Gandalf's demands in order to regain it (*Hobbit* 262). Ingratitude is the second of the malignancies associated with Greed and, again, Thorin's behavior toward Bilbo clearly shows this in the same incident of the Arkenstone. Forgetting all his promises of service, gratitude, and reward as well as the deeds performed by the hobbit, Thorin sends him away with threats of physical violence. The third and final vice resulting from Greed is robbery, of which all the dwarves, but especially Thorin, are guilty as they are determined to hold off the armies of men and elves rather than part with any of Smaug's treasure—even though Tolkien clearly states that much of it was the rightful property of the elf king and the men of Dale (250). Earlier, Smaug mentions this in his questioning of Bilbo while planting doubts about the arrangement he made with the dwarves. While waiting for Dain to arrive, Thorin schemes to keep even the fourteenth part of the trove, which he promised in exchange for the Arkenstone. Interestingly, though, Thorin eventually realizes the evil of his besetting sin and the harm it has caused. In what is perhaps the most moving moment of the entire story, the dying King under the Mountain asks forgiveness of Bilbo Baggins and clearly admits, "If more of us valued food and cheer and song above hoarded gold, it would be a merrier world" (273).

Although the order and number of the Deadly Sins has changed a number of times, according to one of the traditional arrangements, Pride is the most ancient of evils and the worst of these offenses. It was, after all, the sin of Lucifer, Son of Morning and the brightest of the angels, who would not be subservient to lesser creatures, and also of Adam and Eve, who would be like gods, knowing both good and evil. Appropriately, then, Tolkien devotes the most time to this wrong and its representatives, mortal men and wizards who appear in the bodies of old men.

Saruman is overcome by pride when he entraps Gandalf at Orthanc, demanding cooperation in his plans to dominate Middle-earth. Saruman's long disquisition on the exercise of power refers to the old order and formal alliance that must be swept away along with sneering asides about the fading races, which Saruman views with contempt (*FR* 339–40). His argument, in spite of Tolkien's denials (*FR* 11–12), definitely echoes Hitler's justifications for World War II. Saruman's claim that he is best fitted to wield the power of the Ring and pathetic attempt to set himself up as a secondary Dark Lord, complete with ring, tower, and orcs, particularly disgusts Gandalf. "We must have power," Saruman insists, "power to order all things as we will, for that good which only the Wise can see." But Gandalf is certain that there will be no "we" when he hears Saruman's bold declaration: "I am Saruman, the Wise, Saruman Ring-maker, Saruman of Many Colors!" (339).

This same vanity and vainglory are seen in the behavior of Denethor, Steward of Gondor, when he speaks to Gandalf, who has just arrived in the Citadel. After a long rehearsal of his own accomplishments, Denethor dismisses the advice of the wizard and concludes:

> Pride would be folly that disdained help and counsel at need; but you deal out
> such gifts according to your own designs. Yet the Lord of Gondor is not to be

made the tool of other men's purposes, however worthy. (*RK* 29)

Even his use of the title betrays him, for as Gandalf reminds him on more than one occasion, he is the *Steward* of Gondor and therefore answerable to a superior. This lesson, however, is lost on the broken old man, which is made clear in the episode in the Fen Hollen when Denethor again reacts angrily to Gandalf's attempts to remind him of his station:

> But I say to thee, Gandalf Mithrandir, I will not be thy tool! I am Steward of Gondor of the House of Anárion. I will not step down to be the dotard chamberlain of an upstart. Even when his claim is proved to me, still he comes but of the line of Isildur. I will not bow to such a one, last of a ragged house long bereft of lordship and dignity. (*RK* 153)

Yet, as Steward, it was his prime responsibility to return the throne to its rightful heir. Through his portrayal of Denethor's actions, Tolkien reflects the impulse of medieval writers to descry sin and wrongdoing.

As in his description of Greed, Gower also lists some of the attendants that usually accompany Pride. The worst of these is disobedience of which several examples are evident in Tolkien's story. Boromir, son of Denethor, brazenly disobeys the instructions given to the members of the fellowship never to attempt to handle the Ring and to protect and aid the ring-bearer; at Amon Hen, he attacks Frodo in hopes of gaining the ring for himself:

> How it angers me! Fool! Obstinate fool! Running willfully to death and ruining our cause. If any mortals have claim to the Ring, it is the men of Númenor, and not Halflings. It is yours by unhappy chance. It might have been mine. It should be mine. Give it to me! (*FR* 518–19)

Saruman is likewise guilty of this wrong since the Valar sent him to aid the peoples of Middle-earth in their struggles against the Dark Lord. In his disobedience, he sought an alliance with Sauron intending to become a second Ringlord. Denethor also disobeys his oath as Steward, assuming to himself powers that he would never have even if he reigned as king, as Gandalf sternly reminds him in the Hallows of Gondor:

> Authority is not given to you, Steward of Gondor, to order the hour of your death. . . . And only heathen kings, under the domination of the Dark Power, did thus, slaying themselves in pride and despair. (*RK* 152)

Gower next lists Complaint as an attendant of Pride. Boromir's behavior displays this wrong: he constantly complains of the suffering he and his city have gone through already in defense of the Southern Kingdom. More tellingly, as Faramir reports, Boromir had whined to his father that those who have served as Stewards as long as their family should become Kings. Denethor is not entirely corrupted by his own pride and corrects his son's misapprehension (*TT* 346).

Presumption also attends on Pride in the *Confessio Amantis* and in the incidents involving Denethor and Saruman cited above. The most obvious example, however, occurs in the behavior of Grima Wormtongue in the Court of Theoden (*TT* 143–44). Supposedly the counselor of the King of the Golden Hall, he presumes to speak for the Lord of the Mark, even giving orders to Éomer and then imposing restrictions on the actions of the visitors to the court. Not satisfied with enfeebling Theoden to the point of inactivity, Grima behaves as if he were already on the throne. Gandalf, impatient at bandying words with the sycophant, unleashes his power and leaves Wormtongue groveling on the floor in a serpent-like position while the wizard stands over him, denouncing the traitor's actions.

Boastfulness is the last of the flaws connected to Pride, and again Tolkien gives us several examples of it in the behavior of Boromir, Saruman, and Denethor, all of whom we have already seen commit the greater sin of arrogance. Each of these characters takes credit for and brags of accomplishments that they actually have only helped to achieve. Boromir, for instance, boasts of many victories that were really won as much through the bravery of the men of Minas Tirith and the courage of his brother Faramir as by his efforts. As with the dwarves and Greed, Tolkien has a mortal man demonstrate Pride's opposing virtue: Humility. Aragorn, though the uncrowned King of Gondor and heir to the lines of Isildur and Anárion, offers to accompany the hobbits in his guise of a ranger to serve and protect them. "'I am Aragorn, son of Arathorn; and if by life or death I can save you, I will'" (*FR* 232). Even after he has triumphed on the Pelennor Fields and the crown is his, Aragorn will not accept the throne until all things are reordered in Minas Tirith and shuns any pomp and ceremony when entering the city (*RK* 162–64).

The third of the Deadly Sins is Envy, and its representative race are the Elves. At first glance, this might seem to be a contradiction, for the Elves are the Children of the Stars, and presented as the favored race created by Erú and nurtured by the Valar. But sin can wear a face of beauty, as demonstrated by the sin of Lucifer, Son of Morning, who was the most beautiful of all the angels until he fell into hell and became Satan. The history of the Elves includes several transgressions: the theft of the light of the Two Trees by Fëanor, and the departure of the Noldor from Valinor against the command of the Valar. In the Second Age, there is the deception of Sauron, which tempted the elves to reveal the secrets of ring-making, which led to the troubles of the Third Age. Envy, however, appears in *Hobbit* when Thranduil, Legolas's father, is envious of the elf lords of old whose treasuries bettered his own (163). He was likewise jealous of the dwarves who held all the riches of Smaug —including some that were rightfully his. In this same vein, we see one of the lesser vices of Envy described by Gower—Detraction or denigration of others. Several times during the action of *LR*, various elves (including the Lord Celeborn, consort of Galadriel) speak disparagingly of the dwarves or make references to imagined wrongs in the past (*FR* 445, 462).

It is their immortality, however, that makes the Elves especially liable to Envy. Although they can be wounded or killed as in the great battles of the past of

Middle-earth, Elves can live forever, slowly aging, but never growing old, suffering neither sickness nor other weaknesses of the flesh. In a world of constant mutability where everything else ages and dies, such a gift can lead to boredom or stagnation or the desire to dominate the lesser races. As Tolkien explains in a letter to Michael Straight, immortality led to the elvish melancholy that appears many times in the trilogy; as they form alliances with and get to know members of the other races, the mortals die and new generations come along (*Letters* 236). This becomes a great burden as ages pass and the world changes around them, but they remain constant. This leads to two of the weaknesses displayed by the Elves—constantly looking to the past and an unwillingness to change. Thus, Sam and the Company felt like they were walking in a past age in Lothlórien, and Galadriel fears the probable results of the successful achievement of the Quest of Mount Doom (*FR* 474).

Envy is also very evident in the Elves' resentment of the Gift of Men from Ilúvatar—which is death. Even in *Silm*, the Valar perceived that the Elves' immortality was no gift in a Middle-earth that was itself mortal. With his younger children, mortal men, Erú was more careful and gave them the chance to leave the circles of the world forever. Even in their afterlife, the Elves will not be reunited with the other races as seen in the Choice of Luthien, who gives up her immortality in the Undying Lands to spend an eternity with Beren in the Halls of Mandos (*FR* 259–60). This is likewise why the final parting of Arwen and Elrond is so bitter—because it is forever. Ironically, the men of Middle-earth do not often see Death as a "gift" and envy the Elves because they are immortal. This even led to the downfall of Númenor when Ar-Pharazôn sought to wrest immortality from the Valar (*Silm* 334–37).

The Elves' envy also manifests itself in a vice Gower associates with that sin: withdrawal. Since they cannot relate successfully with mortals, the Elves have begun to withdraw—not only into their secret enclaves, but also out of Middle-earth and into the Undying Lands. "'They are sailing, sailing, sailing over the Sea, they are going into the West and leaving us'" remarks Sam, even before the adventure begins (*FR* 70). With few exceptions, the Elves have withdrawn so far that they have lost interest in Middle-earth, viewing themselves almost as exiles. When Gildor Inglorion and his company encounter Frodo, Pippin, and Sam on their second night out, he is reluctant to part with much knowledge or advice and tells the hobbits bluntly

> The Elves have their own labors and their own sorrows, and they are little concerned with the ways of hobbits, or of any other creatures on earth. Our paths cross theirs seldom, by chance or by purpose. (*FR* 121)

This sentiment is echoed in an almost cruelly pointed statement made by Lindir in the House of Elrond: "It is not easy for us to tell the difference between two mortals. ... To sheep other sheep no doubt appear different, or to shepherds. But Mortals have not been our study. We have other business" (*FR* 309–10). Still, as in the case of the first two Deadly Sins, Tolkien again shows us one of the representative race overcoming this vice when Glorfindel expresses the elven willingness to assist the quest of the ring, despite the chance that in the One Ring's destruction, the power of the elven rings will fail and with it, the future of the race in Middle-earth: "'Yet all the Elves are willing to endure this chance, . . . if by it the power of Sauron may be broken and the fear of his dominion be taken away forever'" (*FR* 352).

The next of the Deadly Sins to enter in Langland's work is Sloth who appears

> all beslobbered with his gummy eyes. "I shall have to sit down," he said, "or I'll fall asleep. I cannot stand or prop myself up all the time, and you can't expect me to kneel without a hassock. If I had been put to bed now, you'd never get me up before dinner was ready, not for all your bell-ringing—not unless nature called." (72–73)

Tolkien's venerable Ents demonstrate this sin. Treebeard tells Pippin and Merry that many of his race have grown sleepy, almost "treeish" and have taken to standing by themselves, "half-asleep all through the summer" (*TT* 92). This inactivity, this lack of resolve has left the Ents forgotten by many of the other peoples of Middle-earth. And the Ents' sloth has also given Sauron and his minions their opportunity. Langland's description of this sin gives its attendant evils more emphasis than any other. He first lists delay as one of the characteristic malignancies of Sloth; Treebeard makes clear that his is one of his own faults: "But Saruman now! Saruman is a neighbour: I cannot overlook him. I must do something, I suppose. I have often wondered what I should do about Saruman" (*TT* 89–90). Upon hearing Pippin and Merry's story, delay comes to an end. Treebeard announces that he has summoned an Entmoot, something "which does not often happen nowadays" (*TT* 97–98), but which he now feels is overdue.

The second evil of Sloth is forgetfulness, a natural result of inertia. When he first meets the hobbits, Treebeard has trouble remembering the old lists of the creatures of Middle-earth. He has likewise almost forgotten what the Entwives look like and has problems remembering their names. The next wrong associated with Sloth is negligence, of which Treebeard accuses himself and his fellow Ents, who have failed in their duties as shepherds of the trees. In the face of the attacks and maraudings of Saruman and his orcs, they have been negligent too long, such as Skinbark, who was "wounded by the Orcs, and many of his folk and his tree-herds have been murdered and destroyed" (*TT* 92). In reaction, he went up in the high places amid the birches and would not come down. Treebeard then explicitly indicts himself for idleness, a fault Langland also associates with Sloth:

> Many of those trees were my friends, creatures I had known from nut and acorn; many had voices of their own that are lost for ever now. And there are wastes of stump and bramble where once there were singing groves. I have been idle. I have let things slip. (*TT* 91)

Again, though, the race chosen to illustrate Sloth also demonstrates its opposite virtue. Treebeard grows so angry at the treachery of Saruman that he rouses up all his fellow Ents and they set out to redress the wrongs done against them and their trees: *"To Isengard! ... We go, we go, we go to war, to hew the stone and break the door; For bole and bough are burning now, the furnace roars—we go to war!"* (*TT* 106). Note how Tolkien encourages moral behavior here and elsewhere by *showing*, rather than *exhorting*, virtue in action; this technique appears less didactic than what the medieval sources have done.

Next in Langland's parade of evil is Gluttony, who

> could neither walk nor stand without his stick. And once he got going, he moved like a blind minstrel's bitch, or like a fowler laying his lines, sometimes sideways, sometimes backwards. And when he drew near to the door, his eyes grew glazed, and he stumbled on the threshold and fell flat on the ground. (71)

In Tolkien's world, the hobbits sometimes display this vice, for we learn early in *Hobbit* that Bilbo (and all hobbits) expect frequent, full meals. Indeed, Mr. Baggins is so flummoxed after Gandalf's initial visit that he has to calm his nerves with some more cake. We hear about his well-stocked larder during the unexpected party and listen to Bilbo's complaints throughout the story that he has missed so many meals that he has lost count and wishes to be back in his cozy hobbit hole—eating. The first incident in *FR* is the parallel long awaited party at which it "snowed food and rained drink" and from which many of the guests had to literally be carried home because they were so satiated (60). Later on in the adventure we are told that hobbit children learn to cook as soon as they learn to read (if not before) because food and eating are such important parts of their existence. When Frodo and Sam are alone in the wilds with only Gollum as their guide, Sam notes his master's gauntness and decides that he must cook something nourishing (*TT* 325). This love of food and drink explains the characteristic plumpness of most adult hobbits, justifies the reference to Bilbo's bulging waistcoat, and anticipates the description of a dumpling-shaped Mr. Baggins running down the road after the departing dwarves.

In his panegyric on the Deadly Sins, Chaucer's Pardoner has a lot to say against the activities and attitudes of some individuals who seem "to make their god their belly." As well, the Pardoner points out the connection of Gluttony to other evils:

> O gluttony, with reason we complain!
> O if one knew how many a malady
> Must follow such excess and gluttony,
> To eat with moderation he'd be able
> Whenever he is sitting at his table.
> > (*Tales* 341)

Tolkien is also aware of this, for the hobbits' girth seems to be connected with their indolence; when we see them at home, they appear to spend most of their time eating, drinking, and attending parties. Plumpness prompts their aversion to adventures. The well-fed and cautious Mr. Baggins dismisses Gandalf with a curt, "we have no use for adventures. Nasty, disturbing things! Make you late for dinner!" (*Hobbit* 16). Both Bilbo and Frodo, as their adventures go on, shed their excess weight due to short rations and activity. In Elrond's house, Frodo speaks as he sees his reflection in a mirror: "'Yes, you have seen a thing or two since you last peeped out of a looking-glass'" (*FR* 295). Attendant on this loss of weight seems to be a growing willingness to go on adventures and even behave heroically if the situation demands without so much as a backward glance at their well-stocked holes. In the woods, on the second night of their journey to Crickhollow, the hobbits meet Gildor, who tells them the "'wide world is all about you: you can fence yourselves in, but you cannot for ever fence it out'" (*FR* 120). As they shed their excess weight, the hobbits develop constancy, bravery, and a sense of moral responsibility that enables them to go out on adventures and indeed do great things. Perhaps this is what Tolkien himself had in mind when his narrator comments on halflings: "There is a seed of courage hidden (often deeply, it is true) in the heart of the fattest and most timid hobbit, waiting for some final desperate danger to make it grow" (*FR* 192).

> It is not seldom that one sees
> The rage of lechery today,
> Take what it will, and where it may.
> For love, which is devoid and bare
> Of reason, as all men declare,
> When heedlessness and folly fire
> Its wild voluptuous desire,
> Spares not a thought for kin or kind.
>   (Gower 260)

Thus John Gower introduces the figure of Lechery into his work. Tolkien gives this sin sketchy treatment. Its representative is again a mortal man, albeit a twisted caricature of one. Grima Wormtongue, already examined as a figure of presumption, assumes the power and authority of his Lord, Theoden. Worse still, he has betrayed the master and the people he was supposed to serve. He did, indeed, fill the role of counselor to the Lord of the Riddermark of Rohan, but the advice he gave was dictated by Saruman to assure the inactivity and, eventually, the fall of the Rohirrim. Gandalf theorizes correctly that Wormtongue's promised reward included a vast share of the treasury of Meduseld, and more importantly the hand of Éowyn on whose person Grima had long cast lecherous eyes and lascivious looks. The wizard further charges, moreover, that Wormtongue had "haunted her steps" (*TT* 153), which sounds like stalking. A major difference in Tolkien's treatment of this vice is that there is no repentance on the part of an offender. Grima is twice given the opportunity to renounce his wrongs and join the forces of the free peoples. But each time he chooses to continue in the evil life, and he eventually is shot down by the hobbit archers for his murder of Saruman on the very doorstep of Bag End (*RK* 318, 365).

Anger, the seventh of the Deadly Sins, first appears in Gower's *Confessio Amantis* so described:

> If thou wouldst know all sins,
> Most alien to the law is one
> Well known on earth to human-kind
> Since ever men had swords to grind:
> And, in the power of this Vice,
> Good friends have often, in a trice,
> Been maddened by the merest chance.
> And yet the Vice does not enhance
> Men's pleasure: where it most achieves,
> There also most mankind it grieves.
> (123)

Tolkien chose to depict Anger in the figures of the Goblins and Orcs, who seem to be in a constant rage at the other races of Middle-earth or with each other. Treebeard explains that the orcs were made by Morgoth in the Great Darkness as counterfeits of the elves. As the Children of the Stars were noble, logically the orcs were villainous. When they first appear in *Hobbit*, the Great Goblin gives a howl of rage and gets so angry that he jumps off his throne and rushes at Thorin (71). In the camp of the orcs who capture Merry and Pippin, Grishnákh and Uglúk perfectly manifest the noisy and brawling irritability that characterizes this race at all times: "'Curse you! You're as bad as the other rabble; the maggots and the apes of Lugbúrz'" (*TT* 66). In Cirith Ungol, Shagrat and Gorbag aim their wrath and rancor against one another as often as against Frodo and Sam:

> "Got you Gorbag!" cried Shagrat. "Not quite dead, eh? Well, I'll finish my job now." He sprang onto the fallen body and stamped and tramped it in his fury, stopping now and again to stab and slash it with his knife. (*RK* 218)

Finally, on the crest of the Morgai, Sam and an exhausted Frodo listen to the angry words of a soldier orc and a small tracker until the fury of the smaller goads him into shooting his comrade with an arrow (*RK* 242–43). Since they exist in a world so full of mistrust and violence, it is easy to understand why Orcs are so easily made angry.

Attendant on anger are two ancillary vices—hatred and war. The hate orcs feel for the other races of Middle-earth is clearly described in both *Hobbit* and *LR*. In *Hobbit*, Tolkien informs us that "Goblins are cruel, wicked and badhearted. . . . They did not hate dwarves especially, no more than they hated everybody and everything" (69). In *RK*, after we have encountered many more of this vile folk, Frodo further explains:

Orcs have always behaved like that, or so all tales say, when they are on their own. But you can't get much hope out of it. They hate us far more, altogether and all the time. If those two would have seen us, they would have dropped all their quarrel until we were dead. (249)

As for their practices of violence and war, goblins "don't care who they catch as long as it is done smart and secret and the prisoners are not able to defend themselves" (*Hobbit* 69). In a manner similar to Wormtongue and his wrongs, the orcs are given the chance to repent of their evil and escape punishment. This occurs at the Battle of Helm's Deep when Aragorn warns them to withdraw or "'[n]ot one will be left alive to take back tidings'" (*TT* 178). Like Wormtongue, the orcs refuse this offer—and the result is the same: death at the hands of those against whom they felt such anger.

In the tradition of Gower, Langland, and Chaucer, then, Tolkien did indeed "reflect and contain in solution elements of moral and religious truth" in an effort to foster virtuous behavior as some medieval writers did through the ancient device of the figures embodying the Seven Deadly Sins. By depicting the vices and virtues of his characters, Tolkien encourages his readers to adopt a new awareness of right and wrong so that by the end of the books, their understanding is very different from when they started. At the conclusion of *Hobbit*, Gandalf remarks to Bilbo, "You are not the hobbit that you were," (281) and in the final pages of *LR*, Saruman says to Frodo, "'You have grown Halfling, ... you have grown very much. You are wise." (*RK* 364). If Tolkien has been successful in his use of these medieval figures of sin, these observations are true of the readers as well.

WORKS CITED

Baltimore Catechism. New York: W. H. Sadler Inc., 1945.

Bloomfield, Morton. *The Seven Deadly Sins*. East Lansing, MI: Michigan State College P, 1952.

Chaucer, Geoffrey. *The Canterbury Tales*. Ed. Ronald L. Ecker and Eugene J. Crook. Palatka, FL: Hodge and Braddock, 1993.

Day, David. *A Tolkien Bestiary*. New York: Ballantine, 1979.

Foster, Robert. *A Guide to Middle-earth*. New York: Ballantine, 1971.

Gower, John. *Confessio Amantis*. Trans. Terrence Tiller. Baltimore: Penguin, 1963.

Helms, Randel. *Tolkien's World*. Boston: Houghton, 1974.

Holman, C. Hugh. *A Handbook to Literature*. Indianapolis: Bobbs-Merrill, 1980.

Kocher, Paul H. *Master of Middle-earth*. Boston: Houghton, 1972.

——. *A Reader's Guide to THE SILMARILLION*. London: Thames, 1980.

Langland, William. *Piers the Plowman*. Trans. J. F. Goodridge. Baltimore: Penguin, 1966.

Noel, Ruth S. *The Mythology of Middle-earth*. Boston: Houghton, 1977.

Purtill, Richard L. *J.R.R. Tolkien: Myth, Morality and Religion*. New York: Harper, 1984.

Reilly, Robert J. "Tolkien and the Fairy Story." *Thought* 38 (1963): 89–106.

Robertson, D. W. *A Preface to Chaucer*. Princeton: Princeton UP, 1962.

Tyler, J.E.A. *The New Tolkien Companion*. New York: St. Martin's, 1979.

7

Is Tolkien a Renaissance Man? Sir Philip Sidney's *Defense of Poesy* and J.R.R. Tolkien's "On Fairy-Stories"

Tanya Caroline Wood

> Suddenly he said: "Of course you don't suppose, do you, that you wrote all that book yourself?'. . . . I think I said: "No, I don't suppose so any longer." I have never since been able to suppose so. (*Letters* 413)

What kind of direct or indirect 'help' did Tolkien receive in writing "On Fairy-Stories" ("OFS", *Essays* 109–61)? Tolkien's praise and defense of fairy-stories is similar to Sir Philip Sidney's *Defense of Poesy* (*DOP*), especially in terms of the use of classical rhetoric, which they both studied at Oxford.[1] Like Sidney, Tolkien mixes the encomium, which praises and elevates its subject, with aspects of the defense, which vindicates an accused subject. Epideictic rhetoric is the dominant mode of the Renaissance (Vickers 18), a period with which Tolkien has already been linked. Rose A. Zimbardo argues that Tolkien utilizes the medieval/ Renaissance principles of *discordia concors*, imitation, and mutability in *LR*, and points out that Sidney and Tolkien share the conception of the artist as creator of a better world (63–64). R. J. Reilly also notes that Tolkien's "OFS" has "specifically Christian implications" that the critical tradition "has hardly had since Sidney's *Defense*" (90), and that *LR* "is an example of the dictum, so favored by the Renaissance critics, that literature is both *dulce* and *utile*" (103). So is Tolkien a Renaissance Man? The encomium is far more characteristic of Renaissance writing than that of Old English, the medieval period, or the twentieth century. As well, commentators commonly refer to Sidney's *DOP* as the epitome of early modern criticism, and Tolkien and Sidney have much in common. Nonetheless, Tolkien does not refer to Sidney in his published work and there is no firm evidence that Tolkien ever read Sidney.[2] But their similarities do suggest that Tolkien may be more of a Renaissance Man than is usually thought.[3]

Robert Coogan discusses the classical structure for the encomium that Aristotle describes in *Rhetoric* and Aphthonius in *Progymnasmata*, and applies it to *DOP*, arguing against K. O. Myrick's influential analysis of the *DOP* as an example of forensic rhetoric. Aphthonius organizes the encomium into the *prooimion* (introduction), *genos* (discussion of the subject's family), *anatrophe* (upbringing of the subject), *praxeis* (praise of the subject's accomplishments), *synkrisis* (comparison), and *Epilogos* (conclusion) (Coogan 103). Sidney and Tolkien use the basic elements of Aphthonius, with several alterations in order and in emphasis:

Aphthonius	Sidney	Tolkien (page #): section title
Prooimion (intro.)	Prooimion	Prooimion (109): first three paragraphs
Genos (family)	Genos (& synkrisis)	Genos (109–10): Fairy-story
Anatrophe (upbringing)	Praxeis (& synkrisis)	Anatrophe/ "Digressio" (110–19): Fairy-story
Praxeis (deeds)	Refutatio	Genos (& synkrisis) (119–29): Origins
Synkrisis (comparison)	Anatrophe/Digressio[4]	Refutatio (129–145): Children, Fantasy
Epilogos (conclusion)	Epilogue	Praxeis (145–54): Recovery, Escape, Consolation
		Epilogue (155–57)

Although Aphthonius does not specifically refer to the *digressio*, classical writers particularly recommend pleasant digressions to leaven longer encomiums (Hardison 30). Theodore C. Burgess in his study of classical writers and theorists on the encomium notes that "[a]lmost all writers upon the encomium . . . speak directly or indirectly of the great freedom allowed in applying rhetorical precepts" (121). In the second section,"Fairy-story," Tolkien begins with definitions, part of establishing the *genos* of the fairy-story, digresses with the *anatrophe* of English fairy-stories, then applies a major *synkrisis* of fairy-stories to neighboring genres, before moving back to the question of *genos*. Both Tolkien and Sidney place their *synkrisis* earlier than the classical order, and as part of another section rather than as a separate section. Sidney and Tolkien also devote considerable space to the *refutatio*, usually part of forensic rather than epideictic rhetoric. Although Coogan argues that the *refutatio* has a place in Aristotle's model for the encomium, providing that controversial material is handled delicately (105), Sidney's *refutatio* shows too much vehemence and too little delicacy for *DOP* to be considered solely as an encomium. Any absolute adherence to any one rhetorical system is unlikely for Sidney, since in Renaissance literary practice there was never any rigid system of genres with form strictly corresponding to subject (Colie 114–15). Thus, Sidney and Tolkien both use the formal order of the encomium loosely and mix the encomium with the defense.

Aristotle's *Rhetoric* states that any encomium must emphasize the virtue and importance of the subject (91) and that amplification (heightening and exaggeration) is the rhetorical figure "most suitable" to the encomium since it invests the subject with "beauty and importance" (105). Coogan argues that Sidney's telos is "the triumph and coronation of poetry," which gains the laurel as the "King" of literature (99). Thus, when Coogan analyzes Sidney's verbal register, he finds such words as "highest knowledge," "venerable," "valiant," "noblest," "courage," "excellent," "ornament," "heavenly," "excellent," "reverence," "highest," "triumphers," "peerless," "faithfulness," "treasure-house," and "golden" (102, 104). Aristotle notes that the useful moral virtues—wisdom, courage, magnificence, magnanimity, prudence, and liberality—are particularly important in the encomium (91). These virtues are apparent in Sidney's vocabulary, with emphasis on the virtue of the singular magnificence appropriate to a "King." In "OFS," Tolkien also follows Aristotle's recommendations by mentioning "virtue" (116, 139), "inherent morality" (118), "wisdom" (137), "dignity" (137), "virtuous and noble" (151), "permanent and fundamental" (149), "heroic" (148), "ideal" (138), "purity" (143), "pure" (139), "humility and innocence" (136), "clean" (146), "higher" (139), "practical" (148), "richness" (109), "richer" (135), "wealth" (145), and "bounty" (156). Tolkien's overall aim is to argue that fairy-stories are "not a lower but a higher form of Art, indeed the most nearly pure form, and so (when achieved) the most potent" (139). Sidney and Tolkien share similar vocabulary, but Sidney emphasizes the peerless nature of poetry and Tolkien emphasizes Christian virtues. Both follow Aristotle's recommendations: to emphasize morality and to use amplification.

Sidney and Tolkien begin their encomium with the *prooimion*, or introduction to the theme of praise, which earns the goodwill of the audience, and establishes the character of the speaking persona. Aristotle advises the speaker to first "give the key-note, and then attach the main subject" (427) and states that peripheral material is appropriate to the encomium (429). Sidney's keynote is an anecdote describing his horsemanship lessons in Italy and his horse-obsessed teacher Pugliano, which leads to his main subject—that poetry is at least as praiseworthy as horses. Tolkien's *prooimion* has something of Sidney's playfulness and also emphasizes a journey; Tolkien is a romantic adventurer in the "perilous" land of Faërie (109). He then states the intellectual reason for his quest by posing a set of three questions: "What are fairy-stories? What is their origin? What is the use of them?" (109). These three questions help determine the basic structure of "OFS" (just as three tasks, riddles, or problems often structure fairy-stories). In the encomium, Burgess notes that "[o]ne of the most common features was a profession of inadequacy before a subject so vast" (122). Hence, Tolkien represents himself a "wandering explorer (or trespasser)" in the "wide and deep and high" land of Faërie (109). The tongue-tied, "unprofessional," and "impertinent" Tolkien can only offer the "hints" of answers from his limited gleanings of the vast number of fairy-stories extant (109). Further on, he declares that he is "unlearned" (120) and "ill-instructed" (138), even as he demonstrates precisely the opposite. Sidney's humility is similarly ironic. He tells us that his praise of poetry is driven by his own "self-love" (3), and that he finds himself a person who has "(I know not by what mischance) in these my not old years and idlest times . . . slipped into the title of a poet" (4). His irony is clear as Sidney goes on to define poetry as the antithesis of selfishness and idleness, linking it to patriotism, heroism, and intense labor. Thus, in the *prooimion*, Sidney and Tolkien both use peripheral journeying anecdotes to introduce their theme and share an ironic posture of humility.

Next, Tolkien turns to the dictionary to pin down the precise *genos*, or identity, of the fairy-story. The *OED* is unhelpful and indeed misleading because of the *anatrophe*, or upbringing, of fairy-stories in England. Tolkien rejects the *OED*'s definitions of "fairy" and its associates as literally belittling, a shrinkage that Tolkien suggests is the result of the great voyages of the explorers that made the world seem too small to hold full-grown fairies (111). Tolkien's "true" tradition is represented by the *Beowulf* poet, the *Gawain* poet, Gower, and Spenser. Tolkien consistently refuses to expurgate the darker side of fairy-stories (such as Grendel) in favor of prettiness. Alongside their positive qualities, fairy-stories can be also "perilous" (109), "indescribable" (114), "shadowy" (114), "dangerous" (109, 147), "gruesome" (128), and "as hideous as a nightmare" (151). Fairy-stories may contain "dungeons" (109), "illusions" (116), "peril" (109, 135, 137), "strangeness" (109), "horror" (122, 128), "regret" (129), "sorrow" (137), and "dark significance" (141). Tolkien expresses a particular dislike for the work of Michael Drayton and William Shakespeare because he thinks that they ignore this ambivalence and trivialize elves and fairies into "flower-and-butterfly minuteness" (111–12). For Tolkien, the English literary tradition (especially anything involving Shakespeare) is generally impoverished. In a letter to Milton Waldman he states, "I was from early days grieved by the poverty of my own beloved country: it had no stories of its own (bound up with its tongue and soil), not of the quality that I sought, and found (as an ingredient) in legends of other lands" (*Letters* 144). This critique of the upbringing of fairies in English literature is presented as a digression (113). Sidney's famous *digressio* is similar. Sidney adumbrates Tolkien's concerns about the sparse English tradition, as he examines the luminaries of English poetry, finding something to praise in Chaucer, Surrey, *Mirror for Magistrates*, Spenser, and *Gorboduc*, but much more to blame (46–47). Both Sidney and Tolkien try to redress this lack by writing themselves. Sidney—"sick among the rest"—hopes that his provision of neoclassical rules will improve English poetry and his own (53). In a letter to Jane Neave, Tolkien declares that *LR* is a "practical demonstration of the views that I expressed" in "OFS" (*Letters* 310). Tolkien and Sidney write a *digressio* on the poor upbringing of fairy-stories/poetry in England and suggest that literature is in need of some correction in theory and in practice.

Tolkien still needs to define his difficult and elusive subject clearly. A fairy-story must first take place within the indescribable realm of Faërie but must not be confused with other genres; consequently, Tolkien uses *synkrisis* (comparison). He excludes from the fairy-tale stories that contain diminutive beings, "traveller's tales" (115), the "preposterous" science fiction aspects of *The Time Machine* (115–16), dream narratives (116), and beast fables (117–18). The distance of time and space creates some of the required difference (as with *LR*), and any "inherent morality" in a tale can also bring it closer to the fairy-story (118). In contrast, Sidney uses *synkrisis* to dismiss poetry's competitors. He memorably caricatures the astronomer who "looking to the stars might fall into a ditch" (14), the mathematician who "might draw forth a straight line with a crooked heart" (14), and the historian "loaded with old mouse-eaten records" (15). Only the poet, Sidney argues, can combine the specific example with the underlying abstract moral concept. Tolkien is not as absolute as Sidney in his dismissal of his literary neighbors as "the borders of the fairy-story are inevitably dubious" (116). Also,

Tolkien's task is to establish the value of fairy-stories *within* fiction, rather than Sidney's task to justify fiction itself. Sidney's project is more difficult for he is surrounded by a Puritan and anti-literary milieu, including Lord Leicester's circle, which favors translation and history over secular poetry (Soens xv), and Oxford, which favors logic (Coogan 113). Both writers nonetheless use *synkrisis* to separate their subjects from other surrounding genres, although Tolkien's concern is the question of identity whereas Sidney's concern is the dismissal of the competition.

Tolkien establishes he identity of fairy-stories by further attention to *genos* (family) in "Origins." He is particularly concerned with the "ancestral inventor," or the founder of each branch of the tree of tales (121). This inventor is a "sub-creator" of a world radically different from material fact, which still takes its forms and words from materiality, and recombines them:

> We may put a deadly green upon a man's face and produce a horror; we may make the rare and terrible blue moon to shine; or we may cause woods to spring with silver leaves and rams to wear fleeces of gold, and put hot fire into the belly of the cold worm. But in such 'fantasy', as it is called, new form is made; Faërie begins. (122)

Sidney's view of poetry is strikingly similar. Harry Berger describes Sidney's approach as *counterfactual* in which the writer experiences a certain freedom and autonomy from reality, and Berger calls this a defining characteristic of the Renaissance imagination (8). Sidney's poet builds "upon the depth of nature," inventing "forms such as never were in nature, as the heroes, demigods, cyclops, chimeras, furies, and such like" (9). In Sidney's famous formulation,

> Nature never set forth the earth in so rich a tapestry as diverse poets have done, neither with so pleasant rivers, fruitful trees, sweet-smelling flowers, nor whatsoever else may make the too-much-loved earth more lovely. Her world is brazen, the poets only deliver a golden. (9)

When Sidney examines Greek etymology, he finds that the word for "poet" (*poiein*) means "to make" (8). A "maker" was also a medieval/Renaissance term for a poet. For Sidney, the poet remakes nature into "another nature" (9) and does not merely paint the visible (12). Tolkien might have used the term "maker" to stress his emphasis on *inventive* fantasy, which he describes as "making and delight" (143). Tolkien links this "making" to the God-like powers of the writer of the fairy-story: "[W]e make in our measure . . . because we are made: and not only made, but made in the image and likeness of a Maker" (50). Sidney also comments that man has gained "divine breath" from the "Heavenly Maker" who created poets and "made man in his own likeness" to make in turn (10). Both Sidney and Tolkien argue that the writer makes a new reality, using the God-given powers of the creator.

Once Tolkien identifies the imaginative processes of this "ancestral inventor," the emphasis shifts to the ancient lineage of his subject. Sidney also focuses on the *progonoi* (ancestry) of poetry, one of the possible subdivisions of the *genos* (Coogan 103). Sidney argues that poetry is "the first light-giver to ignorance" and extends as far back as the written word (4), from the ancient Greeks and Romans, to barbarians such as the Irish, Welsh, Turks, and Indians (6–7). Tolkien argues that fairy-stories are ubiquitous, existing "wherever there is language" (121) in Greek, Roman, Norse, Swahili, and even in French. The subset of terms used by Tolkien includes "universally" (121), "very ancient" (121), "ancient" (129), "antiquity" (128), "abyss of time" (18), "distant time" (18), "distance and great abyss of time" (128), "Other Time" (129), "outside Time" (129), "old" (128, 129, 131, 134), and "older" (139). Fairy-stories have a genealogy in England that extends back to *Beowulf* and beyond (116). As Coogan points out, Sidney emphasizes place and time in praising the universality and lineage of poetry (103–4). Tolkien follows the same strategy with the fairy-story.

Tolkien's next step in the sections on "Children" and "Fantasy" is to include the *refutatio*, which usually occurs as a stage in forensic rhetoric and is a defense of a client against the accusations of opponents. Tolkien includes the *refutatio* because he must defend fairy-stories from the wide-spread belief that they are suitable only for children. Andrew Lang, as the editor of fairy-stories intended for children, represents this view. Tolkien, despite his admiration for Lang's abilities, thinks that fairy-stories cut off from an adult audience are "ruined" (131). Tolkien, to his later regret, wrote *Hobbit* for children (*Letters* 218) but designed the heroic epic *LR* for a "more grown up" audience (*Letters* 42).[5] Sidney certainly aims to elevate poetry from its position as the "laughingstock" of children (4), but he still sees poetry as the "first nurse whose milk by little and little enabled [children] to feed afterwards of tougher knowledges" (4). Tolkien rejects any automatic association between children and fairy-stories. This link is not "of the same order as the connexion between children's bodies and milk" (130). Instead, Tolkien argues that although children are capable of entering a secondary world that is "true" in terms of the laws of that world, they are no more capable of belief in it than an adult, and they also need this escapism much less (133). Children also prefer the black and white of absolute moral judgments rather than the moral ambivalence of fairy-stories (137). Finally, Lang's description of the childhood appetite for fairy-stories fails to match with Tolkien's experience. Tolkien suggests that either Lang is mistaken or that "children differ considerably" (134). Tolkien's is a fundamentally different perspective from Sidney's view of poetry as suitable for infant pedagogy.

Fairy-stories clearly have an important place for Tolkien in human development, in later adolescence, and early adulthood. Tolkien maintains in the section on "Children" that his own interest in fairy-stories did not come from childhood but "was wakened by philology on the threshold of manhood, and quickened to full life by the war" (135). Tolkien was just under sixteen when he first started studying philology (Carpenter 34) and twenty-four when World War

I broke out. Tolkien links his taste for fairy-stories to his developing masculinity—one older meaning of the word "quickened" suggests the physical 'quickening' of male desire—as well as to a possibly "escapist" reaction to the war. There seems to be a dormant association in Tolkien's mind between fairy-stories and adult sexuality shown in the use of "lover" (109), "primal desire" (116), "primal 'desires'"(117), "the satisfaction of certain primordial human desires" (116), "longing" (152), "heart's desire" (154), "desire" (134, 135, 143, 151), "desirability," (135) "desires" (116), "desired" (135), "desirable" (134), the "imaginative satisfaction of ancient desires" (153), and "potent" (122, 126, 127, 133, 139, 140). Of course, when taken in each separate context, the primary meaning of these words and phrases is not sexual. However, to insist that words can have only one meaning disregards the subtle connotations of language. This association between fairy-stories and adult sexuality is explicit when Tolkien comments that "the story-maker who allows himself to be 'free with' Nature can be her lover not her slave" (147). Fairy-stories are represented as the direct result of heterosexual intercourse between (male) writer and (female) Nature. Tolkien certainly insists that reading fairy-stories is part of becoming adult; men should not read them as "boys who would not grow up" (138). Instead, children should read fairy-stories as they would wear "clothes [that] should allow for growth" (138). As a boy moves into adulthood, he should also move into an increased understanding of the fairy-story, which teaches "callow, lumpish, and selfish youth [that] peril, sorrow and the shadow of death can bestow dignity, and even sometimes wisdom" (137). Thus, Tolkien views fairy-stories as especially appropriate to aid sexual, social, and intellectual maturation in young men.

Females appear to have no proactive place in Tolkien's conception of reading and writing. The reader is implicitly male; Tolkien does not call women reading fairy-stories as if they were children again, girls who would not grow up. Presumably Tolkien was heterosexual (a safe assumption); thus his writer is also implicitly male, the "lover" of Nature, and not "her" slave (53). Tolkien's Nature is passive and submissive, to be "made free" with and then to be transcended by the male imagination. Tolkien, in a letter to his son Michael, makes explicit his view of the natural "servient, helpmeet instinct" in women, and their subsequent intellectual passivity:

> [I]t is their gift to be receptive, stimulated, fertilized (in many other matters than the physical) by the male. Every teacher knows that. How quickly an intelligent woman can be taught, grasp his ideas, see his point—and how (with rare exceptions) they can go no further. (*Letters* 49)

Women may be "fertilized" by the male teacher, just as nature is fertilized by the male writer to produce the fairy-story, but women are usually incapable of originality. Thus, most women cannot invent a fantasy world, and can not function as the creators of "potent" (and therefore masculine) fairy-stories to teach the next generation of males. Women are marginalized outside Tolkien's economy of male to male pedagogy. Tolkien's exclusion of women is also demonstrated by his own life, in which his intellectual and social needs were largely fulfilled by men (Carpenter 144). This homosociality can also be seen in the all-male fellowship in *LR*. Where Tolkien comfortably masculinizes the audience, the writer, and the written product in "OFS," Sidney's audience is often explicitly female (as in the *Old Arcadia*). Lynn Dickson points out that Sidney represents the act of writing as feminine and accompanied by considerable anxiety (42). For example, Sidney portrays poetry both positively as a nursing mother (*DOP* 4) and negatively as dangerous siren (*DOP* 34; Dickson 43). Tolkien's notions subtly position females as pleasant but rarely central, whereas Sidney's attitude is more involved, troubled, and ambivalent.

Tolkien continues his *refutatio* in his section on "Fantasy," using a variety of strategies that Sidney also shares. Sidney first attacks the malice and stupidity of his opponents; "poet-haters" are "smiling railers" who "prodigally spend a great many wandering words in quips and scoffs" and they "correct the verb before they understand the noun" as their "scoffing comes not of wisdom" (32–33). Tolkien also attacks his prosecutors, who are stupid and stricken with "error and malice" (139). They lack the kind of imagination that can appreciate the "arresting strangeness" of fantasy (139). Both writers use *ad hominem* tactics against their detractors, although Sidney's language is more vehement and abrasive.

However, the *refutatio* should follow forensic logic, and a common strategy is to undermine the premises of the opponents' position. One such premise for Sidney is that poetry is an inferior art form (Coogan 105). Tolkien also undermines the inferiority associated with the "fantastic" and suggests that fantasy is inappropriately subordinated to the "imagination"; instead, Tolkien redefines the imagination as mere "image-making," rather than any more exalted use (138–39). When imagination combines with "freedom from the domination of observed fact," the result is fantasy (139). When fantasy achieves an "'inner consistency of reality',"' it becomes "Art" with a capital "A" (140). Because Faërie is a realm of complexity, it is difficult to produce, and often deteriorates into mere "fancy," particularly in painting and drama (including pantomime and Shakespeare). Tolkien, in a letter to Dora Marshall, emphasizes "[t]he labour!" involved with *LR* (*Letters* 209). Sidney seeks to raise the status of poetry "which is among us thrown down to so ridiculous an estimation" (8) by emphasizing the difficulty of poetic production, the need for rules, imitation, and practice. Both Sidney and Tolkien reevaluate the devalued terms of "poetry" and "fantasy" respectively and emphasize the difficulty of the production of good work.

In the *refutatio*, Sidney negates another premise of his opponents: that poetry lies (Coogan 105). Tolkien, like many other defenders of literature, counters the same argument against fairy-stories. Sidney directly confronts Plato, the great enemy of Renaissance poetics, who accused poetry of being "the mother of lies" (*DOP* 34) whereas Tolkien confronts only the shadow of Plato's opinion, first in one of the *OED*'s definitions of the fairy-story as a "falsehood" (110) and then in a correspondent's equation of fantasy as "'[b]reathing a lie though silver'" (143).

The depreciative tone Tolkien finds associated with "fantasy" is an ancient one. When Sidney carefully separates those "*phantastike*" poets who distort fact, "infect the fancy with unworthy objects" (37), and "build castles in the air" (10), from his "*eikastike*" poets who figure forth good things (37), he uses Platonic terms, as discussed by Italian critics such as Tasso in the 1580s (Soens xxxi-ii). In Plato's view, the primary world is noumenal, existing as an ideal behind the distorted material world (or secondary world). The world of poets is an even more distorted vision of the primary world, and therefore represents "lies" in a fundamental sense (Soens xxxii). Neither Sidney nor Tolkien argues that poetry and fantasy are free from abuse; man is fallen for both. Sidney asks "what, shall the abuse of a thing make the right use odious?" (37) and distinguishes between "meaner" artists "who counterfeit only such faces as are set before them" and more creative artists (12). Tolkien also acknowledges that "the creative desire is only cheated by counterfeits" (143). Sidney marshals an impressive series of arguments against Plato, asserting that poetry "nothing affirms and therefore never lies" (35), Plato was a poet himself (40), poets cannot be banished for wantonness because no licentiousness is possible in Plato's ideal community (40–41), and Plato rejected only *abusive* poets, who imitate already existing pagan ideas, from his *Republic*. Sidney finally enlists Plato as "an ally of the poetic cause" (Roe 103). Sidney apparently agrees with Plato's negative opinion of poetry when he suggests that fantastic poetry can delude and bewitch by "infecting us with many pestilent desires, with a siren's sweetness drawing the mind to the serpent's tail of sinful fancies" (34). By criticizing the fantastic, Sidney attempts to silence the moral objections of puritan critics; he acknowledges their accusations as partially true, but confines them to one illegitimate branch of poetry. Tolkien defends fantasy against accusations that it has anything like a siren's fatal allure when he insists that fantasy "does not seek delusion, nor bewitchment and domination; it seeks shared enrichment, partners in making and delight, not slaves" (143). For Tolkien, a partnership of equality between the reader and writer of fantasy escapes the kind of deceitful seduction and slavery that Sidney attaches to "phantastike" poetry. Both writers use similar strategies to defend against Plato's charge of lying, but part of Sidney's defense is to assault the fantastic, the same branch of literature that Tolkien defends.

Sidney and Tolkien do share one notable defensive strategy against Plato's attack on poetry: they insist that poetry and fairy-stories go back to Plato's noumenal ideal world, rather than distorting the already secondary material world by another level of lies. Soens explains that Sidney's poet, endowed with divinely given natural reason, "can see the 'Ideas' of the virtues as they may be conceived to exist in Plato's ideal world," and can recreate them as an equivalent to Eden (x). Tolkien also alludes to Eden when he mentions that fantasy can fulfill the desire to talk to animals, which is an imperishable human need "as ancient as the Fall" (152). When Tolkien describes sub-creative art as having "'the power of giving to ideal creations the inner consistency of reality'" (138), the "ideal" is initially puzzling for it can not be explained in terms of the world of Faërie, an ambivalent place. Yet when Tolkien remarks that fairy-stories can offer a vision of "primary truth" (156) and a "sudden glimpse of the underlying reality or truth" (155), the genesis of "ideal" becomes apparent. Tolkien's fantasy worlds, a reflection of God's truth, are a Christian version of Plato's underlying ideal world. Tolkien maintains in a letter to Milton Waldman that he always "had the sense of recording what was already 'there', somewhere: not of 'inventing'" (*Letters* 145). Rather than belying this underlying reality, fantasy is fundamentally in harmony with God's primary world because "we make still by the law in which we're made" (144). In each *refutatio*, Sidney and Tolkien assert that their detractors are biased, and that their subjects are the superior art form and hold profound truth.

The *praxeis*, or praise of the subject's accomplishments, is particularly central to the encomium, and the positive effect of the praise of virtue on the morals of the audience is its vital impetus (Aristotle 101). The classical encomium seeks to engender virtue above all. To this end, the deeds of the subject praised may not be exactly the absolute truth but can be amplified or expanded (Hardison 30). Tolkien scatters praises of fairy-stories throughout "OFS" but concentrates them in "Recovery, Escape, Consolation," and in the "Epilogue." In the former section, Tolkien begins to answer directly the question on the praxis of fairy-stories that he initially poses: "What is the use of them?" (109). First of all, Recovery is the "regaining of a clear view" of what would otherwise seem "the drab blur of triteness and familiarity" (146). Fantasy even becomes an agent of insurrection because the fantasist may "rouse men to pull down the street lamps" (149). Although street lamps are a particularly ugly symptom of the industrial era for Tolkien, he seems unlikely to be encouraging street-protests, so the exaggeration of the encomium is probably in effect. Secondly, fantasy may allow the escape from the body, which suffers "hunger, thirst, poverty, pain, sorrow, injustice, death" (151). Tolkien redefines the value of commonly used terms. His definition of "escape" does not equate with cowardice; instead, the terms and phrases associated with "escape" are "freedom" (139), "freed" (146), "open your hoard and let all the locked things fly away" (147), "wild" (153), "free and wild" (147), "wildness" (149), "fly" (149, 151), "not a slavery to [fact]" (144), and "free as a fish" (151). Although Sidney also argues for a writer's access to freedom from fact—unlike a philosopher or a physician, a poet refuses to be under any "subjection" to nature (9)—Tolkien extends this freedom to include both a recovery of reality and an escape from it.

Tolkien's final pitch for the value of fairy-stories involves "the Consolation of the Happy Ending," or "Eucatastrophe," an echo of the promise of the resurrection of Christ (156). Thus, the consolation offered by fairy-stories alludes to the joy of God and God's redemption of mankind, which is so emphasized in the epilogue. Tolkien's text takes on the "inherent morality" that Tolkien has already defined as part of the fairy-story (118), which must nonetheless exist independently of tiresome preaching (111). In a letter to Peter Szabó Szentmihályi, Tolkien writes that he aims at "literary *pleasure*" and adds a disclaimer, "I neither teach nor preach," reflecting his hostility to the charge of didacticism (*Letters* 414). This attitude is also reflected in Tolkien's rather disingenuous reformulation of the primary humanist and classical *praxeis* of literature, to "teach and delight," contained in Sidney (*DOP* 12). Tolkien's "making and delight" (143) stresses invention and implicitly denies the overt pedagogical and moral motives of the Christian humanists. The *praxeis* of Sidney's poetry pleasure is utopian; "to lead and draw us to as high a perfection as our degenerate souls . . . can be capable of" (*DOP* 13; see Soens xi); despite his denials, Tolkien's overall aim is similar. For example, in a letter to Peter Hastings, Tolkien notes that in his writing he tries to show "the elucidation of truth, and the encouragement of good morals in this real world, by the ancient device of exemplifying them in unfamiliar embodiments, that may tend to 'bring them home'" (*Letters* 194). For Sidney, as well, this moral improvement is vital, as one Cyrus in poetry can breed a thousand in the material world. As is entirely appropriate in the encomium, Tolkien both teaches and possibly (although not tiresomely) preaches in the *praxeis*, a potent rhetorical combination that Sidney shares.

In the *praxeis*, Tolkien's description of the gospels as the greatest fairy-story of them all allows an encomium of superlative force in the epilogue. Toward the end of "Recovery, Escape and Consolation" and in the epilogue of "OFS," Tolkien's evangelism and his encomiastic rhetoric reach a climax. Divine words of praise weave a tapestry of extraordinary density with words and phrases such as "keeping promises" (152), "observing prohibitions" (152), "the Escape from Death" (153), "consolation" (153), "*Eucatastrophe*" (153), "deliverance" (153), "denies . . . universal final defeat" (153), "sudden and miraculous grace" (153), "greater" (154, 155), "powerful and poignant" (154), "gleam" (154, 155), "satisfaction" (155), "one facet of a truth incalculably rich" (155), "supreme" (156), "redeemed" (156), and "Joy beyond the walls of the world" (153). The repeated use of the terms "joy" and "joyous" are particularly notable examples of the repetition characteristic of the encomium. Tolkien's repetition of "true" and "truth" before the epilogue (113, 116, 132, 133, 144, 153, 155) becomes confirmed within it (155, 156). The epilogue abandons the strictly logical approach of his *refutatio* and takes a leap of faith to link the happy ending of the fairy-story to the hope and joy offered by Christianity. While large claims are entirely appropriate in the encomium, they must be believable; hence Tolkien acknowledges that it may be "presumptuous" in making this connection (155). He even suggests that once man is finally redeemed all "tales may come true," and fairy-stories will be reshaped just as man will be reshaped (156). The enormity of this suggestion (will Aragorn, Frodo, and Bilbo walk the earth?) is inherent in the encomium. Tolkien's claims go far beyond the more prosaic function of Sidney's epilogue. Alongside a summary of his arguments, Sidney returns to his original self-mocking tentativeness describing *DOP* as "this ink-wasting toy of mine" (55) and ironically threatening the anti-poetaster with the "want of a epitaph" (56). For Tolkien, any rejection of the Incarnation (and implicitly the fairy-story) leads to "sadness or to wrath" (156) away from the hope promised by happy endings. These are much larger consquences than lack of an epitaph. Although Tolkien initially gives fairy-stories a moral neutrality—they are "not the road to Heaven; nor even to

Hell" (110)—this view finally disappears in the evangelical fervor of the epilogue. For Sidney, poetry is king, but for Tolkien, fairy-stories are divine.

So is Tolkien a Renaissance Man? Certainly, in the sense that he is not so much a specialist as his own often vigorously stated prejudices (against Shakespeare or classical studies) would imply. But the answer to this question in the literary and philosophical terms of the Renaissance is more equivocal. The chivalric code, the ladder of love, the overt sensuality, and the celebration of man's mastery over nature that often characterize the Renaissance are almost absent in Tolkien. After all, more than 350 years separate Sidney's and Tolkien's works, and so it is natural that there are many differences between the two writers. In fantasy, Sidney strategically denounces the very same genre that Tolkien seeks to defend. Tolkien also concentrates on evangelism in his epilogue, whereas Sidney returns to irony. Tolkien ends with an overtly Christian message, perhaps hoping to convert Christians into readers of fairy-stories and vice versa. Sidney's tone is also more satiric and vehement than Tolkien's more academic approach, especially in the *synkrisis*. Tolkien's paean of praise to fairy-stories is, if anything, more of an encomium than Sidney's *DOP*. Sidney and Tolkien also disagree on questions of pedagogy; Sidney's poetry is the educator for all ages, and, although Tolkien does not exclude children from reading fairy-stories, he believes such tales are more appropriate for adults, with particular reference to the education of young men. They also differ in their attitudes to women; where Sidney sees writing itself as feminine and ambivalent and often has a specifically female audience in mind, Tolkien sees the task of writing as a masculine mastery of nature, in which the central concerns are passed from male writer to male reader. In this latter sense, Tolkien may have been more of a Renaissance man than Sidney.

Still, Tolkien shares much of the stock in the "soup" of story ("OFS" 120) with Sidney, particularly in terms of the tradition of encomiastic praise: they both emphasize virtue and use amplification to heighten the praise, use peripheral journeying anecdotes to introduce their theme and share an ironic posture of humility, use *synkrisis* to separate their subjects from other surrounding genres, emphasize place and time in praising the universality and lineage of poetry, and emphasize the accomplishments of their subjects. The speaking personae of Sidney and Tolkien are also characteristic of the encomium. As Coogan says of Sidney, the audience recognizes the writer as a "truly noble character who provides and preserves good things . . . who seeks to produce virtue . . . and who does things not for his own sake" (108–9). Both use the formal order of the encomium loosely and mix the encomium with the defense. In each *refutatio*, Sidney and Tolkien assert that their detractors are biased, that their subjects are the superior and most difficult art form, and that their subjects do not lie. Outside these characteristics of the encomium/defense, Sidney and Tolkien both write a *digressio* which emphasizes the sparseness of the English tradition and seeks to improve it.

Finally, Tolkien's use of the word of God to justify literature is more characteristic of the Renaissance than the post–Enlightenment. This logocentrism provides a firm ground, enabling the transcendent praise of a literature that recreates a counterfactual reality, enabled by God's creation of man in his own likeness. Ironically, the encomium is one of the few types of poetry that Plato allows inside his *Republic* (Hardison 26). Sidney and Tolkien vigorously use this approved form to argue that poetry and fairy-stories are superior forms of art since they re-create God's primary reality rather than belie it. Sidney's adumbrates many of Tolkien's ideas, which indicates that either that Tolkien was influenced by Sidney (an argument difficult to prove) or that they have a similar literary heritage. Either way, Tolkien did not write all of "OFS" himself. Part of Tolkien's legacy is classical rhetoric and Renaissance philosophy. He is a Renaissance Man in the sense that he shares some of the period's informing ideals in terms of the recreative imagination, classical rediscovery, and Christian humanism. If not of direct lineal descent, Sidney and Tolkien display the kinship of a common ancestry.

NOTES

1. Tolkien said, "My love for the classics . . . took ten years to recover from lectures on Cicero and Demosthenes," implying a later rediscovery (Salu and Farrell 12).

2. Lorise Topcliffe, a librarian at Exeter College where Tolkien spent his undergraduate years, found that Tolkien, during his time as a literature and language undergraduate, took out only books on "grammar, the history of the language and a bit of Shakespeare" (e-mail to the author: 2 Feb. 1998). Wayne Hammond, who has some "fragmentary" notes on Tolkien's library, also reports that neither he nor fellow scholar Christina Scull has any knowledge that Tolkien read *DOP* (e-mail to the author: 18 Feb. 1998).

3. Perhaps Tolkien's relationship to the Renaissance is underinvestigated because of his denunciations of Shakespeare. Commentators have so closely associated Shakespeare with "Renaissance literature" that a rejection of Shakespeare too easily becomes a rejection of everything the period represents; for example, Carpenter comments that for Tolkien "English literature ended with Chaucer" (70). This observation aside, Tolkien praises Gower, Spenser (*Essays* 111–12) and even (although not wholeheartedly) Shakespeare (*Letters* 88).

4. Coogan does not specifically place the *anatrophe* within Sidney's scheme. Sidney's (like Tolkien's) digression does fulfill the requirements of the *anatrophe* as it addresses the question of the upbringing and possible rebirth of literature in England.

5. Sidney also follows this trajectory. He writes the *Old Arcadia* for women. He dismisses it (either modestly, disingenuously, or sincerely) as "a trifle, and that triflingly handled" (3), before he writes the second epic *New Arcadia* for a more general audience.

WORKS CITED

Aristotle. *Aristotle's "Art" of Rhetoric*. Trans. John Henry Freese. New York: Putnam, 1926.

Berger, Harry. *Second World and Green World: Studies in Renaissance Fiction Making*. Berkeley: U of California P, 1988.

Burgess, Theodore C. "Epideictic Rhetoric." *Studies in Classical Philology* 3 (1902): 89–248.

Carpenter, Humphrey. *J.R.R. Tolkien: A Biography*. London: Unwin, 1977.

Colie, Rosalie L. *The Resources of Kind: Genre Theory in the Renaissance*. Berkeley:

U of California P, 1973.

Coogan, Robert. "More Dais than Dock: Greek Rhetoric and Sidney's Encomium on Poetry." *Studies in the Literary Imagination* 15.1 (1982): 99–113.

Dickson, Lynn. "Sidney's Grotesque Muse: Fictional Excess and the Feminine in the *Arcadias*." *Renaissance Papers* (1992): 41–55.

Hardison, O. B. *The Enduring Monument: A Study of the Idea of Praise in Renaissance Literary Theory and Practice*. Chapel Hill: U of North Carolina P, 1962.

Reilly, R. J. "Tolkien and the Fairy-Story." *Thought* 38 (1963): 89–106.

Roe, John. "The Poetry of Sidney, Shakespeare, Chapman, and Donne." *Platonism and the English Imagination*. Ed. Anna Baldwin and Sarah Hutton. Cambridge: Cambridge UP, 1994. 100–16.

Salu, Mary, and Robert T. Farrell, eds. *J.R.R. Tolkien, Scholar and Storyteller: Essays in Memoriam*. Ithaca and London: Cornell UP, 1979.

Sidney, Philip. *The Old Arcadia*. Ed. Katherine Duncan-Jones. Oxford and New York: Oxford UP, 1973.

——. *Sir Philip Sidney's Defense of Poesy*. Ed. Lewis Soens. Lincoln: Nebraska UP, 1970.

Soens, Lewis. Introduction. *Sir Philip Sidney's Defense of Poesy*. ix–xlii.

Vickers, Brian,ed. and Introduction. *Rhetoric Revalued*. New York: Medieval and Renaissance Texts, 1982.

Zimbardo, Rose A. "The Medieval-Renaissance Vision of *The Lord of the Rings*. [sic]" *Tolkien: New Critical Perspectives*. Ed. Neil D. Isaacs and Rose A. Zimbardo. Lexington: UP of Kentucky, 1981. 63–71.

8

Weaving Nets of Gloom: "Darkness Profound" in Tolkien and Milton

Debbie Sly

From the first appearance of *LR* in 1954, comparisons have been drawn between Tolkien's work and that of Milton, in some cases to support claims for Tolkien's status as a great writer or to undermine them by suggesting his inferiority. Two of its earliest and most distinguished readers made the comparison, although the conclusions they drew from it were very different. W. H. Auden, reviewing *RK* in January 1956, discussed the representations of "the conflict between Good and Evil" in Tolkien's trilogy and *Paradise Lost* (*PL*), and decided that although in general Tolkien cannot be ranked with Milton, "in this matter he has succeeded where Milton failed" on the grounds that Tolkien's supreme deity, unlike Milton's God, does not directly intervene in the struggle (5). Only seven months later, Edwin Muir expressed reservations about precisely this element in the trilogy, writing that "his good people are consistently good, his evil figures immovably evil, and he has no room in his world for a Satan both evil and tragic" (7).

More recently, Colin Duriez has pointed out "the important parallels between Tolkien's fiction and Milton's great work," suggesting that such a comparison brings out "the freshness and depth of Christian meaning in Tolkien's work" (147). It is certainly instructive to compare Tolkien's work, in particular *Silm*, with Milton's *PL*, not to make value judgments of this kind, but to explore more fully the complexity of Tolkien's creativity. Both texts reflect what might be termed a creative struggle between religious orthodoxy and aesthetic imperatives, though these factors operate very differently in each case.

Paradoxically, what Tolkien and Milton have most in common as artists, their devout Christianity, also divides them: Milton rewrites Genesis from a radically Protestant and Renaissance perspective, whereas Tolkien's Roman Catholicism inspires a version of the universe that is at times distinctly medieval, although it also reflects the cataclysmic events of the twentieth century. The Protestant reverence for the "Word" limits Milton's options to a considerable extent, while

Tolkien's relationship to it is, Deborah and Ivor Rogers have argued, "of a median sort" (79). Although Tolkien describes *LR* as "a fundamentally religious and Catholic work" (*Letters* 172), he elsewhere insists that it is "fatal" for art, and perhaps especially for his own brand of "myth and fairy-story," to be "explicitly" religious (*Letters* 144). Freed from any requirement to reproduce the insistently linear narrative of Christianity, Tolkien's mythology is characteristically cyclical in structure, involving not a single Creation and a single Fall (for Satan's and Man's are united in what Aristotle would term the "action" of *PL)*, but a long series of creations and falls. At the center of Milton's poem is a concern with the theological implications of sexuality, a concern most clearly seen in the twinned figures of Eve and Sin. Tolkien's cosmogony avoids any reference to possible sexual aspects of the creative process, but *gender* is of aesthetic importance. And whereas both *PL* and *Silm* are confronted with the problem of the aesthetic representation of evil, especially of its seductive aspects, and of explaining its apparent necessity to God/Ilúvatar's plan, they deal with them in significantly different ways.

One of the most striking aspects of Tolkien's cosmos is its apparent freedom from the physical laws that (as far as we can tell) govern our universe—and have provided over the centuries a series of challenges to the cosmology established by the Judaeo-Christian tradition. In *PL*, Milton describes a realistically "globous earth" (5; 649), but Arda is created flat and is remade as a sphere only after the downfall of Númenór. This event (one of that series of falls referred to above) exemplifies the complex relationship between the necessities of physics, theology, and aesthetics in Tolkien's work. On the original flat earth, it is a physical possibility for Men to travel to the blessed realms in the West, although they are forbidden to do so; the privileged Edain are even allowed to dwell in "the Land of Gift" (313), closer to those realms than to their original home in Middle-earth. However, the abuse of that privilege by the Númenóreans results in its withdrawal and a physical change in Arda, so that although the Dúnedain (their descendants in Middle-earth) are still drawn to the West, even "those that sailed furthest set but a girdle about the Earth and returned weary at last to their beginning; and they said: 'All roads are now bent'" (339).

Traditionally, the discovery of the shape of our planet has come to represent intellectual progress—and has been seen (whether accurately or not) as characteristic of modern as opposed to medieval thought: thus derogatory references are made to "flat earthers." For Tolkien, however, the roundness of the earth symbolizes *limitation*—its containment of Man's corporeal existence —although this limitation is itself, paradoxically, limited: the Eldar who remain in Middle-earth are not limited by it, being able still to sail to Valinor; thus alternative models of the world co-exist to represent differing levels of spirituality.

The complex interaction in *PL* of the conventions of epic heroism, Renaissance humanism, and Protestant individualism produce in Satan the powerful and ambivalent figure so seductive to Romantic readers, such as Blake and Shelley. As Stanley Fish points out, readers may experience the same temptation as Eve (237);

being, unlike Eve, already fallen, it is even less surprising if they (and Edwin Muir) find Satan tragic, even attractive, rather than repulsive, a "hero of the fallen imagination," as Kenneth Gross has called him (318). For Satan is the first individual encountered in the poem, and Milton allows him to upstage every other character with an extended exploration, not just of non-problematical sinful elements in Satan's nature, such as pride and anger, but also of disconcertingly human ones, such as pain, remorse, and frustration. Book 1 culminates in the famous portrait which has spawned a hundred darkly brooding literary offspring:

> . . . his face
> Deep scars of thunder had intrenched, and care
> Sat on his faded cheek, but under brows
> Of dauntless courage, and considerate pride
> Waiting revenge; cruel his eye, but cast
> Signs of remorse and passion to behold
> The fellows of his crime.
> (1; 600-606)

Tolkien does not intend to confront readers with their fallen natures in this way by making evil so attractive *in its incarnations* (though I must confess to a sneaking liking for Gollum). In his response to W. H. Auden's review of *RK*, Tolkien denies dealing "in Absolute Evil" on the grounds that no "'rational being'" can be "wholly evil" (*Letters* 243); but he avoids any detailed examination of the nature of either Melkor or Sauron. They are never presented as suffering grief or remorse—when thwarted, they rage or sulk—and their original and fallen natures are represented symbolically in terms of the possession or the forfeiture of fairness. Milton's Satan has subordinates representing different aspects of evil, but their presence, as the quotation above suggests, tends to humanize him. Like the epic hero he so much resembles, Satan consults his lieutenants, but does not shirk responsibility:

> "But I should ill become this throne, O peers,
> And this imperial sovereignty, adorned
> With splendour, armed with power, if aught proposed
> And judged of public moment, in the shape
> Of difficulty or danger could deter
> Me from attempting."
> (2; 445-450)

The relationship between Melkor and Sauron is never explored in this way. Indeed the existence of a lieutenant who merely reproduces his characteristics at a slightly lower level may extend Melkor's power to intervene in Middle-earth, but it tends to lessen his impact on the reader. This would seem to support not only Muir's judgment of Tolkien's achievement, but also the more general one that his universe is based on an unproblematic confrontation between the forces of darkness and the forces of light.

However temptation *does* exist in Tolkien's universe: darkness does indeed have power over the human spirit—but it is not darkness incarnate as an heroically demonic persona, but darkness as an *aesthetic category*, the aspect of darkness that Burke celebrates in his *Philosophical Enquiry into the Origin of our Ideas of the Sublime and Beautiful*. For Burke, of course, darkness is merely a characteristic of the sublime, but his relevance here lies in his focus on the pleasurable (or otherwise), rather than the spiritual and moral, effects of his categories. He praises Milton's descriptions of both Death and Satan, not for their power to inspire either admiration or disgust for what they represent, but for their power *per se*; they are cited purely as exemplars of Milton's skillful use of "a judicious obscurity" (Burke 59–62).

A few years after the initial publication of *LR*, Tolkien provided a strikingly specific account of the origin of his work in a letter to his son Christopher:

> Nobody believes me when I say that my long book is an attempt to create a world in which a form of language agreeable to my personal aesthetic might seem real. But it is true. An enquirer (among many) asked what L.R. was about, and whether it was an 'allegory.' And I said it was an effort to create a situation in which a common greeting would be *elen síla lúmenn' omentielmo* [sic—this appears as *omentielvo* in *LR*], and that the phrase long antedated the book. (*Letters* 264–65)

Tolkien's primary interest in language and its reciprocal relationship with mythology is well known and has been widely discussed; I wish to explore the clue that this "common greeting," which means "a star shines on the hour of our meeting" (*FR* 90), offers to that "personal aesthetic." I have suggested that his cosmos is not bound by known physical laws in that Arda is not necessarily round; further evidence of this is provided by the peculiar nature and role of light. Tolkien's account of the creation of light is complex, unorthodox ,and, like the rest of the narrative, cyclical. In *PL,* following Genesis, God's primary act is the performative utterance that brings light into being. This act is presumably preceded by darkness—as it is in Milton's version: "darkness profound / Covered the abyss" (7; 233–34). In *Silm*, darkness is decidedly belated, coming into being *after* the initial vision of the making and marring of Arda: "But even as Ulmo spoke, and while the Ainur were yet gazing upon this vision, it was taken away and hidden from their sight; and it seemed to them that in that moment they perceived a new thing, Darkness, which they had not known before except in thought" (21). In one sense, this is more logical in symbolic terms than the process described in Genesis: if darkness represents evil, and evil enters the cosmos with the first rebellious thought of Melkor, then darkness must indeed be subsequent to the light that represents divine power. This possibility is, however, problematic in conceptual terms because it seems to require some third option, neither light nor darkness, to exist before creation.

The making of Tolkien's Arda is associated with the creation of light, in that it comes into being as "a light, as it were a cloud with a living heart of flame," an image recalling Milton's description of the first appearance of light "in a cloudy tabernacle" (7; 248). But after that, Tolkien's cosmology departs from the Christian one. At once Melkor begins his meddling, kindling "great fires" in rivalry (22); when these fires are subdued, a new light source becomes necessary. The Valar then create their first "great lamps," Illuin and Ormal, "and the light of the Lamps of the Valar flowed out all over Earth, so that all was lit as it were in a changeless day" (39). These lamps are broken by Melkor, darkness returns, and the Valar have to rebuild a second "blessed" realm, from which darkness is again excluded by the creation of the "Two Trees of Valinor" (43). At this point in Tolkien's narrative a subtext becomes perceptible. Although their light is secondary (even tertiary, in that it replaces that of Illuin and Ormal, which were themselves not part of the first stage of creation) and exists in a world already blighted by Melkor's fall and its results, it seems to be *more beautiful* than that of the original "Lamps." The "changeless day" of the Spring of Arda is replaced by a more subtle illumination:

> In seven hours the glory of each tree waxed to full and waned again to naught;
> and each awoke once more to life an hour before the other ceased to shine. Thus
> in Valinor twice every day there came a gentler hour of softer light when both
> trees were faint and their gold and silver beams were mingled. (43)

Darkness, in this cosmos, should have no place in such a blessed realm—yet this dimming of light which is a reminder, even an acknowledgment of its existence, is a moment of significant beauty, of *aesthetic* rather than theological power.

With their gold and silver beams, the Trees are the origins of the familiar light sources in our world; yet even after the Trees' destruction (Melkor again), the creation of the Sun (Tolkien's description of it as a "second-best thing" [*Letters* 148] seems an understatement) and Moon is not immediate. For Middle-earth is awaiting the appearance of the Firstborn and must lie under "'the shadow of Melkor'" (58) in order that, in the words of Mandos, "'the Firstborn shall come in the darkness, and shall look first upon the stars'" (55). This is one of the most significant departures from Christian orthodoxy: if darkness symbolizes evil, then the Elves, unlike Adam and Eve, would appear to be created *fallen*. How is this to be reconciled with the insistence that they represent a *higher* form of existence, unless Tolkien is making an implicit distinction between religious and aesthetic experience? For both within and outside *Silm*, Tolkien makes this point: Ilúvatar himself foretells that "they shall have and shall conceive and bring forth more beauty than all my Children" (47); Tolkien explained to Naomi Mitchison that "they represent really Men with greatly enhanced aesthetic and creative faculties" (*Letters* 176). Starlight would seem to represent a supreme aesthetic experience, and one that defines the nature of the elves: Varda makes "new stars and brighter against the coming of the Firstborn" (55), and the Valar name the elves Eldar, "people of the stars" (57). The conflict suggests that the demands of religious orthodoxy are less easily reconciled to Tolkien's "personal aesthetic" than he and many commentators have acknowledged.

It is necessary at this point to examine his account of creation and to relate it, as he did himself in many of his letters, to the concept of "sub-creation" described in "On Fairy-Stories." Here, famously, Tolkien offered a definition of the successful "story-maker":

> He makes a Secondary World which your mind can enter. Inside it, what he relates is 'true': it accords with the law of that world. You therefore believe it, while you are, as it were, inside. (*Essays* 132)

In *Silm*, Tolkien's supreme deity, Ilúvatar, initiates creation in two originating acts: "He made first the Ainur, the Holy Ones, that were the offspring of his thought, and they were with him before aught else was made. And he spoke to them, propounding themes of music; and they sang before him, and he was glad" (15). While Ilúvatar continues to change "the themes of music," the process of transforming these themes into material form belongs to the Ainur. As Tolkien remarks, they "took part in the making of the world as 'sub-creators'"(*Letters* 284), charged with the responsibility of bringing into being everything except "the Children of Illúvatar," the "races of Elves and Men."

There are some parallels here between Milton and Tolkien. In *PL*, the creation of the cosmos does not begin until God has not only created its elaborate hierarchy of "Thrones, dominations, princedoms, virtues, powers," (5; 601) but has also, in the lines described by Alistair Fowler as "among the most controversial in the poem" (295n), "begot whom I declare / My only Son" (603–4). Christ then materializes the divine will in the act of creation, which otherwise is closely modelled on Genesis. However, there is no equivalent to Christ in *Silm* (although "Ilúvatar" does mean "'Father of All'" [404]), and the important role played by music in Tolkien's creation seems to be drawn from a very different cosmogony, that of the followers of Pythagorus, in which creation is visualized in distinctively abstract terms. These are in marked contrast with the Judaic insistence on creation as the single-handed act of a solitary male deity, an insistence that censors, as it were, earlier accounts in which creation is imagined in terms of a sexual act involving male and female elements. Such an insistence seems to lie behind Milton's reference to an original begetting of Christ that does not require the participation of Mary. The rejection of sexuality characteristic of early and medieval Christianity reflects the part played in the formation of the doctrine of the immortality of the soul by the Greek Platonic tradition derived from Pythagorus (Boman 53). Although there is some debate about the relationship between early Christianity and later Hellenism[1], the Pythagorean cosmos is the most likely source for Tolkien's process of creation, which moves from the abstraction of music to the materiality of physical *making,* carefully avoiding even metaphoric references to paternity.

Yet this avoidance of the sexual is paradoxically linked to an assertion of the power of *femininity* in which theology and aesthetics again appear to be in conflict.

Although the Valar, unlike Milton's angels, divide themselves into masculine and feminine beings, the division is based on gender rather than any biological concept of sexuality, and its implications are metaphorical and aesthetic, rather than physical:

> [W]hen they desire to clothe themselves the Valar take upon them forms some *as of* male and some *as of* female; for that difference of temper they had even from their beginning, and it is but *bodied forth* in the choice of each, not made by the choice, *even as* with us male and female may be shown by the raiment but is not made thereby. (*Silm* 23; emphases added)

The comparison with human sexuality is just that, an analogy to enable "us" to understand difference through similarity; for the Valar, bodies are an option, not the necessity for existence. In contrast, Raphael's description of angelic sexual activity, in Book 8 of *PL,* comes as something of a surprise, given the absence of any female angels, and seems entirely inspired by Milton's concern with the theological rehabilitation of sex within the institution of marriage.

The Valier represent, not a femaleness necessary to a creativity based on the model of sexuality, but *femininity* associated with particular spheres of influence, most notably in the case of Varda. Responding to the suggestion of a Jesuit friend, Tolkien acknowledged the resemblance of Galadriel, the dominant female figure in *LR*, to the figure of the Virgin (*Letters* 172), and the similarity is even more marked in the case of Varda, whom the elves call "*Elentári*, Queen of the Stars," and whom they invoke in the hymn, "*O Elbereth! Gilthoniel!*" (*FR* 114). Varda is, however, a more powerful figure than the Christian Mary, in that her status is derived from a more direct association with divine power. Mary is only the *bearer* of the source of light, the necessary female participant in the incarnation of Christ (which for Milton is separate from his origin), while of Varda, Tolkien states in *Silm*, "In light is her power and her joy" (28). Not only does she create the stars but it is she who fills the first two Lamps of the Valar with light (39), and although the secondary light of the Two Trees is created by Yavannah, it seems significant that she also is a Valar in feminine form. Despite this difference, the elves' reverence clearly has its origin in Tolkien's response to Mary: in the letter cited above, he wrote that "all my own small perception of beauty both in majesty and simplicity" was founded on the figure of "Our Lady" (*Letters* 172). Such a claim seems to counter my argument that for Tolkien, aesthetic and spiritual experience blend readily in the cult of the Virgin. It is significant, however, that Tolkien attributes to her his sense of *beauty* rather than of holiness.

Still, there is a negative side to such an idealization. Mary's elevation has tended to coexist with a paranoid distaste for the female body that finds its expression in the writing of many of the fathers of the early Church; a detailed analysis of this aspect of Catholic theology can be found in Marina Warner's *Alone of All Her Sex* (1981). A similar concern can also be found in those Protestant writers who idealize the female, such as Spenser and, of course, Milton. In

Tolkien's work, too, there is a dark "Other" to the beauty, wisdom, and virtue of Varda and Galadriel. Anne C. Petty suggests that in *LR* the lethal female spider Shelob and Galadriel "are binary opposites in Tolkien's conception" (81); such an opposition is also implicit in Brenda Partridge's "No Sex Please—We're Hobbits," in which she analyzes the sexual symbolism surrounding both Galadriel and Shelob, comparing the latter in particular with Milton's "Sin" (187–89). Just as Varda represents a far greater feminine power than Galadriel, so Shelob's horror is but a shadow of that of her progenitrix in *Silm,* Ungoliant:

> In a ravine she lived, and took shape as a spider of monstrous form, weaving her black webs in a cleft of the mountains. There she sucked up all the light that she could find, and spun it forth again in dark nets of strangling gloom, until no more light could come to her abode; and she was famished. (86)

Although I agree with Partridge that Tolkien's female monsters share the horrible physicality of Milton's Sin, I think there are important differences in their function. Sin, with her father/lover Satan and their offspring Death, form what Fowler calls "a complete anti-Trinity" (129n); they are part of an elaborate series of "fallen" equivalents balancing the celebration of chaste marital sex in *PL* with dire warnings against lust, incest, and other undesirable activities. Sin, originally, like her father, "in shape and countenance bright, / Then shining heavenly fair" (2; 756–57), but deformed by the process of giving birth to Death, can trace her genealogy back through Satan to God. She is therefore in theological terms a safely subordinate figure, as Eve is in comparison with the largely non-Biblical figure of Mary, whose place in Roman Catholic doctrine dates mainly from the fourth century C.E., and has been linked by some commentators to the need to counter the influence in Mediterranean culture of the Magna Dea.[2] Ungoliant's origins are less clear:

> The Eldar knew not whence she came; but some have said that in long ages before she descended from the darkness that lies about Arda, when Melkor first looked down in envy upon the kingdom of Manwë, and that in the beginning she was one of those that he corrupted to his service. (85)

There is a potential for confusion here: if Ungoliant has "descended from darkness," she is already a product of Melkor's fall, rather than being, like Sauron, created unfallen by Ilúvatar. But if this is the case, there is no need for her to be "corrupted to his [Melkor's] service." Significantly, Tolkien does not suggest that she was, like Sauron, one of the Maiar, "the people of the Valar, and their servants and helpers" (33), and no meaning is offered for her name in the index to *Silm* (unlike the other powers of evil in the text), although in a letter to Naomi Mitchison, Tolkien explains that "*Ungol*" is Elvish for "spider" (*Letters* 180). Her end is as obscure as her beginning: "Of the fate of Ungoliant no tale tells" (95).

Although her femininity is (like Varda's) symbolic, in that her "lust" (unlike Sin's) is for light to spin into those nets of gloom, at times Tolkien's description comes close to making her power of negation so strong it is in danger of becoming a positive force. From weaving "an Unlight, in which things seemed to be no more, and which eyes could not pierce, for it was void" (86), Ungoliant goes on to produce a "Darkness" which "seemed not lack but a thing with being of its own: for it was indeed made by malice out of Light, and it had power to pierce the eye, and to enter heart and mind, and strangle the very will" (89). Again, it is significant that in all the explanations of the role and nature of evil in his work Tolkien offers in his letters, there is virtually no discussion of Ungoliant; she is (in the letter cited above) referred to only briefly as "the primeval devourer of light" who "assisted the Dark Power" (*Letters* 180). This may be because her nature undermines his repeated assertions that evil is a negative force that cannot create, only corrupt (*Letters* 178, 195). (In its curious combination of reticence, rhetoric, and revulsion, Tolkien's attitude is reminiscent of that of another, more influential, portrayer of femininity, Sigmund Freud.) Ungoliant, then, is a problematic figure in *theological* terms; she seems to exist beyond theology's powers of explanation, wrapped in her self-engendered obscurity. Yet in *aesthetic* terms, as a source of darkness, she appears to be the necessary counterpart to Varda, creator of the stars, whose beauty is invisible without those "black webs."

That sub-creation is inevitably enmeshed in this apparent contradiction is demonstrated by the exemplary act from which the title of *Silm* derives. In his reference to the Valar as "sub-creators," Tolkien is possibly making a fairly grandiose claim for his genre—as indeed Milton does, confessing to his own presumption in pursuing "things unattempted yet in prose or rhyme" (1; 16), and repeatedly drawing parallels between divine and human creation by his use of the word "author."[3] However, the elves are most obviously intended as a model for creative aspiration, and their "sub-creative function" is "chiefly symbolized" by the making of gems—especially the eponymous *Silmarilli*, or "Primeval Jewels" (*Letters* 148).

Fëanor's obsession with the Silmarils, causing both his fall and that of his sons, raises a further possible discrepancy between theological and aesthetic imperatives. Milton's Adam and Eve fall because Satan tempts them to accept something that has been explicitly forbidden and to which they have no right, something moreover that is incompatible with a state of unfallen-ness and has nothing to do with beauty, but everything to do with *power*—as Satan's invocation to the Tree of Knowledge indicates: "O sacred, wise, and wisdom-giving plant, / Mother of science, now I feel thy power / Within me clear" (9; 679–81). The Fëanorians fall because of their desire for the *beauty* of jewels that contain the unfallen Light of the Two Trees but that appear otherwise functionless, adding nothing to the power of their possessor, and that are "hallowed" by Varda—an apparently validation of their creation (78).

The fact that Fëanor also made them, and thus has some claim to them, further complicates the situation. Melkor's involvement, too, is different from Satan's in that although he poisons the relationship between Fëanor and the Valar, this is because he also desires the jewels for himself. And although these events are the forerunners of a long series of acts of treachery and violence, in the words of

Fëanor, "the deeds that we shall do shall be the matter of song until the last days of Arda" (104). They will certainly be the matter for the pen of J.R.R. Tolkien, who is, even more than the Valar, the sub-creator of Arda, and of the Silmarils and the evils that follow them. Sunshine and the harmless pleasures of life are not the stuff of 'high' art—the lives of hobbits are the subject of epic only when one of them accidentally falls victim to the desires inspired by the Ring.

All foregoing analysis suggests that aesthetic experience at the higher, Elven, level *requires* the existence of darkness. Art is born not so much out of a *conflict* between good and evil, which implies ultimate victory by one side (a victory that is, moreover, predetermined in Christian doctrine) but from their *coexistence*, and that implicit in the elves' devotion to Varda is an acknowledgment of the engendering darkness of Ungoliant. This is not quite the same as accepting that the possibility of evil is necessary for the exercise of freely willed virtue, and thus an appropriate subject for art, which is Milton's point in "Areopagetica" when he praises Spenser for exposing Sir Guyon (and of course the reader) to the temptations of "the cave of Mammon and the bowr of earthly blisse that he may see and know, and yet abstain" (213).

When Tolkien declares that there "cannot be any 'story' without a fall" (*Letters* 147), he means, of course, that all stories must reflect what for him is the essential truth about humanity: it is fallen. However (like the ambiguous instructions above the West-door of Moria) the statement has another, very simple meaning: without the Fall, there could be no stories, no art of any kind. Indeed, not only may evil be a prerequisite for aesthetic experience and its production through art, but the origins of evil, as emblematically seen in "darkness profound," may be linked to the sub-creative impulse itself. Melkor's first sin is to insert his own discordant theme into the music of Ilúvatar. Tolkien, too, despite his explicit commitment to "fundamentally religious and Catholic," sub-creation, introduces a "discordant" theme, but one, I would argue, that adds considerably to the affective power of his work, just as the "discordant" attraction of Milton's Satan has, for so many readers, enriched *Paradise Lost*.

NOTES

1. For a summary, see "Christianity," *Encyclopaedia Britannica*, 15th ed. (1974).

2. See, for example, Geoffrey Ashe, *The Virgin* (37), and Michael P. Carroll, *The Cult of the Virgin Mary* (75).

3. For an extended analysis of this aspect of *PL,* see Marshall Grossman, *"Authors to Themselves": Milton and the Revelation of History.*

WORKS CITED

Ashe, Geoffrey. *The Virgin*. London: Routledge, 1976.
Auden, W. H. "At the End of the Quest, Victory." *New York Times Book Review*. 22 Jan. 1956: 5.
Boman, Thorlief. *Hebrew Thought Compared with Greek*. London: SCM, 1960.

Burke, Edmund. *A Philosophical Enquiry into the Origins of our Ideas of the Sublime and Beautiful.* London: Routledge, 1958.

Carroll, Michael P. *The Cult of the Virgin Mary.* Princeton: Princeton UP, 1986.

Duriez, Colin. "Sub-creation and Tolkien's Theology of Story." *Scholarship and Fantasy.* Ed. K. J. Battarbee. Proceedings of the Tolkien Phenomenon, May 1992, Turku, Finland. Turku: U of Turku, 1993. 133–50.

Encyclopaedia Britiannica. "Christianity." 15th Ed. 1974.

Fish, Stanley. *Surprised By Sin.* London: Macmillan, 1967.

Fowler, Alastair (ed.) *Paradise Lost.* By John Milton. London: Longman, 1971.

Gross, Kennneth. "Satan and the Romantic Satan: A Notebook." *Re-membering Milton.* Ed. Mary Nyquist and Margaret Ferguson. London: Methuen, 1987. 318–41

Grossman, Marshall. *"Authors to Themselves": Milton and the Revelation of History.* Cambridge: Cambridge UP, 1987.

Milton, John. "Areopagetica." *Selected Prose.* Ed. C. A. Patrides. Harmondsworth: Penguin, 1974. 196–248.

——. *Paradise Lost.* Ed. Alastair Fowler. London: Longman, 1971.

Muir, Edwin. "Strange Epics." *Observer* 22 Aug. 1956: 7.

Partridge, Brenda. "No Sex, Please—We're Hobbits: The Construction of Female Sexuality in *The Lord of the Rings.*" *J.R.R. Tolkien: This Far Land.* Ed. Robert Giddings. London: Vision, 1983. 179–97.

Petty, Anne C. *One Ring to Bind Them All: Tolkien's Mythology.* Tuscaloosa: U of Alabama P, 1979.

Rogers, Deborah Webster, and Ivor A. Rogers. *J.R.R. Tolkien.* Boston: Twayne, 1980.

Warner, Marina. *Alone of All Her Sex.* London: Picador, 1985.

9

Gagool and Gollum: Exemplars of Degeneration in *King Solomon's Mines* and *The Hobbit*

William N. Rogers II and Michael R. Underwood

As scholar and philologist, J.R.R. Tolkien was necessarily concerned with the sources that underlay the Old English and Middle English texts he worked with, but in his famous essay "*Beowulf*: The Monsters and the Critics," he emphasizes interpretation, not the mosaic of sources behind the text. For a variety of reasons, criticism of Tolkien's own imaginative work has also tended to reach for larger meanings—psychological, moral, and religious—rather than dwell on the minute particulars of sources. Tolkien's indebtedness to the heroic literature and "linguistic matter" of northern Europe was so overwhelming—and so openly acknowledged—that for his early critics it was easy to consider the matter of sources open and shut. In the case of *Hobbit*, for instance, Tolkien said that "*Beowulf* is among my most valued sources" (*Letters* 31).

Yet in recent years critics have drawn attention to a wide range of sources very much closer in time to Tolkien than the heroic literature that was his professional interest. William H. Green in *The Hobbit: A Journey into Maturity* suggests as important sources for that work George MacDonald's *The Princess and the Goblin* (1872), William Morris's medieval romances, S. R. Crockett's *The Black Douglas* (1899), and E. A. Wyke Smith's *The Marvellous Land of the Snergs* (1927). He also cites works with which Tolkien expressed a "familiarity"—Lewis Carroll's *Alice in Wonderland* (1865), Kenneth Grahame's *The Wind in the Willows* (1908), Joel Chandler Harris's *Brer Rabbit* (1906), H. G. Wells's *The Time Machine* (1895), and Robert Louis Stevenson's *Treasure Island* (1886). Among other "important" influences (6), Green draws special attention to Sir Henry Rider Haggard's *King Solomon's Mines* (1885). Jared Lobdell in *England and Always: Tolkien's World of the Rings* discusses the "writers whose influence Tolkien himself acknowledged, or to whose works he referred, or whose works he conspicuously echoed"; he reports that "the list [of such writers] is not long, and the first name on it, Sir Henry Rider Haggard, is almost certainly the most important" (6). Humphrey Carpenter also puts Haggard's name in a "short list" of "comparatively recent authors [who] made their mark on [Tolkien]"—William Morris, Andrew Lang, George MacDonald, Rider Haggard, Kenneth Grahame, and John Buchan (172).

Although Tolkien himself, in letters and interviews, acknowledged writers whose work had "interested" him over the years, he sought to make clear that "influence" in his case was something other than a discrete matter of one-to-one correspondences.   His well-known—and obviously carefully thought out —reflections on this subject were recorded by Humphrey Carpenter:

> One writes . . . a story not out of the leaves of trees; still to be observed, nor by means of botany and soil-science; but it grows like a seed in the dark out of the leaf-mould of the mind: out of all that has been seen or thought or read, that has long ago been forgotten descending into the deeps. No doubt there is much selection as with a gardener: what one throws on one's personal compost-heap; and my mould is evidently made largely of linguistic matter. (126)

Nonetheless, when queried late in life, Tolkien put particular emphasis not on the "linguistic matter" in his "compost-heap," but on the "interest" generated by one particular writer—H. Rider Haggard: "I suppose as a boy *She* interested me as much as anything—like the Greek shards of Amyntas, which was the kind of machine by which everything got moving" (Lobdell 7).[1]

Despite this unambiguous admission by Tolkien and the previously cited acknowledgments by critics that Haggard influenced Tolkien, the thematic and other links between these writers have largely remained unexplored. The whole range of influence existing between these writers is not pertinent to this essay, but only one specific link. It is a particularly striking connection that draws together two memorable characters, both freighted with implications of degeneration and loss of moral purpose and direction. The contention here is that there exists a close relationship between the most memorable character in *Hobbit* other than Bilbo Baggins himself—the comic-sinister, bright-eyed, slinking riddler Gollum—and the equally memorable Gagool, a fiendish and deadly presence, in *King Solomon's Mines* (*Mines*). Our concern is not source hunting as an end in itself, but rather how a source influences a writer's imagination and how that source finds a congruent place in the particular cultural and ideological meanings of the "borrowing" text.

Sir Henry Rider Haggard (1856-1925) wrote narratives in late-Victorian and Edwardian England, of which *She* and *Mines* are the most famous, that characteristically involve a small band of male comrades setting out on perilous, fantastic, but (especially for the young in spirit) quite compelling adventures.[2] Such fictions that updated the Medieval-Renaissance quest romance strongly appealed to Tolkien, first as a boy who probably first read Haggard in the early years of the new century and then later when he began writing fiction himself. Haggard's enormously successful *Mines* has remained in print ever since its publication in 1885. As late-Victorian boys' adventure fiction, it has been patronized and dismissed because of its formulaic elements, stereotypical characterizations, and improbable and incredible plot; but from its first appearance its psychological depths have held the attention of thinkers as central to twentieth-century thought as Freud and Jung. (In recent years critics of postcolonial discourse have singled it out for particular consideration.) Haggard, never a writer who labored over his prose, admitted that he wrote this work in an enveloping rush of inspiration, scarcely putting the pen down and quite consciously trying to tap deep inner sources—what might be called archetypal patterns in the subconscious mind. It is a text that with a driving narrative and symbolic, almost dreamlike landscape holds the attention of the naive as well as the theoretically sophisticated reader.

Mines comprises a series of adventures, each in some way more challenging than the one before. Allan Quatermain, the narrator, is a much-experienced white hunter in Africa; but contrary to what might be expected, he is middle-aged, below average height, slight of build, and avowedly unheroic. He is reluctantly drawn into the quest of a young Englishman, Sir Henry Curtis, to find a brother lost in an unknown region of Africa, where he was searching for the long-lost diamond mines of King Solomon. Quatermain, along with Sir Henry and the naval officer Captain Good, a mysterious African called Umbopa, and other African helpers, ventures where "no man has gone before," at least not to return. The company hunts big game, marches into a trackless desert, and survives heat and thirst only to face death from starvation and cold while climbing over a mountain barrier. Their descent into fertile, well-tended lands leads to the realm of the Kukuanas, a warrior state ruled by fearsome King Twala, who when first met is flanked by his malicious son Scraggra and the mysterious adviser Gagool. Shortly after this, it is revealed that Umbopa, the mysterious African, is in fact Ignosi, the wrongfully deposed king of Kukuanaland. His efforts to regain the throne lead to a ferocious, hand-to-hand battle of massed armies—those loyal to the rightful king Ignosi against the many more loyal to the evil Twala. This epic battle, in which Quatermain and his companions play a conspicuous part, leads to the victory of Ignosi. The self-confessedly unheroic Allan Quatermain fights alongside the others, although he is knocked unconscious and (as narrator) can recount the concluding events of the battle only second-hand. Ignosi the rightful king and his men triumph; the evil Twala is killed in single combat with Sir Henry.

However, this is not at all the end of the adventure. The mines—and their secret depths—remain to be explored and exploited. The white men and a Kukuana girl named Foulata, who loves Captain Good, set off for the mines accompanied by Gagool, their sinister guide. In the caves, a horrific place of entombment for the kings of the Kukuanas, and in an inner chamber full of diamonds of the most incredible size, Gagool attempts to trap them forever by releasing an immense stone door. However, she is delayed by Foulata, whom she kills before she is herself crushed by the descending door. Escaping the tomblike inner chamber, the three adventurers receive the blessings of King Ignosi, carry away a rich sampling of diamonds, and—to tie up all loose ends!—find Curtis's long-lost brother. Quatermain leaves Africa to live near Sir Henry in the peaceful English countryside.

As these abbreviated details of plot and characterization suggest, connections of various sorts are evident between *Mines* and *Hobbit*. Although he does not go into specifics, Green argues that the works share "dozens of motifs" (6). Among these would probably be the following: an unheroic and unassuming narrator who is both resourceful and brave when faced by crisis; a band of questers whose journey has comic elements (Captain Good is forced to display himself in Kukuanaland without trousers, with only one side of his face shaved, and a monocle in one eye); a narrator who is knocked unconscious during a climactic, epic battle; perilous wanderings in caves with an immense treasure as the goal; and a return to a pastoral landscape of peace and contentment. These parallels, though not definitive proof of Tolkien's imaginative appropriation of Haggard's African narrative, since Haggard himself draws on already-existing formulaic elements and patterns, provide a sort of matrix that gives an extra degree of plausibility to the intimate connection, argued here, between two characters, one in Haggard, the other in Tolkien. Gagool in *Mines* and Gollum in *Hobbit* are both etched, disturbingly and permanently, in the mind of any reader of these "fantasies."

When Quatermain first catches sight of Gagool, she appears to be "a withered-up monkey [that] crept on all fours into the shade of the hut and squatted down" (140), but shortly afterward he dwells, fixedly, on ambiguous descriptive details that position her closer to the non-human ("monkey-like," a "furry covering," "the hood of a cobra") than the fully human:

> The wizened monkey-like figure cre[pt] up from the shadow of the hut. It crept on all fours, but when it reached the place where the king sat, it rose upon its feet, and throwing the furry covering off its face, revealed a most extraordinary and weird countenance. It was (apparently) that of a woman of great age, so shrunken that in size it was no larger than that of a year-old child, and was made up of a collection of deep yellow wrinkles. Set in the wrinkles was a sunken slit, that represented the mouth, beneath which the chin curved outward to a point. There was no nose to speak of; indeed, the whole countenance might have been taken for that of a sun-dried corpse had it not been for a pair of large black eyes, still full of fire and intelligence, which gleamed and played under the snow-white eyebrows, and the projecting parchment-coloured skull, like jewels in a charnel-house. As for the skull itself, it was perfectly bare, and yellow in hue, while its wrinkled scalp moved and contracted like the hood of a cobra. (147)

When Gagool finally speaks, it is with a repetitive urgency and a bloody ferocity: "The figure . . . suddenly projected a skinny claw armed with nails nearly an inch long, and . . . began to speak in a thin, piercing voice—'Listen, O king! Listen, O people! . . . Listen, all things that live and must die! Listen, all dead things that must live again—again to die! Listen, the spirit of life is in me, and I prophesy. I prophesy! I prophesy!'" (147–48). Gagool's is a creed of blood and death, in both of which she rejoices. She proclaims her great age—centuries in length—and speaks of the history of the Kukuanas as she has seen it, her words full of menace and foreboding. Quatermain is appalled: "The words died away in a faint wail, and the terror seemed to seize upon the hearts of all who heard them, including ourselves. The old woman was very terrible" (148). This "terrible" quality is firmly emphasized in the final chapters of the novel when she has been captured and is confronted by the new king Ignosi, who says, "'Yet I will slay thee. See, Gagool, mother of evil, thou art so old thou canst no longer love thy life. What can life be to such a hag as thee, who hast no shape, nor form, nor hair, nor teeth—hast naught, save wickedness and evil eyes? It will be mercy to slay thee, Gagool.'" To this she replies with a relentlessly materialistic view of life:

> "Thou fool," shrieked the old fiend, "thou accursed fool, thinkest thou that life is sweet only to the young? It is not so, and naught thou knowest of the heart of man to think it. To the young, indeed, death is something welcome, for the young can feel. They love and suffer, and it wrings them to see their beloved pass to the land of shadows. But the old feel not, they love not, and, *ha! ha!* they laugh to see another go out into the dark; *ha! ha!* they laugh to see the evil that is done under the sun. All they love is life, the warm, warm sun, and the sweet, sweet air. They are afraid of the cold and the dark, *ha! ha! ha!*" and the old hag writhed in ghastly merriment on the ground. (252–53)

At this point, prodded by a spear, she agrees to lead the white men to the "place where the stones are"; but in her head and heart are plans for revenge.

To relate Gagool to Gollum five considerations are relevant: (1) Gagool is human, but so distorted and changed by time as to be only a kind of parody of human life; she is frequently described in terms of animals—monkeys, snakes, vultures, a dog, and so forth; she is also described as a "fiend." (2) Although her body has shrunken—indeed, fallen away—in her extreme age, her eyes are large and bright, "gleaming," "full of intelligence and insight"; these, along with her speech, are what especially define her. (3) She conceals herself in a cloak, appears only with the king, and revels in a night-time "witch-hunt," when she dispenses death as she alone sees fit. (4) Her manner of speech is "prophetic," full of repetitions and oddly unsettling "hee-hees" and "ha-has"; the combination of an ancient (female) body, glittering, intelligent eyes, and a cackling malignity that at times causes her to writhe on the ground is arresting and unsettling. (5) But of special importance and resonance is her materialistic philosophy of life—one that is devoid of idealism or any sense of the spiritual; she revels in a strictly materialistic view of life, as indicated in her words to Twala, finding a sufficiency in life itself and the physical world (the "warm sun and sweet air"), and a delight in bringing death to the young. A terrible greediness and self-referencing accords convincingly with her desiccated, death's-head appearance. As she becomes more and more like a mummy, skin stretched tightly over a skull, her will to survive seems to have grown ever stronger.

To contextualize and understand Gagool's deeper significance for Haggard and his contemporary readers, the anxieties faced by late-Victorians should be considered, if only briefly. By 1885, the year *Mines* was published, the confidence of the mid-Victorian years of the Great Exhibition of 1851 had given way to uncertainties and doubts engendered by many circumstances: economic recession; the challenge of the continental powers, especially Germany; scientific materialism; perceived cultural decline; and fears of moral "decadence." A poem such as "Recessional" by Haggard's good friend Rudyard Kipling articulates the "imperial anxiety" present even at Queen Victoria's Diamond Jubilee: "If, drunk with sight of power, we loose / Wild tongues that have not Thee in awe, / Such boasting as the Gentiles use/ Or lesser breeds without the Law—/ Lord God of Hosts, be with us yet . . . ."

Gagool's malign words—symbolically underlined by her horrific appearance —embody fears and anxieties prevalent throughout Europe as the nineteenth century drew to an end. In 1895 when the German journalist Max Nordau's polemic against his times appeared in English translation, his one-word title—*Degeneration*—put the darkest construction on "The Psychology of Mysticism," "Tolstoism." "The Richard Wagner Cult," "Ibsenism," "Friedrich Nietzsche," and "Zola and His School." As early as 1873, however, English aesthetic critic Walter Pater in his notorious, later suppressed "Conclusion" to *Studies in the Renaissance* had expressed a view of life that emphasized the moment of experience—which he saw as a summation of energies coming together briefly before inevitably dissipating—as against a ripe summation of wisdom and carefully meditated (religiously hopeful) philosophies of life: "Not the fruit of experience," he wrote, "but experience itself, is the end. A counted number of pulses only is given to us of a variegated, dramatic life. How may we see in them all that is to be seen in them by the finest senses? . . . To burn always with this hard, gemlike flame, to maintain this ecstasy, is success in life" (188–89). For Pater, certainly, the moments of experience to be most appreciated were aesthetic. For Gagool, who might be thought of—in the terminology of Harold Bloom—as a creative "misreader" of Pater, the moments of experience that she revels in, as referred to earlier, are both hedonistic (delight in "warm sunlight and sweet air") and amoral (delight in seeing others die). Seen in the context of Haggard's times, Gagool's for-the-moment hedonism embodies the "worst case" fears of "earnest" Victorians who feared that religious faith and morality were being lost in the closing decades of the old century.

Complementing Pater's "new hedonism" were the conclusions of the increasingly powerful nineteenth century discourse of science. In his well-known lecture "The Physical Basis of Life" (1868), Thomas Henry Huxley, "Darwin's Bulldog," drew attention to "the advancing tide of matter [that] threatens to drown [the] souls of many of the best minds of these days" (21). In 1895, H. G. Wells's *The Time Machine*—the work of a young writer trained in science—set forth a future in which humankind has evolved into two distinct but dependent forms: the childlike Eloi who cavort on the green surface of the earth, enjoying "Paterian" moments of intense, but ephemeral experience, and the cruel, technologically adept

Morlocks, who dwell in caves and emerge only at night. In a perverse symbiosis, the Morlocks harvest the Eloi, who are their source of protein. In "On Fairy-Stories" Tolkien speaks of the Eloi and Morlocks as creations that "live far away in an abyss of time so deep as to work an enchantment upon them" (*Essays* 115–16). These words and the contrast in *The Time Machine* between innocent pastoralism and brutal "subterraneanism" suggest that Wells's short novel might have played a role in Tolkien's juxtaposition of shire-dwelling hobbits and cave-bound goblins.

Of all the sources of scientific anxiety from the mid-nineteenth century on, Darwin's "Theory of Evolution" was the most profoundly disorienting and the most fiercely resisted. Darwin originally called his theory "descent with modification" and shunned using "evolution as a description of his theory . . . [since] evolution already had a . . . a vernacular meaning that "embodied a *concept of progressive development*—an orderly unfolding from simple to complex. . . . Thus evolution, in the vernacular, was firmly tied to a concept of progress" (Gould 34–35). "Progress"—which implies some guiding hand, some teleological end of the process—was meaningless in Darwinian discourse. As a "theory of local adaptation to changing environments, [Darwin's Theory] proposes no perfecting principles, no guarantee of general improvement . . ." (Gould 45). In certain cases, Darwin argued, adaptation will involve the loss of features no longer necessary. The blind lake fish that Gollum catches with his long fingers are perfect examples of such "degenerative" adaptation. Gagool and Gollum both can be seen as having "adapted" to their environments and innate characters (their souls) in the sense of *devolving* not only physically, but also *morally*, having lost ethical and altruistic capacities. Gagool has become more animal-like and even reptilian as her life extends beyond all due limits; Gollum, also over a long period of time, departs from the physical features of his hobbit kind.

Gollum reflects important elements of Gagool's character, as well as her philosophy of negation. Like Gagool, there is something compelling in a sinister way about Gollum, as Tolkien himself acknowledged when he took up the character again in *LR* and remarked that in the writing "Gollum continues to develop into a most intriguing character" (*Letters* 81). He is "intriguing" despite being only tangentially described. Since he lives deep in a tangle of caves under a mountain, on an island in a cold lake, and in total darkness, he is present more as a voice—humorous, childish, and malign—than as a well-defined physical presence. Yet certain physical details are emphasized. In *Hobbit*, he is first described as "old Gollum, a small slimy creature" with "two big round pale eyes in his thin face" (77). As Bilbo appears at the shore of the lake, Gollum is looking for "blind fish, which he grabbed with his long fingers as quick as thinking" (77), but then he watches "Bilbo now from the distance with his pale eyes like telescopes" (77). Later these phrases appear: "Gollum with his bright eyes" (89); "his eyes gleamed cold in his head" (90); "his eyes went green" (90). Bilbo considers, yet then most signficantly rejects, a physical attack that would both blind and kill Gollum: "He must stab the foul thing, put its eyes out, kill it" (92). Sight and blindness, both literal and metaphoric, appear throughout the descriptions of Gollum.

Living alone, in crushing isolation, Gollum talks to himself as to a special friend, styling himself "'my precious'" (78)—a name he comes to apply as well to the ring that grants invisibility. When he reflects on his fate should the ring fall into the hands of the goblins, his self-referencing voice finds its characteristic timbre, replete with "gollum, gollum" sounds made by gulping and swallowing, here intensified because of excitement and fear:

> "Ssss, sss, gollum! Goblinses! Yes, but if it's got the present, our precious present, then goblinses will get it, gollum! They'll find it, they'll find out what it does. We shan't ever be safe again, never, gollum! One of the goblinses will put it on, and then no one will see him. He'll be there but not seen. Not even our clear eyeses will notice him; and he'll come creeping and tricksy and catch us, gollum, gollum!" (89)

When he can, Gollum supplements his usual diet of "blind" fish with small goblins. (Bilbo would serve as another welcome supplement.) Cunning, untrustworthy, without a conscience and devoid of all pity, he is a threat that Bilbo overcomes through his cleverness and sheer good (or providential) luck. Bilbo wins—albeit with cunning of his own—the riddling contest, and uses the ring of invisibility to good effect. His surprising athleticism comes to his aid as he leaps seven feet over Gollum while narrowly (or providentially) avoiding the roof of the cave. However, although Bilbo, who has every reason to hate Gollum, could well have used "Sting" to kill him, he hesitates as he recognizes that Gollum "was miserable, alone, lost. A sudden understanding, a pity mixed with horror, welled up in Bilbo's heart: a glimpse of endless unmarked days without light or hope or betterment, hard stone, cold fish, sneaking and whispering" (92).

This rather mysterious "understanding" and "pity" is understandable when it is revealed in *LR* that Gollum is akin to hobbits—something that Bilbo, at a deep level, senses. As a young hobbit, Gollum left the pathways of normal life, moved underground, and in time adapted to a dark, constricted, "hopeless" environment. Gollum has so shrunken in spirit and degenerated physically and morally that only vestiges of hobbit nature remain, such as a liking for riddles. He appears quite diminished when Bilbo has escaped his clutches with the ring: "He had lost: lost his prey, and lost, too, the only thing he had ever cared for, his precious" (91). A material thing—not a living being—is what he most cares for. Yet he remains "of hobbit-kind," as Gandalf explains to Frodo in *FR* (80). Douglas Anderson quotes a 1963 letter from Tolkien to his publisher regarding Gollum's appearance: "[He] should not be made a monster, as he is by practically all other illustrators in disregard of the text"; according to Anderson, a description of Gollum drawn from various writings by Tolkien would be this: " He should be a slimy little creature no larger than Bilbo: thin, with a large head for his size; large protuberant eyes; a long skinny neck; and thin, lank hair. His skin was white, and evidently he wore black garments. His hands were long and his feet webby, with prehensile toes" (94). Of particular significance in this description is that Gollum should be "little," "no larger than Bilbo"—akin to the hobbits despite his degenerated state.

Specific points of connection between Gagool and Gollum, following the same sequence used when describing Gagool's characteristics, are as follows: (1) He is of hobbit nature, but so distorted and changed by the circumstances of his way of life that he exists as an odious parody of the comfort-loving, convivial hobbits, just as Gagool is an obscene parody of human (and female) form. Hobbit holes are snug, warm, and well furnished; Gollum's cave is pitch black, cold, stark and frightful. Hobbits enjoy good food and tobacco; Gollum eats only cold, blind, slimy lake fish, with a small goblin as a rare treat. Changes over time have made Gollum into something of an anti-hobbit—a dark doppelganger of his engaging kind. (In this respect Stevenson's *Dr. Jekyll and Mr. Hyde*, another possible influence on Tolkien, comes to mind.) (2) Gollum's "small" body is not described, but, as in the case of Gagool, his eyes are referred to several times in the relatively few pages when he is introduced; adapted to the darkness, they are large, "bright," and expressive. (3) Like Gagool his speech is full of repetitions and sibilants —childlike, darkly humorous, and malevolent. (4) Also like Gagool, Gollum's view of life, as it can be inferred from his behavior, is narrowly materialistic and completely self-centered. In effect buried under a huge weight of indifferent, obdurate matter, without a view of the sky and the sun, the source of life, Gollum comes to "care for" and identify with one thing—the golden ring—that he calls by the same name he gives himself: "precious." Gollum's life and outlook is, in heightened, quasi-symbolic form, that of the materialist—a prisoner of "matter," ever fearful, finding no comfort or salvation, his only point of reference himself and his ring, which is a surrogate for himself; significantly, the ring is an object that gives him a degree of freedom through releasing him—through invisibility—from the prison of his body and its material essence. (5) Even the names Gagool and Gollum are quite similar, beginning with the same consonant, having two syllables, and being made up of six letters.

Of course, Gagool and Gollum are not identical in every respect, nor should we expect them to be, given Tolkien's creative ingenuity. One major difference is that Gagool is female and as such taps end-of-the-century anxieties about female power and its threat to "helpless" males.[3] Another is that Gagool derives part of her power from her association with the ruler of Kukuanaland—King Twala—whereas Gollum shuns the goblin rulers of the caves in which he lives. However, the points of connection are many, as indicated above—size, eyes, voice, speech patterns; and, most significantly, in view of the ideational basis of the works in which they appear, they possess a self-referencing belief in materialism and the insatiable claims of the naked ego. Both characters serve as foils for the protagonists of their respective works, heightening the pluck, good humor, courage, and idealism of Quatermain and his companions and similar qualities in Bilbo.

For Haggard and Tolkien, Gagool and Gollum may well have embodied an extreme opposition to their own fundamentally religious outlooks. Although

Haggard was by no means a regular churchgoer or orthodox believer, he had a spiritual, vitalistic outlook that reached beyond the confines of any one church. As such, he was like many Victorians who had lost the particular doctrinal and sacramental forms of Christianity, but retained, or struggled to retain, something of a spiritual "essence." Tolkien, a Roman Catholic since 1900 when his mother converted, was a traditional, orthodox "believer" throughout his life (Carpenter 31). Though he was quite unlike his friend C .S. Lewis in not writing directly or polemically about his faith, belief in a sacramental Christianity was central to him and to his creative work. A soldier in World War I and a worried father whose son was a combatant in World War II, Tolkien faced the monstrous, collective horrors—and evil—of the twentieth century. *Hobbit* and *LR* are works that ultimately express a triumph of what is positive, indeed spiritual, against the forces of denial and death. Thus not surprisingly in creating Gollum out of the "leaf-mould" of his childhood reading, he may have been influenced by Haggard's Gagool not only for her obvious theatricality, but for how she expresses the negation of a strictly material view of life.

When at the end of *Mines* the evil scheme of Gagool to trap the adventurers is averted, if barely, she is crushed—both physically and symbolically—by the immense (material) weight of a great stone door: "She is under—ah, God! Too late! Too late! The stone nips her, and she yells in agony. Down, down, it comes, all the thirty tons of it, slowly pressing her old body against the rock below. Shriek upon shriek, such as we had never heard, then a long sickening *crunch*, and the door was shut just as we, rushing down the passage, hurled ourselves against it" (280). In a similar way, though not as graphically rendered, Gollum is left alone in his benighted material world, surrounded by—indeed, crushed by—rock, cold, and darkness. For Haggard and Tolkien a strictly material conception of life involved darkness, misery, degeneracy, and death in dreadful forms; yet when they created characters to give bodily form to a terrible denial of life's bounty and fulfillment, they gave fictional immortality to two beings that remain in mind long after readers have finished *King Solomon's Mines* and *The Hobbit*.

NOTES

Rogers would like to offer thanks to Ms. Amanda Louise Plain, a student in William Rogers's English 544: British Literature, 1890–1918, Fall 1997, at San Diego State University. She brought to his attention what she perceived as the similarity of Gagool and Gollum, and in time that insight led to a conference paper and this essay. To Daniel Timmons, a most supportive editor, the authors owe many thanks for helpful suggestions and criticisms. As a personal aside, Rogers notes, "I look back with intellectual delight on the many coffee-sipping conversations Michael Underwood and I had about Gagool, Bilbo, and other matters, academic and personal, during the 1997–98 and 1998–99 academic years at SDSU; a collaboration could not have been carried out more smoothly and cordially than ours!"

1. Tolkien originally made this remark in a phone interview to Henry Resnik (40); as

well, the first edition of *The Hobbit* [Tolkien, J.R.R. *The Hobbit; or, There and Back Again.* Boston: Houghton, 1938] was checked and the authors found that Tolkien's earlier description of Gollum also reflects the essence of Gagool.

    2. A helpful introduction to Haggard is Norman Etherington, *Rider Haggard* (Boston: Twayne, 1984). Dennis Butts's Introduction to his edited edition of *Mines* (New York: Oxford, 1989) is clearheaded and quite informative about Haggard, his work in general, and the novel itself.

    3. Bram Dijkstra's books, *Idols of Perversity: Fantasies of Feminine Evil in Fin-de-Siecle Culture* (New York: Oxford UP, 1986) and *Evil Sisters: The Threat of Female Sexuality and the Cult of Manhood* (New York: Knopf, 1996), make clear the various manifestations of male anxiety about the "new woman" and predatory female figures that proliferated toward the end of the nineteenth century.

WORKS CITED

Anderson, Douglas A., ed. *The Annotated Hobbit*. By J.R.R. Tolkien. Boston: Houghton, 1988.

Carpenter, Humphrey. *The Inklings: C. S. Lewis, J.R.R. Tolkien, Charles Williams, and Their Friends.* 1978. New York: Ballantine, 1981.

———. *J.R.R. Tolkien: A Biography.* London: Allen & Unwin, 1977.

Gould, Stephen Jay. *Ever Since Darwin: Reflections in Natural History*. New York: Norton, 1977.

Green, William H. *The Hobbit: A Journey into Maturity.* New York: Twayne, 1995.

Haggard, H. Rider. *King Solomon's Mines.* 1885. Oxford: Oxford UP, 1989.

Huxley, Thomas Henry. *Selections from the Essays of Thomas Henry Huxley.* Ed. Alburey Castell. New York: Appleton, 1948.

Lobdell, Jared. *England and Always: Tolkien's World of the Rings.* Grand Rapids, MI: Eerdmans, 1981.

Nordau, Max. *Degeneration.* New York: Appleton, 1895.

Pater, Walter. *The Renaissance: Studies in Art and Poetry. The 1893 Text.* Ed. Donald L. Hill. Berkeley: U of California P, 1980.

Resnik, Henry. "An Interview with Tolkien." *Niekas* 18 (1967): 37–47.

Wells, H. G. *The Time Machine.* 1895. New York: Bantam, 1968.

10

"Joy Beyond the Walls of the World": The Secondary World-Making of J.R.R. Tolkien and C. S. Lewis

David Sandner

Fantasy authors have often described the imaginative conception of their creations.[1] J.R.R. Tolkien and C. S. Lewis have been particularly expressive and earnest when discussing the inspiration for their fantasy works. Lewis claims that *The Lion, The Witch and The Wardrobe* "all began with a picture of a Faun carrying an umbrella and parcels in a snowy wood" (*On Stories* 53). Lewis entered Narnia when an image fixed itself in his mind, and only afterward did he invent a story (and a world) to go with his odd and incongruous image. The first line of *Hobbit* reportedly entered Tolkien's head, seemingly unconnected to anything else, when he sat correcting "School Certificate papers in the everlasting weariness of that annual task" (*Letters* 215). As Tolkien remembers it, "One of the candidates had mercifully left one of the pages with no writing on it (which is the best thing that can possibly happen to an examiner) and I wrote on it: 'In a hole in the ground there lived a hobbit'"(Carpenter 172). Tolkien further comments: "I did not and do not know why. I did nothing about it for a long time, and for some years I got no further than the production of Thror's Map" (*Letters* 215); still, he has claimed that "[n]ames always generate a story in my mind. Eventually I thought I'd better find out what hobbits were like. But that's only the beginning" (Carpenter 172). But beginnings are important in fantasy because the reader arrives in a Secondary Realm where fairy-stories happen much as the authors themselves arrived at the improbable beginnings of their stories: with a sense of surprise and full with possibilities. Tolkien and Lewis are similar in their desire to evoke the reader's wonder of *Faërie*.[2] However, their realizations of this "Joy Beyond the Walls of the World" are distinctive, most noticeably in the depth of their Secondary Realms and treatment of allegory.[3]

For Tolkien, in "On Fairy-Stories" "Fantasy" is identified by its "arresting strangeness" (*Essays* 139). The wonder the authors felt right at the beginning

—at the very moment they wandered into their particular "Perilous Realm" through the happy discovery of the image of a faun or the sentence about a hobbit—must be conveyed to the reader throughout if the fantasy story is to succeed. Fantasy responds to a basic yearning, but not necessarily by providing satisfaction to that yearning. As Tolkien writes of his own reading of fantasy stories, "If they awakened *desire*, satisfying it while often whetting it unbearably, they succeeded" (134). Fantasy succeeds for Tolkien not by satisfying his sense of wonder, but by awakening it, and, what is even better, by "whetting it unbearably."

In his critical writings Lewis claims that fantasy works on the reader not by what it delivers in exciting turns of the plot, but by what it suggests, and that suggestion is present from the first page, or even before the first page. Lewis observes:

> *The Well at the World's End* [by William Morris]—can a man write a story to that title? Can he find a series of events following one another in time which will really catch and fix and bring home to us all that we grasp at on merely hearing the six words? . . . And I must confess that the net very seldom does succeed in catching the bird. (*On Stories* 17–18)

For Lewis, *The Well at the World's End* does not catch "the bird," but few of the moment-by-moment plots of even the best fantasy stories live up to his expectations before he begins to read. Furthermore, Lewis concludes that although the net of story can never finally catch "the bird," the heart of fantasy lies precisely in our thwarted desires, that "image of truth" (19). Fantasy expresses, at its best, an unfulfilled (and perhaps unfulfillable) yearning which is itself a kind of satisfaction.

Although Lewis maintains that fantasy never fulfills our expectations, the attempt itself remains worthwhile because "I think it is sometimes done—or very, very nearly done—in stories. I believe the effort to be well worth making (*On Stories* 19-20). As Lewis writes about the story as a net, catching the bird becomes of secondary importance and then finally moot. Gradually, the goal becomes not for us to catch the bird, but for it to catch us and lead to "its own country." Even that possibility is not realized "for this essay," and instead Lewis indicates that "the effort" itself is what is worthwhile. Fantasy is important for Lewis not because of what it does but because of what it "very, very nearly" does, the unfulfilled possibilities at its heart, the longing for something beyond that which can be comprehended by the "net" of either story or life.

Similarly, in his famous definition of fairy-stories, Tolkien proposes that fantasy literature attempts to capture "in a net of words" a bird which must slip the net; fantasy is defined by its very inability to be defined, by its quality of longing for something which can only be glimpsed, but never found, in the story itself:

> The definition of a fairy-story—what it is, or what it should be—does not,
> then, depend on any definition or historical account of elf or fairy but upon the
> nature of *Faërie*: the Perilous Realm itself, and the air that blows in that
> country. I will not attempt to define that, nor to describe it directly. It cannot
> be done. *Faërie* cannot be caught in a net of words; for it is one of its qualities
> to be indescribable, though not imperceptible. (*Essays* 114)

Fairy-stories are identified by the presence of *Faërie*, the enchanted realm,
rather than by definition. Tolkien describes fantasy as a wind blowing from
beyond the world, something felt but unseen, which may move the reader to
look for something that cannot be found in the text at all. This quality of *Faërie*
must be present from the beginning and beyond the end.

But how is the writer to achieve this? How does a writer cast the net and
enter a Secondary Realm? For Tolkien, the "net of words" employs "Art, the
operative link between Imagination and the final result, Sub-creation" (139).
When the Sub-creation has "a quality of strangeness and wonder in the
Expression, derived from the Image," Tolkien calls it Fantasy; Fantasy makes a
Secondary World, which for Tolkien can achieve a worthwhile effect only if it
can command a certain Secondary Belief, the "'inner consistency of reality'"
(139–40). If the art of sub-creative fantasy could be absolutely successful in
commanding Secondary Belief, the result would be Enchantment:
"Enchantment produces a Secondary World into which both designer and
spectator can enter, to the satisfaction of their senses while they are inside; but
in its purity it is artistic in desire and purpose" (143). Enchantment is an elvish
craft which Fantasy can never fully attain, "even if the elves are, all the more in
so far as they are, only a product of Fantasy itself" (143). Sub-creation links the
author of a Secondary Realm to Creation itself, asking art to move the artist
beyond the medium, the text bound by its covers, into a direct relationship with
Faërie itself.

Tolkien locates the power of fantasy in language, noting the unusual power
of adjectives to transform whatever they modify, as in the simple pairing of
green sun. Tolkien claims:

> The mind that thought of *light, heavy, grey, yellow, still, swift*, also conceived
> of magic that would make heavy things light and able to fly, turn grey lead
> into yellow gold, and the still rock into swift water. . . . In such "fantasy," as it
> is called, new form is made; *Faërie* begins; Man becomes a sub-creator. (122)

It is characteristic of Tolkien that he began *Hobbit* with the discovery of a
sentence, not, as with Lewis, an image. Responding to and re-wording the text
of a pair of interviewers, Tolkien asked, "[H]ow did linguistic invention lead to
imaginary history?"—and answered himself:

> "The imaginary histories grew out of Tolkien's predilection for inventing

languages. He discovered, as others have who carry out such inventions to
any degree of completion, that a language requires a suitable habitation, and a
history in which it can develop." (*Letters* 375)

Both Tolkien's sentence and Lewis's image set their imaginations in motion,
causing them to wonder and so to discover entire Secondary Realms. However,
for Tolkien, the process of discovery is more detailed and methodical than for
Lewis. Middle-earth, with its languages and so suitable habitations and
histories, stood waiting and ready when Tolkien's sentence about a hobbit
suddenly arrived. But Tolkien did not immediately see any connection between
it and his already realized histories and languages. Only time and reflection
gradually allowed the hobbits a local habitation and a name. And once the
hobbits were grounded in a place, the story itself began to unfold. For Lewis,
the story, in the fragmentary form of images, comes first, and only afterward,
through placing the images in order as if arranging the pieces of a puzzle, does
the story find its broader context.

Tolkien knows the history of Middle-earth before he begins *Hobbit*, whereas
Lewis writes the history of his Secondary Realm only in the last *Narnia* book.
The lamppost, for example, marks the entry into Narnia for both Lucy and
Lewis, and only at the end of the series, in *The Last Battle*, does Lewis discover
how the lamppost itself came to be waiting beyond the wardrobe. Pulled out of
modern London, the lamppost is brought to the beginning of things for Narnia
and planted in the matter of the world itself, where it takes root. In this moment,
Lewis realizes a unity for his Secondary Realm out of his first odd image,
simultaneously connecting the journeys between the two worlds and discovering
the integrity of Narnia itself. Tolkien did not work this way. He needed to
discover the history of Middle-earth out of which his story would spring as a
necessary precondition to beginning at all.

According to Tolkien, fantasy literature—the depiction of a Secondary
Realm—offers the reader three gifts: Recovery, Escape, and Consolation.
Recovery describes the way the presence of *Faërie* not only allows a glimpse of
another world, but also initiates a reevaluation and rediscovery of the mundane
world, of oneself, and of one's place in the world:

> Recovery (which includes return and renewal of health) is a re-gaining
> —regaining of a clear view. I do not say "seeing things as they are" and
> involve myself with the philosophers, though I might venture to say "seeing
> things as we are (or were) meant to see them"—as things apart from ourselves.
> (*Essays* 146)

When we see things again, as "we are (or were) meant to see them," Tolkien
believes that everything is felt to be in proper perspective and in its proper
place. Lewis also claims fantasy has this effect on the reader:

> It stirs and troubles him (to his life long enrichment) with the dim sense of

something beyond his reach and, far from dulling or emptying the actual world, gives it a new dimension of depth. He does not despise real woods because he has read of enchanted woods: the reading makes all real woods a little enchanted. (*On Stories* 38)

In fantasy literature, the world is not simply left behind for pleasing visions of wonder. Instead, the world and the world of *Faërie* merge, as they "are (or were) meant to," and the world becomes "a little enchanted," or perhaps the reader does, revealing "a new dimension of depth." Both Tolkien and Lewis argue that this "new dimension of depth" is presumably already present but unperceived, because the wonder of the world has been taken for granted or even ignored.

The longing for *Faërie*, then, is not a "blind" yearning for a transcendental world, simply beyond or above the "real," but rather offers integration, or reintegration, with the world itself, with "real woods" and the natural world. Tolkien declares:

Faërie contains many things besides elves and fays, and besides dwarves, witches, trolls, giants, or dragons: it holds the seas, the sun, the moon, the sky; and the earth and all things that are in it: tree and bird, water and stone, wine and bread, and ourselves mortal men, when we are enchanted. (*Essays* 113)

Entering *Faërie* does not mean leaving the mundane behind because that realm encompasses all the things of the world and more, the natural and the supernatural. Tolkien reinforces this point by noting the hazard in calling fairies supernatural beings:

Supernatural is a difficult and dangerous word in any of its senses, looser or stricter. But to fairies it can hardly be applied, unless *super* is taken merely as a superlative prefix. For it is man in contrast to fairies, who is supernatural . . . whereas they are natural, far more natural than he. (110)

The promise of *Faërie* for Tolkien is a return to the world from which we have become estranged. Fantasy expresses a yearning for the world itself, in all its lost (or missing or exiled) fullness.

Tolkien calls the second impulse of fantasy "Escape"; he rejects the charge against fantasy that it is, in any simple sense, "escapist." Tolkien denies that fantasy literature is a rejection of the "real" world in favor of a never-never land of wish fulfillment. Humanity, when it is disenchanted, is in a prison of its own devising, cut off from the full experience of the world as we are (or were) meant to see it. Tolkien claims that "Escape is evidently as a rule very practical, and may even be heroic"; if one is unjustly imprisoned, escape is practical and positive: "Why should a man be scorned, if, finding himself in prison, he tries to get out and go home?"; Tolkien believes that fantasy's critics "are, not always by sincere error, confusing the Escape of the Prisoner with the Flight of the

Deserter" (148).   In the "Escape" that Tolkien experiences from fantasy literature, one is not running away but freeing oneself again to be more fully in the world.

Lewis also counters the "popular charge of escapism" leveled at fantasy for children by considering two kinds of "wish-fulfillment," one provided by fantasy literature and the other by "the school story or any other story which is labeled a 'Boy's book' or a 'Girl's book'" (*On Stories* 37-8). The second kind of wishing flatters the ego, sending "us back to the world divinely discontented" by all we cannot be; the first enlarges the imagination, and so, for Lewis, enriches the soul: "For, as I say, there are two kinds of longing.   The one is askesis, a spiritual exercise, and the other is a disease" (39).   Askesis is related to "ascetic," to spiritual discipline in which one denies the simple gratification of one's ego to gain spiritual enlightenment; the escape of fantasy literature for Lewis is a movement away from the desires of the ego toward the yearnings of the soul.

When discussing the "surprise" of the marvelous in works of fantasy, Lewis points out that it is different from the "surprise" of discovering what happens in an unfolding plot.   Fantasy remains surprising because it is the "*quality* of unexpectedness, not the *fact* which delights us" (*On Stories* 39) and leads us to re-read a well-loved romance again and again.   The presence of the fantastic is always the presence of the "other," the presence of what is unknown by definition, what is not only unexpected but unexplainable, always "surprising" in Lewis's terms.   Fantasy invokes mystery, and for Lewis, "Mystery," as the presence of the other, suggests the contemplation of the "other" world of the spirit.

For Tolkien, as well, *Faërie* represents the world of the spirit.   The third impulse of fantasy literature, the Consolation of fairy-story, is provided by what Tolkien calls "*Eucatastrophe*," a spiritual Joy felt at the sudden and miraculous happy ending, the moment when the casting of the net "very, very nearly" catches the bird:

> The consolation of fairy-stories, the joy of the happy ending: or more correctly of the good catastrophe, the sudden joyous "turn" (for there is no true end to any fairy-tale). . . . [I]t is a sudden and miraculous grace: never to be counted on to recur.   It does not deny the existence of *dyscatastrophe*, of sorrow and failure: the possibility of these is necessary to the joy of deliverance; it denies (in the face of much evidence, if you will) universal final defeat and in so far is *evangelium*, giving a fleeting glimpse of Joy, Joy beyond the walls of the world, poignant as grief. (*Essays* 153)

Eucatastrophe, the "sudden turn" of the happy ending, is like Lewis's quality of "surprise" in fantasy literature.   Our astonishment is a sudden gratification of a deeply held yearning for the world of the spirit, for "*evangelium*," a fleeting glimpse of an answer to the question: Is the fantasy story "true?"   Tolkien replies, "In the 'eucatastrophe' we see a brief vision that the answer may be greater—it may be a far-off gleam or echo of *evangelium* in the real world" (155). Tolkien believes that any glimpse of the world of the spirit is tied up with our own fallen state, with "sorrow and failure." Fantasy offers hope, but also a clear vision of the "underlying reality or truth" (155). Fantasy provides "'eucatastrophe',," acting as what Lewis called "a spiritual exercise," as "askesis," moving the reader away from the simple gratification of the here and now to a contemplation of the world of spirit, which, paradoxically, provides a deeper appreciation of the HERE and the NOW, as *Faërie* and the primary world become one: our world, enchanted.

This "fleeting glimpse of underlying truth" occurs not in the story, not between the bounds of its covers, but must be read through the story in the opening offered by its surprising beginning, or its "sudden joyous turn," or by what it suggests in its very title, or in what lies beyond its end. When Tolkien writes about "Consolation" in *Hobbit*, he recognizes it in the scene of the Eagles' arrival when all hope seems lost:

> I knew I had written a story of worth in "The Hobbit" when reading it (after it was old enough to be detached from me) I had suddenly in a fairly strong measure the "eucatastrophic" emotion at Bilbo's exclamation: "The Eagles! The Eagles are coming!" (*Letters* 101)

Still, "Consolation," if Tolkien is right, abides both there and everywhere, waiting only for a discerning reader.

In *The Lion, The Witch and the Wardrobe*, Aslan's return from death signals the moment of a sudden turning, a miraculous grace. In the story, Edmund's life is put in peril because of what is described as the "Deep Magic":

> "Have you forgotten the Deep Magic?" asked the Witch. "Let us say I have forgotten it," answered Aslan gravely. "Tell us of this Deep Magic." "Tell you?" said the Witch, her voice growing suddenly shriller. "Tell you what is written on that very Table of Stone which stands beside us? Tell you what is written in letters deep as a spear is long on the trunk of the World Ash Tree? Tell you what is engraved on the scepter of the Emperor-Beyond-the-Sea? You at least know the magic which the Emperor put into Narnia at the very beginning. You know that every traitor belongs to me as my lawful prey and that of every treachery I have a right to a kill." (113–14)

Edmund has fallen and his life is judged as forfeit. But Aslan offers himself up as a sacrifice instead of Edmund, and the Witch takes him, humiliates him, and kills him. The story reaches its nadir. All seems lost. Susan and Lucy cry over his corpse, only to find it has vanished, and then that Aslan is alive again. If Lewis is correct concerning the net of story, his own fantasy story, like Morris's, like all stories, must fall short of realization, even here at the climax. Instead, such a moment hints at our own desire in the midst of all wrong to have everything set right again.

"But what does it all mean?" asked Susan when they were somewhat calmer.
"It means," said Aslan, "that though the Witch knew the Deep Magic, there is
a magic deeper still which she did not know. Her knowledge goes back only
to the dawn of Time. But if she could have looked a little further back, into
the stillness and the darkness before Time dawned, she would have read there
a different incantation. She would have known that when a willing victim
who had committed no treachery was killed in a traitor's stead, the Table
would crack and Death itself would start working backward. And now—"
"Oh, yes. Now?" said Lucy jumping up and clapping her hands. "Oh,
children," said the Lion, "I feel my strength coming back to me. Oh, children,
catch me if you can!" (132–33)

Lewis's story turns on the resurrection of Aslan, the return of hope with life, the
redemption of Edmund and the reader in a glimpse of the Gospels reenacted.

Tolkien's *Hobbit* contains no moment clearly related to the Gospels, such as
the resurrection of Aslan. The arrival of the Eagles, an example of
"Consolation," seems subtle in comparison to Lewis's. Moreover, Tolkien's
Secondary Realm is certainly more colorful and expansive, and the stories told
within it weave a tighter net, vastly detailed and self-sustaining. Lewis's Narnia
appears to exist for its characters to fulfill its allegorical stories; Middle-earth
has a deep history, never finished in Tolkien's lifetime, which is itself a kind of
consolation. In Lewis, "sudden turns" are more obvious, whereas Tolkien's
"eucatastrophic" incidents run throughout his works like threads in an intricate
tapestry, each moment of grace necessarily understood against a wider backdrop
of meanings and movements. Tolkien's moment is typically more subtle, and
Lewis's more directly allegorical in its retelling of the Christian gospel. With
both authors, however, these moments are born out of desire and hope, an
emotion drawn straight up out of spiritual longing.

The very ability to write fantasy, to create a Secondary Realm, is, for both
Tolkien and Lewis, derived from the same creative energy that made and moves
all; to be a creative artist celebrates the Creation. Summing up Tolkien's
position, Carpenter states:

We have come from God, and inevitably the myths woven by us, though they
contain error, will also reflect a splintered fragment of the true light, the
eternal truth that is with God. Indeed only by myth-making, only be becoming
a "sub-creator" and inventing stories, can Man aspire to the state of perfection
that he knew before the Fall. (147)

Fantasy, as the place of "sub-creation," aspires to the truth of myth; myth
reflects the ideal, "the true light" that must remain but dimly seen in a fallen
world. Lewis comments that the "story of Christ is simply true myth: a myth
working on us the same way as the others, but with this tremendous difference
that *it really happened*" (Hooper xiv). Similarly, Tolkien declares, "The

Gospels contain a fairy-story, or a story of a larger kind which embraces all the essence of fairy-stories" (*Essays* 155).

> The Resurrection was the greatest "eucatastrophe" possible in the greatest Fairy Story—and produces that essential emotion: Christian joy which produces tears because it is qualitatively so like sorrow, because it comes from those places where Joy and Sorrow are at one, reconciled, as selfishness and altruism are lost in Love. Of course I do not mean that the Gospels tell what is only a fairy story; but I do mean very strongly that they do tell a fairy-story: the greatest. (*Letters* 100)

For Lewis and Tolkien, both the true myth of the gospel and the sub-creative use of fantasy in fairy-stories can rouse wonder and awe, leading to the apprehension of spirit. Fantasy is different from gospel because it presents something that did not happen (though Tolkien notes all "tales may come true" [*Essays* 156]). But it works on us like a gospel, not only relating a moral but actually enacting it; as "a splintered fragment of the true light," a fairy-story touches on myth, and for Tolkien and Lewis all myth touches on the true essence of the gospel.

Tolkien and Lewis wandered into their fairy-stories by unforeseen routes, and both indicate that this is the best way to begin a fairy-story, for writing fantasy, like reading it, must involve the spiritual discipline of inspiration. Lewis maintains:

> Some people seem to think that I began by asking myself how I could say something about Christianity to children; then fixed on the fairy tale as an instrument; then collected information about child-psychology and decided what age-group I'd write for; then drew up a list of basic Christian truths and hammered out "allegories" to embody them. This is all pure moonshine. I couldn't write that way at all. (*On Stories* 46)

Once the story itself has come together, the moral possibilities, latent but always present, come through of their own accord. In "On Three Ways," Lewis notes of his own method of writing: "It is the only one I know: images always come first" (*On Stories* 41). Considering the question of whether a children's story should have a moral, Lewis concludes that one should not begin with a moral, since it leads to conscious superiority as the adult teaches the child. Instead, the moral must be there, in the writer and in the story, all along, even when unlooked for: "It is better not to ask the question at all. Let the pictures tell you their own moral. (*On Stories* 41). The only way to go about writing about morals, Lewis indicates, is not to write about them, but to embody them already. A story, if it is a good story, already contains its own moral, a "splintered fragment of the true light."

Similarly, Tolkien comments on his publisher Raynor Unwin's observation that *LR* might be "pure allegory":

[D]o not let Raynor suspect "Allegory". There is a "moral", I suppose, in any
tale worth telling. But that is not the same thing. Even the struggle between
darkness and light (as he calls it, not me) is for me just a particular phase of
history, one example of its pattern, perhaps, but not The Pattern; and the actors
are individuals—they each, of course, contain universals, or they would not
live at all, but they never represent them as such. (*Letters* 121)

Tolkien distinguishes between a story with a moral and an allegory. For him,
the allegory is prescriptive, while the story alone allows the reader to make of it
what they will, or what they can. Paradoxically, only through Story, Tolkien
indicates, can true Allegory emerge:

Of course, Allegory and Story converge. Meeting somewhere in Truth. So
that the only consistent allegory is real life; and the only fully intelligible story
is an allegory. And one finds, even in imperfect human "literature", that the
better and more consistent an allegory is the more easily can it be read "just as
a story"; and the better and more closely woven a story is the more easily can
those so minded find allegory in it. But the two start out from opposite ends.
(*Letters* 121)

One of the aspects of a good allegory is that it is "just a story" at heart. Tolkien
declares: "I dislike Allegory—the conscious and intentional allegory—yet any
attempt to explain the purport of myth or fairytale must use allegorical
language" (*Letters* 145). The way to write an allegory is to tell a good story,
since any true story touches on true myth, and so embodies allegory as it should
be embodied.

Tolkien's and Lewis's discussions of fantasy indicate the ways they would
like to have arrived at their moral stories. Their narratives of the creative
process describe the meanings of their stories perhaps at times more successfully
than the stories themselves. Long after finishing *Hobbit*, Tolkien regretted a
certain tone in it, a certain, as Lewis would have put it, "sense of superiority,"
which crept in because he felt he had written, to some extent, for children
instead of for the sake of the wonderful tale he had to tell. Tolkien comments:

It was unhappily really meant, as far as I was conscious, as a "children's
story," and as I had not learned sense then, and my children were not quite old
enough to correct me, it has some of the silliness of manner caught
unthinkingly from the kind of stuff I had served to me. . . . I deeply regret
them. So do intelligent children. (*Letters* 215)

If a children's story is worth doing, Tolkien claims in hindsight, it is worth
doing for its own sake, because the story is worth telling.

Even knowing Tolkien's suspicions about "children's" stories, Lewis states
that the genre of the "children's story" remains important to him. Lewis notes,
speaking of himself, that "there may be an author who at a particular moment

finds not only fantasy but fantasy for children the exactly right form for what he wants to say" (*On Stories* 36). He does not disparage fantasy literature for adults, but finds the form of fantasy for children sometimes liberating, indicating it curbs the part of him that he calls "the expository demon," who would over explain, and also "imposes certain very fruitful necessities about length" (37). Similarly, Tolkien acknowledges:

> I do not deny that there is truth in Andrew Lang's words (sentimental though they may sound): "He who would enter into the Kingdom of Faërie should have the heart of a little child." For that possession is necessary to all high adventure, into kingdoms both less and far greater than Faërie. But humility and innocence—these things "the heart of a child" must mean in such a context—do not necessarily imply uncritical wonder, nor indeed an uncritical tenderness. (*Essays* 136)

Children's fantasy is best conceived by not writing for children but by having something to say that is best said in a form of literature designed for them. Similarly, a fantasist writes morally not by writing a rigorously conceived allegory, but by writing a story and finding that story and allegory are one.

Secondary Realms apprehend another world, granting a glimpse beyond the walls of the world; paradoxically, Secondary Realms thus reveal the primary world more fully. In Middle-earth, Tolkien wanders farther beyond the fields we know than Lewis; Middle-earth is both a larger and more tightly woven net of story than Narnia. Based on Tolkien's study (and love) of language and linguistics, Middle-earth forms over a longer time and under closer attention. Lewis's allegories are more overt, whereas Tolkien's are more fully integrated with his stories.

Still, Secondary Realms can be realized only as a tragic falling off, as an embodiment of unfulfilled and unfulfillable desire. This falling off occurs not only to stories set in Secondary Realms, but to stories about Secondary Realms. The stories Tolkien and Lewis tell about how they discovered their Secondary Realms and how those realms work become only another layer of story, another allegory, another realization of other worlds and another fall. The bird escapes the net. One discovers the Secondary Realms of *Faërie* mysteriously, glimpsing them in the wardrobe when one least expects it; the appearance of story itself is a "sudden turn," never to be counted on to return, born of a yearning that is at heart "askesis" or "eucatastrophe," a spiritual exercise. As Tolkien observes of himself, "I desired dragons with a profound desire" (*Essays* 135). That is only the beginning. But, in the end, there may be only beginnings.

NOTES

1. For examples of other fantasy authors describing their imaginative conception of their creations, see Robert H. Boyer and Kenneth J. Zahorski, *Fantasists on Fantasy: A Collection of Critical Reflections by Eighteen Masters of the Art.*

2. For studies of secondary world-making as religious fantasy see Gunnar Urang, *Shadows of Heaven: Religion and Fantasy in the Writings of C. S. Lewis, Charles Williams, and J.R.R. Tolkien*, especially chapter 4, and Martha C. Sammons, *"A Better Country": The Worlds of Religious Fantasy and Science Fiction*, especially chapter 1. For an examination of secondary worlds as modern myth-making, see Mark R. Hillegas's *Shadows of Imagination: The Fantasies of C.S. Lewis, J.R.R. Tolkien and Charles Williams*, especially pp. 75-76. For a discussion of Tolkien's and Lewis's secondary worlds as part of "a long tradition of culturally reactionary fantasists that goes back at least to Scott and includes such figures as George MacDonald, John Ruskin, William Morris, Lord Dunsany, and E.R. Eddison," see Lee D. Rossi, *The Politics of Fantasy: C.S. Lewis and J.R.R. Tolkien*, (1-6). For an outline of the conflict between Tolkien and Lewis's theories of secondary worlds "on the one hand and many modern writers and critics on the other," see Richard Purtill, *Lord of the Elves and Eldils: Fantasy and Philosophy in C. S. Lewis and J.R.R. Tolkien*, especially pp. 15–30.

3. For the differences between Tolkien and Lewis on the sub-creation of secondary worlds and its connection to Christianity, see Walter F. Hartt, "Godly Influences: The Theology of J.R.R. Tolkien and C. S. Lewis," and Randel Helms, "All Tales Need Not Come True." For Tolkien's dislike of Lewis's Narnia books, see Humphrey Carpenter, *The Inklings: C. S. Lewis, J.R.R. Tolkien, Charles Williams and Their Friends*, pp. 223–4, 228, 232. For a recent reconsideration of Tolkien's dislike of Lewis's Narnia books (one that "unsettles" more than settles the matter as discussed by Carpenter), see Joe R. Christopher's "J.R.R. Tolkien, Narnian Exile."

WORKS CITED

Boyer, Robert H. and Kenneth J. Zahorski, eds. *Fantasists on Fantasy: A Collection of Critical Reflections by Eighteen Masters of the Art.* New York: Avon, 1984.

Carpenter, Humphrey. *The Inklings: C. S. Lewis, J.R.R. Tolkien, Charles Williams and Their Friends.* Boston: Houghton, 1979.

———. *J.R.R. Tolkien: A Biography.* London: Allen, 1977.

Christopher, Joe R. "J.R.R. Tolkien, Narnian Exile." *Mythlore* 15.1 (55), 1998 Autumn; Vol 15. No. 2 (56), 1998 Winter: 17-23.

Hartt, Walter F. "Godly Influences: The Theology of J.R.R. Tolkien and C. S. Lewis." *Studies in the Literary Imagination* 14.2 (1981): 21–29.

Helms, Randel. "All Tales Need Not Come True." *Studies in the Literary Imagination* 14.2 (1981): 31–45.

Hillegas, Mark, ed. *Shadows of Imagination.* 1969. 2nd ed. Carbondale: Southern Illinois UP, 1979.

Hooper, Walter. Preface. *On Stories and Other Essays.* By C. S. Lewis. San Diego: Harcourt, 1982. ix–xxi.

Knight, Gareth. *The Magical World of the Inklings: J.R.R. Tolkien, C. S. Lewis, Charles Williams, Owen Barfield.* Longmead, UK: Element, 1990.

Lewis, C. S. *On Stories and Other Essays.* Ed. Walter Hooper. 1966. San Diego: Harcourt, 1982.

———. *The Lion, The Witch and the Wardrobe.* 1950. New York: Macmillan, 1988.

Purtill, Richard. *Lord of the Elves and Eldils: Fantasy and Philosophy in C. S. Lewis and J.R.R. Tolkien.* Grand Rapids, MI: Zondervan, 1974.

Rossi, Lee D. *The Politics of Fantasy: C. S. Lewis and J.R.R. Tolkien.* Ann Arbor, MI: UMI Research P, 1984.

Sammons, Martha C. *"A Better Country": The Worlds of Religious Fantasy and Science Fiction*. New York: Greenwood, 1988.

Urang, Gunnar. *Shadows of Heaven: Religion and Fantasy in the Writings of C. S. Lewis, Charles Williams, and J.R.R. Tolkien*. Philadelphia: Pilgrim, 1971.

11

Taking the Part of Trees: Eco-Conflict in Middle-earth

Verlyn Flieger

> In all my works I take the part of trees as against all their enemies. Lothlórien is beautiful because there the trees were loved; elsewhere forests are represented as awakening to consciousness of themselves. The Old Forest was hostile to two-legged creatures because of the memory of many injuries. Fangorn Forest was old and beautiful, but at the time of the story tense with hostility because it was threatened by a machine-loving enemy. . . . The savage sound of the electric saw is never silent wherever trees are still found growing. (*Letters* 419–20)

So wrote J. R. R. Tolkien in a letter to the *Daily Telegraph* in 1972. Readers of his works undoubtedly recognize and almost certainly applaud the sentiments he expresses. In the years since *LR* was published, Tolkien has come more and more to be viewed as a kind of advance man for the Green Movement. Patrick Curry's *Defending Middle-earth: Tolkien, Myth and Modernity* is only the most recent of a number of eco-conscious works that have elected Tolkien banner-bearer for a kind of whole-earth ideology. A recent BBC television program on Tolkien and his work has called *LR* "the epic of the Green Movement."[1]

It is clear that in seeing and protesting the destruction by humanity of the world it inhabits and of which it is a part, in recognizing that the natural world was an endangered enclave in need of protection against encroaching civilization, Tolkien was years ahead of his time. Although there may still be some industrial apologists who will deride him as a "tree-hugger," there are more and more ecologically conscious readers who will applaud him for being just that, since his fiction seems to stand foursquare in defense of trees against their human (or orcish) predators. The names and descriptions of trees in his fiction constitute a catalogue any reader will recognize—Laurelin, Teleperion, the White Tree, Niggle's Tree, the Party Tree, the mallorns of Lothlórien, Finglas, Fladrif, Fimbrethil, Bregalad, Treebeard (these last more properly tree-herds, but for all practical purposes walking, talking trees), and even the avenging Huorns, who after the Battle of Helm's Deep so thoroughly requite their axed and incinerated kindred.

The many book-jacket photographs of Tolkien posed in juxtaposition to a tree, preferably a large and ancient one, are iconographic representations of his relationship to these and other trees that spread their branches throughout his fiction. The real picture, however, is not that simple. It is complicated, contradictory, and deserves more careful scrutiny than it has received up to now.

Since unexamined praise is as useless as unexamined censure, I wish respectfully to suggest that Tolkien, his ecological stance in regard to Middle-earth, and that stance's too-often uncritical characterization and acceptance by his admirers, all warrant a closer look.

In the context of his letter to the *Telegraph,* and with the memory of so many trees to support the position maintained therein, it may come as something of a shock to be reminded that the first real villain to be met with in *LR* is a tree. I except the Black Riders, since at this point in the narrative we have not met, but only seen and heard them. We don't know who or what they are or what they want. But we know more than enough about Old Man Willow: Huge, hostile, malicious, his trapping of Merry and Pippin in his willowy toils, his attempt to drown Frodo, give the hobbits their first major setback, and come uncomfortably close to ending their journey before it has properly started. As if a tree villain were not enough, the villain's habitat, the Old Forest, which on the strength of Tolkien's letter should qualify as venerated Tolkienian ground, is equally malevolent. Not just dark and mysterious and filled with little-understood magic like the Mirkwood of *Hobbit,* the Old Forest is consciously menacing, consciously ill-intentioned toward those humans who invade it. The hobbits' encounter with the Old Forest is the first really dangerous, frightening adventure that they experience in *LR.*

This can hardly be placed under the heading of taking the part of trees, and we are forced to acknowledge a noticeable disjunction between Tolkien's treatment of trees in this early episode—indeed between his portrait of Old Man Willow and those of all his other trees—and the position he takes in his letter, which is very much more what we should expect of him. His assertion in 1972 that the Old Forest's hostility was caused by "the memory of many injuries" is certainly not clear in the Old Forest episode written in 1938 in *The Return of the Shadow* (*Shadow*110), and the discrepancy suggests the possibility, indeed the likelihood that his protective stance had codified in the intervening years, gaining strength and solidity as he reflected on it.

It cannot be denied that as the reader and the hobbits encounter them, the Old Forest and Old Man Willow are negative forces. They are working against the hobbits, and without the timely appearance of Tom Bombadil, the journey of the Ring would be over almost before it started. The Forest, we are told, has long had a bad reputation in the Shire. According to Fatty Bolger, who won't go in it, "stories about it are a nightmare," and it is "quite as dangerous as Black Riders" (*FR* 150). In the course of the hobbits' journey through its tangled pathways the Old Forest trips them, traps them, throws branches at them, blocks their progress, forces them to go where it wants rather than where they want, and does everything in its not inconsiderable power to make them feel unwanted, unwelcomed, and unliked. Pippin's protest that he is "not going to do anything" only antagonizes the Forest, and Merry feels obliged to point out to Frodo that the burden of his little song that "east or west all woods must fail" offends it even further (155, 156). What we are shown at this point in the narrative is Tolkien's version of the standard fairy-tale dark wood on the order of those in "Snow White" and "Hansel and Gretel."

If the Forest is presented as dangerous and threatening, Old Man Willow is shown as worse, for he is beyond threat; he is simply evil. He sings the hobbits into an enchanted sleep, throws Frodo in the water and holds him under, nearly cuts Pippin in half, and swallows Merry whole. Frodo and Sam seriously consider chopping him down or burning him up, and there is no suggestion in the text that either action is ecologically insensitive. Old Man Willow is an enemy, plain and simple. Frodo calls him a "beastly tree" (163), and when Tom Bombadil tells the hobbits that "his heart is rotten," the reader has no reason to disagree (179). This picture of Willow-man simply does not fit with Tolkien's vision of other trees, nor does the Old Forest as here presented fit with his other forests, let alone with his declaration in the letter to the *Telegraph*. Indeed, in a later episode, after the battle of Helms Deep, the Huorns do to the orcs exactly what the Old Forest here tries to do to the hobbits. We must recognize at least a double standard here, if not a fundamental contradiction, which, I suggest, is emblematic of a larger contradiction running throughout the book, a contradiction that Tolkien's admirers may be reluctant to see.

Most readers have accepted both Huorns and Willow-man at face value without stopping to interrogate the apparent contradiction. Jane Chance, for example, compared Willow-man to the Barrow-wight rather than to the Huorns, finding both tree and wight to be death figures, and linking roots (for Willow-man) with graves (for the Barrow-wight); she states unequivocally in *Tolkien's Art* that "Old Man Willow and his malice represent the living embodiment of the parent Tree of Death" (106), presumably in Eden. Chance's reading was consciously Christian, more than a little allegorical, and a great deal more than a little overstated, yet I think it is safe to say that a large portion of Tolkien's audience would at least go with her as far as seeing in Willow-man the embodiment of some kind of evil, if not necessarily the primal Biblical one.

It is worth noting that Paul Kocher's *Master of Middle-earth*, one of the earliest critical books on Tolkien (and perhaps the first to display on its cover a photo of Tolkien next to a huge tree) was also one of the few with good words for Willow-man. Kocher describes Willow-man's hostility as "natural hatred for destructive mankind" (71). While this legitimate defense of Willow-man is in harmony with Tolkien's letter to the *Telegraph* (and indeed with later passages in the book) it is out of kilter with the episode itself, and highlights the contradiction mentioned above, which Tolkien seems never fully to have reconciled. Moreover, the "destructive mankind" that Kocher cites must be extended to encompass destructive hobbit-kind--and this cannot mean just Ted Sandyman and the gang that terrorizes the Shire in the last chapters. It must mean all the hobbits, the good ones as well as the bad ones, all our favorite characters, including Merry and Pippin and Frodo and Sam and his Gaffer.

This is not comfortable for hobbit lovers to see, let alone to acknowledge. For all their exasperating parochialism, the hobbits are by and large and with a few exceptions an endearing bunch, and their Shire is an appealingly nostalgic rural enclave. The "Prologue" to *LR* tells us that hobbits "love peace and quiet and good tilled earth," and that "a well-ordered and well-farmed countryside was their favourite haunt" (*FR* 17). Saruman's attempt to convert this countryside to an industrial state is presented and understood as abhorrent and unacceptable. When the Shire is restored to its former beauty as a peaceful farming community of kitchen gardens, fields, hedgerows, and comfortable pockets of wood and stream for camping out, readers are reassured and comforted that the world is once again as it should be.

It is easy to buy this vision of an idyllic rural world and an ecologically responsible species (the phrases "well-ordered" and "well-farmed" are value laden) without pausing to consider that tilled earth by its nature can have no trees, and that farms must necessarily replace wilderness, which in the Europe on which Tolkien's Middle-earth is based was very likely to be forest. A thoughtful reader would have to acknowledge that much of this well-ordered, well-farmed countryside that is the hobbits' "favourite haunt," even Frodo's peaceful sunlit garden with the sound of Sam's shears in the background, must at some earlier time have been wrested from what Tom Bombadil calls the "vast forgotten woods" (*FR* 179), of which the Old Forest is the sole survivor.[2]

In fact or in fiction, where there are people, trees are in danger—not just from farmers clearing land for crops, but from loggers cutting timber, home-builders replacing trees with houses, road builders laying tracks. The sound of the electric saw, which Tolkien finds so savage, is merely the by-product of a technological advance over the less noisy but equally tree destructive hand-operated saw that was undoubtedly wielded by the hobbits and their predecessors. Here is the sticking point: wild nature and the human community do not coexist easily. Perhaps in an ideal world they should, but in the real world they simply don't. And in Tolkien's fiction, this sticking point leads to an unreconcilable contradiction that puts his beloved Shire-folk in this one respect on a par with his orcs, and in the same respect makes the villainous Old Man Willow and his Forest no more villainous than Treebeard and his Ents. Tolkien's own words are the evidence, as the following passages prove.

> [Saruman] and his foul folk are making havoc now. Down on the borders they are felling trees—good trees. . . . hewn up and carried off to feed the fires of Orthanc. . . . Many of those trees were my friends, creatures I had known from nut and acorn; many had voices of their own that are lost forever now. (*TT* 91)

> [T]he hobbits came and cut down hundreds of trees, and burned all the ground in a long strip east of the Hedge. . . . After that the trees gave up the attack, but they became very unfriendly. (*FR* 154)

> Tom's words laid bare the hearts of trees and their thoughts, which were often dark and strange, and filled with a hatred of things that go free upon the earth, gnawing, biting, breaking, hacking, burning: destroyers and usurpers. It was

not called the Old Forest without reason, for it was indeed ancient. . . . filled with pride and rooted wisdom, and with malice. But none were more dangerous than the Great Willow: his heart was rotten, but his strength was green. (*FR* 179)

All three passages should be familiar to lovers of Tolkien's world. The first is Treebeard's indignant description of the activities of Saruman and his orcs. The second is Merry's account of how the hobbits secured Buckland against the attack of the Old Forest. And the third is Tom Bombadil's revelation of the nature of the Old Forest, its feelings, and a little of its history. Careful consideration of all three is at once confusing and enlightening. The first quotation is both sorrowful and indignant, expressing outrage against destruction and irreparable loss. The second, in contrast, is unemotional: a simple, declarative sentence. It describes the normal (not necessarily "natural") activity of any community in keeping its land cleared for human use. But it fudges the issue, since it does not acknowledge that this activity—that is, the felling and burning of trees—is exactly the same as that described so indignantly in the first quote. Nowadays we call it clear-cutting of old-growth forest, and hard-core conservationists are pretty unanimously against it.

The third quotation is the key to the confusion, and a close reading will show that while the first two passages are in conflict with each other, the third passage is in conflict with itself. In critical terms it deconstructs itself, as careful examination of its language and structure will demonstrate. In the voice of Tom Bombadil, who understands the Old Forest if anyone does, Tolkien begins by telling the hobbits (and us) that the thoughts of trees such as Old Man Willow are often "dark and strange," and "filled with hatred." But almost immediately we are given a legitimate reason for these dark thoughts, this hatred; they are engendered by the activities of "things that go free upon the earth." As used here, "free" is a loaded word, for we are not accustomed to thinking of trees as "unfree," or indeed, connecting them with any concept of freedom versus restraint. We are being reminded of something so obvious that it's easy to overlook: trees cannot run away. If someone starts hacking at a tree with an axe, the rooted tree has to stand and take the blows.

Next we are told in no uncertain terms why things that "go free" fill unfree trees with hatred. This is because of the kinds of things they are free to do. An ascending scale of present participles, increasing in intensity from the merely unpleasant "gnawing, biting," through the destructive "breaking" to the harsh and violent "hacking, burning," describes just what things that go free are free to do to trees that cannot escape them. The sentence is brought to a climax and a close with two nouns carrying unmistakable condemnation: "destroyers" and "usurpers." *Destroyers* is a negative word; nobody likes destroyers. But the word *usurpers* is just as negative if not more so. As employed by an author who believed in hereditary kingship and thought the Norman Conquest was a disaster, it cannot but suggest the unjust, unlawful, hegemonic occupation of territory by those to whom it does not rightfully belong.

But then we are told that the Forest is "filled with pride and malice," and that Willow-man's heart is "rotten." A paragraph that began by describing to its escaped victims a tree's dark, strange thoughts filled with hatred, has doubled on itself to explain that hatred is a reaction (which now seems quite justified) against attack, against the violent usurpation of territory that rightfully belongs to the trees, and has then redoubled to assert that those trees are filled with pride and malice. The narrative voice seems to be arguing both sides of the question. Now revisit the second quote cited above, Merry's matter-of-fact account of how the hobbits cut down "hundreds of trees and burned all the ground in a long strip," and see how that matches with the "hacking" and "burning" of the third quote. The two passages describe the same activities in very nearly the same terms. Who, then, are the destroyers and usurpers? We cannot escape the conclusion that some of them, at least, are hobbits. Pursuing this line of argument, we can see in their actions a provocation at least for the malice and hatred of the Forest, if not for the rottenness of Willow-man's heart.

What the hobbits do to the Old Forest, cutting down and burning hundreds of trees, is no less than what Saruman's orcs do to Fangorn. Moreover, what the Old Forest tried but failed to do to the Shire is no more than what the Ents succeed in doing to Orthanc. As Merry describes the trees at Orthanc, "[t]heir fingers, and their toes, just freeze onto rock; and they tear it up like bread-crust. It was like watching the work of great tree-roots in a hundred years, all packed into a few moments" (*TT* 213). Merry is dramatizing and speeding up the natural activity of trees, but is not underestimating its effects. What happens at Orthanc is not merely *like* the work of great tree roots, it *is* the work of great tree roots. The result of that work is the transformation of Saruman's military-industrial complex into forest, into the Treegarth of Orthanc. Treebeard's domain has now overrun and replaced Saruman's.

To accept Fangorn Forest as somehow different in quality from the Old Forest, to see the Ents as heroes while at the same time seeing Willow-man as a villain "filled with pride and malice," we must ignore the motivation specifically accorded the trees by Tom Bombadil, and close our eyes to the identical actions taken in their own defense by the two forests. These parallels, which I am neither inventing nor exaggerating but simply abstracting from their emotional context, make it plain that Tolkien is sending mixed signals here, or at the very least that he is making it more difficult to distinguish the good guys from the bad guys than one might wish.

Why did the hobbits cut down hundreds of trees and burn the ground? Because, as Merry tells it, the trees "attacked the Hedge: they came and planted themselves right by it and leaned over it" (*FR* 154). By planting themselves, the trees are by natural means extending their domain into the Shire, or at least into Buckland, in the same way the Ents overrun Orthanc. Both forests are doing essentially the same thing, and that is only what it is the nature of forests to do

—to plant themselves, to reproduce and grow and in so doing to extend their territory. This is arbitrarily characterized as a good action when done by the Ents and their army of trees, and a bad action when done—for the very same reasons—by the trees of the Old Forest. Treebeard nostalgically describes to Merry and Pippin the results of unhampered growth by trees.

> Aye, aye, there was all wood once upon a time from here to the Mountains of Lune, and this was just the East End. Those were the broad days! Time was when I could walk and sing all day and hear no more than the echo of my own voice in the hollow hills. The woods were like the woods of Lothlórien, only thicker, stronger, younger. (*TT* 84)

Sounds wonderful, doesn't it? A huge, unspoiled, old-growth forest never touched by the hand of man. Treebeard is describing exactly the kind of "vast forgotten woods" of which Tom Bombadil says the Old Forest is the survivor. What we have here is not just an unreconciled contradiction; it is essentially a double standard: the chopping and burning of trees is presented as villainous when done by orcs in Fangorn, but when done by hobbits in the Old Forest the same activities are not only made acceptable, they are necessary for "a well-ordered and well-farmed countryside."

The temptation for readers anxious to smooth away such discrepancies—if indeed they notice them at all—is to substitute motives for results. Orthanc is an engine of war fueled by the trees that the orcs chop and Saruman burns, and so the Ents are justified in attacking it. The Shire is an agrarian community threatened by the encroachment of the Old Forest, and so the hobbits are justified in clearing the ground along the Hedge. What is overlooked in such reasoning is that no matter who is doing the chopping, or for what purpose, the effect on the trees—which grow according to nature rather than operating from motives in the human sense—will be the same, and it will be destructive. "I am not altogether on anybody's *side,* " Treebeard tells Merry and Pippin, "because nobody is altogether on my *side*" (*TT* 89). He is more right than the romantic reader would like to think.

Conversely, no matter which forest is expanding—whether it is Fangorn or the Old Forest—trees will take possession, and the effect on the countryside will be the same. If we accept at face value Tolkien's presentation of both cases, we would have to conclude that what is right for Fangorn is wrong for the Old Forest, or that what is bad for the Ents is good for the Shire, whereas an alternate view of the situation might be that what Fangorn does to the orcs is just what the Old Forest tries to do to the hobbits. Or to put it yet another way, the only real difference between Treebeard and Old Man Willow is that one is fond of the hobbits and the other tries to eliminate them.

Before we come to such a conclusion, however, we should look again, and carefully, at a tale that grew in the telling, and acknowledge in Tolkien's defense that these apparently competing episodes were developed at very different times in the chronology of composition, and out of very different parts of their author's imagination. With the pursuing Black Riders transformed from what was originally to have been the pursuing Gandalf into a shadowy, ill-defined menace, the story needed a more palpable, perhaps less obviously supernatural, obstacle for his heroes to confront. Moreover (and this, I think, is crucial to the apparent contradiction), when Tolkien created Old Man Willow and the Old Forest, Treebeard and Fangorn did not yet exist.

Willow-man and the Old Forest belong to what Christopher Tolkien characterizes in *Shadow* as the "first phase" of his father's laborious rewriting process, whereas Fangorn and Treebeard began to take shape in the "third phase," during which the character of Treebeard altered drastically. Both Fangorn and Treebeard make their first appearance in Gandalf's account to Frodo, when the latter awakes in the house of Elrond, of the reasons for his disappearance. "I was caught in Fangorn," says Gandalf, "and spent many weary days as a prisoner of the Giant Treebeard" (363). Neither a tree nor a good guy as yet, this Treebeard is unmistakably a villain whose imprisonment of Gandalf adumbrates the more purposeful imprisonment by Saruman that eventually replaced it. Treebeard's next appearance is in "a scrap" of narrative in "ornamental script," which began as a letter dated July 27–29 1939, but which chiefly describes Treebeard as Frodo first encounters him. Here, according to Tolkien's notes, "Frodo meets the Giant Treebeard in the Forest of Neldoreth: . . . he is deceived by the giant who pretends to be friendly, but is really in league with the Enemy" (*Shadow* 384). Treebeard speaks "out of the treetop," and has a "thick gnarled leg with a rootlike foot and many branching toes" (383, 384). Tree-*like* he may be (or be becoming), but he is still a giant, while Fangorn has been at least temporarily replaced by the forest of Neldoreth.

By the time Merry and Pippin escape the orcs and arrive at Fangorn Forest in what Christopher Tolkien calls the "fourth phase," many things had changed. Tolkien's comment in a letter to W. H. Auden that "Fangorn Forest was an unforeseen adventure" (*Letters* 216–17) almost certainly refers to the hobbits' encounter with a Treebeard now not only completely treeified, but radically reimagined. Indeed, it is tempting to speculate that the apparently self-contradictory speech of Tom Bombadil quoted above may have been one cause, at least, of the change in his character. The shift in consciousness that comes halfway through the Bombadil paragraph may have led to the development of a tree guardian who speaks for the trees in their own voice. We can grant, then, that perhaps not only the tale but also its author's consciousness did indeed grow in the telling, and that during that telling some inconsistencies were left unattended, which is not unimaginable in so long and complex a narrative as *LR*.

Nevertheless, the evidence I have cited shows plainly that Tolkien had written himself into what, when it is divorced from the undeniable spell of the story, is clearly an untenable position. He has espoused two unreconcilable attitudes with regard to nature wild and nature tamed—by which I mean nature cultivated according to human standards. The first response of Merry and

Pippin to Fangorn Forest is revealing in this regard. Merry calls it "frightfully tree-ish." Pippin finds the forest "dim and stuffy," calls it "[u]ntidy" and "shaggy," and compares it to the Old Took and his old room at Tuckborough, "where the furniture had never been moved or changed for generations," and where both the Old Took and his old room "got older and shabbier together." He cannot imagine what spring would look like, "still less a spring cleaning" (*TT* 74–77). The parallels between Treebeard and the shabby Old Took and between the Took's old room and the shabby old Fangorn Forest are inescapable and intentional. But we must remember that the spring cleaning that Pippin finds so hard to imagine is a human concept and a human activity. It is not the nature of trees to tidy up.

The obvious contrast is with Lórien, where the trees are neither untidy nor shaggy, but columnar—tall and shapely, with branches high above the ground. There is no underbrush. The smooth trunks of the trees are silver, their unfading leaves gold. They are the habitat of people, of Elves, who build dwelling-places among their spreading branches. Caras Galadon is a city of tree trunks standing orderly and harmonious. It is as much a garden as a forest, or better yet, a city that is its own garden. The flet where Celeborn and Galadriel meet the Fellowship is built around the central trunk, the central column, of a great tree (*FR* 458–59), and Tolkien's description of it recalls the Party Tree built into the tent at Bilbo's farewell gathering (*FR* 48–49). (Both images recall the Barnstokk, the great tree at one end of King Völsung's hall in the Norse *Völsunga Saga*, a story with which Tolkien was well acquainted.) The whole effect of Lórien is aesthetically pleasing. It is civilized, cultivated in all senses of that word, as different a world from Fangorn Forest as can be imagined and still be called a wood.

One vision, that of Fangorn, is of nature let alone, existing in a state of wildness entirely untouched by the destructive "two-legged creatures" that Tom Bombadil talks about. The other vision, that of Lórien, is of nature transcended. Lórien is a faery forest that is unlikely to be found in a natural state on earth. It is an enchanted and enchanting correlative of the Entwives and their ordered, tended gardens. Tolkien admired both visions. He wanted both visions. But he was honest enough to acknowledge—or to have Treebeard acknowledge for him—that the latter vision was bound to overwhelm and replace the former.

> "Of course it is likely enough, my friends," [Treebeard] said slowly, 'likely enough that we are going to *our* doom: the last march of the Ents. But if we stayed at home and did nothing, doom would find us anyway, sooner or later. That thought has long been growing in our hearts; and that is why we are marching now." (*TT* 108)

The paradox may be expressed briefly as follows: civilization and nature are at undeclared war with one another. To make a place for itself, humankind will tame a wilderness whose destruction and eventual eradication, however gradual, is at once an inevitable consequence and an irreparable loss. I believe that Tolkien agreed with each of these positions at one time or another, but that he also felt too many of them at the same time for his own peace of mind or for the inner consistency of *LR*.

Taking *LR* entire and as it stands, we will be less than honest readers if we allow ourselves to gloss over the undeniable similarities between Willow-man and Treebeard in both motivation and action, and the similarities in consequences between the tree chopping of orcs and the tree chopping of hobbits, activity for which one group is blamed while the other is commended. We have been a little too ready to want it both ways, to stay in the narrative moment and allow the narrator the benefit of the doubt, and in so doing forget what it may be inconvenient or uncomfortable to remember.

There are, to be sure, a few places in which Tolkien does directly address both the problem and his own ambivalence, but even then he offers no convincing final answer. One instance is in *Silm*. In the chapter titled "Of Aulë and Yavanna" Tolkien imagines a conversation between Aulë, the smith-Vala and creator of the axe-wielding Dwarves, and his spouse, Yavanna, the mistress of the trees and "the lover of all things that grow in the earth" (30).

> "I hold trees dear [says Yavanna, who fears the axes that her husband makes for his Dwarves]. Long in the growing, swift shall they be in the felling. . . . Would that the trees might speak on behalf of all things that have roots, and punish those that wrong them!" (52).

In answer to her prayer Manwë apparently solves the problem by creating the Shepherds of the Trees, the Ents. "Now let thy children beware!" Yavanna tells Aulë. "For there shall walk a power in the forests whose wrath they will arouse at their peril." Aulë's response is typical: "'Nevertheless they will have need of wood,'" he says and goes on sharpening his axes (46).

Another instance occurs in the posthumously-published fragment "The New Shadow," which Tolkien said he abandoned because "it proved both sinister and depressing," and showed "Gondorian boys playing at being Orcs and going round doing damage" (*Letters* 344). Part of the damage the Gondorian boys do is to steal unripe apples to play with. An argument over the morality or immorality of this arises between Borlas, the owner of the apple trees, who describes "pulling down unripe apples to break or cast away" as "Orcs' work," and Saelon, the apple stealer, who points out with some logic that if "it was wrong for a boy to steal an apple to eat then it is wrong to steal one to play with. But not more wrong " (*The Peoples of Middle-earth* 412). Borlas replies that

> fruit is fruit, and does not reach its full being until it is ripe; so that to misuse it unripe is to do worse than just to rob the man that has tended it; it robs the world, hinders a good thing from fulfilment. Those who do so join forces with all that is amiss, with the blights and the cankers and the ill winds. And that was the way of Orcs. (413)

Saelon points out the obvious—that Borlas's answer is entirely human-centered, and thus fails to take into account the feelings of the trees in question.

> "And is the way of Men too. . . . To trees all Men are Orcs. Do Men consider the fulfilment of the life-story of a tree before they cut it down? For whatever purpose: to have its room for tilth, to use its flesh as timber or as fuel, or merely to open the view? If trees were the judges, would they set Men above Orcs, or indeed above the cankers and blights? What more right, they might ask, have Men to feed on their juices than blights?" (413)

A judicious reader would have to concede that Saelon has a point. In his even handed treatment of the debate thus far, Tolkien seems to be fairly representing both sides of the question. To humans, waste (picking unripe apples) is wrong, while to trees "all Men are Orcs."

The debate becomes lopsided, however, with Borlas's reply, that "if a man eats [a tree's] fruit he does it no injury" for "it produces fruit more abundantly than it needs for its own purpose: the continuing of its kind" (413). This begs the question, since by the same token—the over abundance of the fruit—a boy who steals some of it to play with does the tree no injury either. Moreover, Borlas's ensuing argument that "the proudest tree is not wronged, if it is bidden to surrender its flesh to warm [a] child with fire" (413) again substitutes motives for results, as was the case with the parallel situation of Orcs and Ents. The tree is going to die whether it is proud or humble (and the man who chops it down to burn will not know which it is), but to warm a child is not necessarily more virtuous than to warm an adult.

I do not mean to suggest that Tolkien was exceptional in falling into inconsistency in this matter. He was not. But his own excellence betrays him. Because of the very believability, the "inner consistency of reality" of the world he created, he has always been and continues to be held to a higher standard than most authors. We require of fiction that it be consistent, a demand we rarely make of real life and would not get if we did demand it. We have especially required of Tolkien that his sub-creation—so vivid and convincing that many of his readers pretend to live there—stick to its own norms, when the wonder is that he managed to achieve as much consistency within it as he did. The problem of how to live on earth without changing it, of how to answer growing human needs without sacrificing to them some portion of the natural environment, is unsolvable. If we live and work and eat and build, even if we plant and prune and tend and cherish, it is inevitable that we alter nature, and in that alteration it is also inevitable that some of the things we would wish to preserve will be irretrievably lost.

Tolkien recognized this reality when he spoke in the voices of both Merry and Treebeard, of both Aulë and Yavanna, of both Borlas and Saelon, and most poignantly in the voice of Théoden, who upon first seeing the Ents, comments ruefully to Gandalf: "May it [i.e. the war] not so end that much that was fair and wonderful shall pass forever out of Middle-earth?" (*TT* 192). Théoden was right and Tolkien knew it, and together with Théoden and Treebeard he mourned the passing of much that was fair and wonderful. Yet war is not the only destroyer, but is simply the one most obvious and most obviously evil. There are others less obvious and therefore more insidious. It is not just the orcs and their axes that will finally overcome Treebeard and eradicate Fangorn. It is also the Entwives and their human counterparts—the gardeners and tillers of the soil —who will ultimately crowd out the wilderness.

The poignant duet between Ents and Entwives that Treebeard sings to Merry and Pippin, the debate between wild and tamed nature over whose "land is best" with its beautiful descriptions of each, ends with the argument unresolved, with winter come, darkness fallen, the bough broken, and labor past (*TT* 95–96). The promise that the song holds out of a land in the West "where both our hearts may rest" may be impossible to fulfill in Middle-earth.

NOTES

1. *An Awfully Big Adventure* produced by Julian Birkett (London: British Broadcasting Corporation, 1997). In spite of its title, Jonathan Curry's book does not so much defend Tolkien's Middle-earth as use Tolkien's Secondary World as the springboard for a defense of our more ecologically endangered Primary World.

2. It is not clear how much of the wresting was done by hobbits. Tolkien said in a letter that "it was a well-tended region when they took it over" (*Letters* 196), but stated in the prologue to *LR* that "the land . . . had long been deserted when they [i.e. the hobbits] entered it" (*FR* 22). The phrase "long deserted" carries with it the implication that nature (i.e., trees) must have begun to reclaim the land.

WORKS CITED

An Awfully Big Adventure. Prod. Julian Birkett for BBC Television. London: British Broadcasting Corporation, 1997.

Chance, Jane [Nitzsche]. *Tolkien's Art: A Mythology for England.* London: Macmillan, 1979.

Curry, Patrick. *Defending Middle-earth: Tolkien, Myth and Modernity.* New York: St. Martin's, 1997.

Kocher, Paul. *Master of Middle-earth: the Fiction of J. R. R. Tolkien.* Boston: Houghton Mifflin, 1972.

12

Women Fantasists: In the Shadow of the Ring

Faye Ringel

Since the American paperback publication of *LR* in the 1960s, J.R.R. Tolkien's sub-creation Middle-earth has left the realm of art and attained the status of primary belief. It is difficult to imagine what our world would be like without his writings, impossible to imagine what fantasy literature would be like without his fiction and his theory of sub-creation. While Tolkien's influence can be discerned in many disparate writers, a group of women fantasists who came of age in the late 1960s have contended all their writing lives with the shadow of Tolkien. In print and in interviews, they have acknowledged what is evident in their fiction: their debt to Tolkien's authentic Secondary World, the inevitability of his plot, the magic of his words, the languages and history of Middle-earth. Yet as American women of contemporary times, these writers have declared their uneasiness with what they see as certain of Tolkien's premises: his acceptance of limitations on women's roles, as well as traditional hierarchies of class. Like their male counterparts, these female fantasists have struggled to give fresh perspectives to a genre defined by Tolkien's prominent and enduring stature.

Patricia McKillip, Rosemary Edghill, Delia Sherman, and Greer Ilene Gilman represent a few of this generation of women fantasists. Though at first glance Tolkien's influence on their work may not seem readily apparent, these writers, now in mid-life and mid-career, agree that they cannot imagine those careers without Tolkien. They have defined themselves, in part, by writing against the Tolkienian grain. According to the theory Harold Bloom set forth in *The Anxiety of Influence* and *A Map of Misreading*, these "strong poets" have *swerved* from their precursor.[1] While writing within the genre defined by *LR*, these female fantasists have produced strong, difficult, and original fantasy.

As adolescents in the 1960s, all four women discovered Tolkien—as did the rest of our generation. Unlike other young devotees of Middle-earth, who either abandoned literary fantasy or sought to duplicate Tolkien's unique creation,

Gilman, Edghill, Sherman, and McKillip grew into writers of voice and vision. Still, reading Tolkien was not the only reason they became fantasy writers. Many were already medievalists who had grown up reading otherworld fantasy for children—George MacDonald, C. S. Lewis, E. Nesbit, Lewis Carroll—so that it seemed as though Middle-earth were inscribed on our inner landscapes: reading *LR* for the first time, we thought we had dreamed it into being. Patricia McKillip, born in 1948, recalls the stunning shock of encountering first *Hobbit* and then *LR* in a Catholic school library. There had been nothing like it in her reading experience: she remembers that she had so little context in which to place these books that she "thought this might be history," but found nothing about Middle-earth in the textbooks recounting our world's history. Then she discovered Tolkien's own sources, the Eddas, the sagas, the Celtic myths—and she knew she had reached her realms of gold. Her reaction, like that of so many adolescent readers: "I was blown away and immediately wanted to write a fantasy trilogy."[2]

Although the literary genre of fantasy for adult readers emerged only after the success of *LR*, the revival of romance in prose narrative did not begin with Tolkien: many critics trace it to William Morris and George MacDonald. There is no agreement as to what to call the genre: modern fantasy, epic, heroic, quest, or high fantasy—all have been suggested. The terms "neo-medieval" or "medievalizing" fantasy appear more useful.[3] Those who write in this genre have deliberately recalled and revived medieval patterns of narrative and content and in so doing have isolated themselves from the literary mainstream of the twentieth century. Nevertheless, the popularity of Tolkien has wrought miracles of acceptance for such writers.

Tolkien has provided both the theoretical and the literary underpinnings of the genre. His essay "On Fairy-Stories" establishes the terms "Sub-creation," "Secondary World," and "Otherworlds." Though Tolkien never explicitly cites Coleridge, his essay seems to echo or respond to parts of chapter thirteen of *Biographia Literaria*, Coleridge's theory of the Primary and Secondary Imaginations. Tolkien would restore Fancy, which he derives from fantasy, to the highest place in the mind of the literary creator: the faculty of fancy in the artist enables him to perform sub-creation:

> He makes a Secondary World which your mind can enter. Inside it, what he relates is 'true:' it accords with the laws of that world. You therefore believe it, while you are, as it were, inside. The moment disbelief arises, the spell is broken; the magic, or rather art, has failed. (*Essays* 133)

Although these words seem to apply to all artists, even realistic ones, Tolkien amplifies the definition; for a Secondary World to become a fantasy requires elements (such as a green sun) not taken from our Primary World, though this Otherworld must be consistent with its own laws: "To make a Secondary World inside which the green sun will be credible, commanding Secondary Belief, . . . will

. . . demand a special skill, a kind of elvish craft" (140). Coleridge's Secondary Imagination also creates a new world: "[I]t dissolves, diffuses, dissipates, in order to re-create or where this process is rendered impossible. . . . [I]t struggles to idealize and to unify. It is essentially vital" (167). Perhaps Tolkien's main point of variance with Coleridge is his insistence on something outside the artist's imagination, that intervention of the elves, "the elvish craft," as being necessary for the writing of fantasy. The sub-created world may govern itself, through the connivance of artist and readers of fantasy, and so the Secondary World becomes essentially believable. For Tolkien, the successful "Otherworld" will govern itself and will approach the condition of myth, inspiring belief entirely separate from the personality of the author.[4]

When defining literary fantasy, critics have followed Tolkien in emphasizing its effect upon the reader. Colin Manlove defines fantasy in terms of its effects on the audience who must accept the magical and not rationalize it away: "A fantasy is: a fiction evoking wonder and containing a substantial and irreducible element of the supernatural with which the mortal characters in the story or the readers become on at least partly familiar terms" (1). Also following Tolkien's rules in "On Fairy-Stories," Patricia McKillip agrees that a firm grasp of reality is vital for the creation of literary fantasy. In an interview for *Faces of Fantasy*, she calls "imagination . . . the golden-eyed monster that never sleeps. . . . It is best fed by reality, an odd diet for something nonexistent; there are few details of daily life and its broad range of emotional content that can't be transformed into food for the imagination" (118).[5] To construct an Otherworld, then, artists must necessarily draw on the materials of their own lives, or else the result will be a pale third-generation copy of Tolkien's sub-creation.

The dangers and seductions of such an Otherworld are set out in Joyce Ballou Gregorian's (1946–1991) novel *Castledown*.[6] The heroine, aptly named Sibyl, discovers a lost manuscript that precipitates her passage from this world to the Otherworld. The following metafictional passage explains the appeal of sub-creation, as it describes the genesis of Gregorian's own fantasy novel:

> "What did you mean when you said it reminded you of something?" Sibyl touched the blue glass ring that hung from a thong around her neck. "You know how I always wear this ring for rehearsals and exams and stuff like that? It's part of a fantasy I started when I was a kid. With a special country. I gave it the name of a place I saw once in an old travel book. Tredana. This is my Tredana ring. I made up lots of things about it, but I never saw the name in print again, until I read this book. That's why the book made me feel funny. When I get home tonight, I'm going to start copying it all out on the typewriter." (40)

Like the author Gregorian, the character Sibyl invented imaginary countries as a childhood pastime. Unlike Tolkien, however, neither author nor character created a new language in which to inscribe the histories of those countries.[7] The power of Gregorian's sub-creation is therefore circumscribed by a childish flatness of language.

The question remains: How to create an original otherworld within a genre with such strong conventions? For an answer, we can turn from Tolkien to Harold Bloom. Bloom's theory of poetic influence explains why in their surface features works of literature may not resemble their supposed sources or precursors. According to Bloom, "Poetic Influence—when it involves two strong, authentic poets, always proceeds by a misreading of the prior poet, an act of creative correction that is actually and necessarily a misinterpretation" (*Anxiety* 30). He expresses this procedure in Oedipal terms, the rebellious son (for example, Wordsworth or Wallace Stevens) killing his poetic father (Milton or Emerson) through misreading, to forge original art. Bloom employs the term "clinamen" or "swerve" for this process of "poetic misreading or misprision" (*Anxiety* 14). For the women fantasists, their struggle, their "agon" in Bloom's lexicon was not with the kindly family-loving Oxonian pipe-smoking Professor Tolkien, or even with the patriarchal Inklings as poetic precursors, but with Middle-earth itself, with the reality of that sub-creation, the languages, the archetypes given form and flesh. How could they travel through realms of imagination without merely retracing the steps of Bilbo and the Dwarves, of Frodo and his companions?

Since the 1970s, many women have taken up the challenge of sub-creation. I have chosen to focus on only a few, though I could have included many others: Esther Friesner, Ann Downer, Elizabeth Willey, Caroline Stevermer, Pamela Dean, Patricia Wrede, Judith Tarr—so many voices, so little room. Patricia McKillip was the first of this generation to achieve success. After several novels for children, her trilogy of *The Riddle-Master of Hed* (1976), *Heir of Sea and Fire* (1977), and *Harpist in the Wind* (1979) established her reputation. Her publisher Del Rey packaged these books to appeal to Tolkien readers. In the earlier editions, Tolkien and Middle-earth are invoked on the covers ("in the tradition of . . . "); inside, maps, glossary, and typeface make the comparison explicit. However, McKillip was not rewriting Tolkien: she was transforming the universal tropes of myth and legend to her own vision. Whether writing for a Young Adult (YA) or adult audience, McKillip never talks down to readers; she makes great demands in terms of plot, theme, and characterization. Although McKillip continues to create different types of imaginative fiction, including her World Fantasy Award-winning *Winter Rose*, none has matched the success of the Riddle-Master trilogy, which has never been out of print.

The other writers cited here have not experienced similar success. Many of their works are now unavailable, despite awards and critical acclaim. Greer Gilman, formerly part of a Cambridge, Massachusetts, writing group along with Delia Sherman, has published one novel, *Moonwise* (1991), winner of the Crawford Award given by the International Association for the Fantastic in the Arts for best first fantasy novel. Sherman's novels are *Through A Brazen Mirror* (1989) and *The Porcelain Dove* (1993). Rosemary Edghill, a prolific writer in many genres, has published three volumes of a projected Twelve Treasures series of metafictions in the hybrid known as "urban fantasy": *The Sword of Maiden's Tears* (1994), *The Cup of Morning Shadows* (1995) and *The Cloak of Night and Daggers* (1997).[8]

These highly conscious fantasists, with academic training in literary theory and wide reading in and out of the genre, can justly be called postmodern. Like other postmodernists, they depend on readers' familiarity with their tropes—in this case, the tropes shaped by Tolkien. As eluki bes shahar notes, "If it is possible for one man in historical times to deliberately craft an archetype, Tolkien has done so. Like it or not, we're all playing on his field and dialoguing with his assumptions" (e-mail communication). The writers may assent to these assumptions, or premises, or take issue with them.

The first premise, accepted by all the writers, is that fantasy fiction must involve a quest. The quest is the archetypal journey of the hero, seeking an object or (as in *LR*) attempting to destroy one, in the process achieving self-knowledge, power, and, perhaps, the restoration of societal order. The motivation for the twentieth century hero is not, as it sometimes was in the medieval romance, random chance or adventure; instead, something wrong must be put right, and the quest hero, however unlikely, seems destined to accomplish the deed. In *LR*, the childlike, ordinary hobbits, not the hubris-filled humans, must principally save the world; for the writers considered here, it is women, young or middle-aged, who must heed the call to adventure. The disparate visions of Edghill, Gilman, Sherman, and McKillip are united by the archetype of the woman as quest hero.

Edghill's women fit no heroic image: these librarians, medical assistants, and fantasy writers join with warriors and elves traveling between our World of Iron and Elphame, searching for magical sword, cup, cloak, saving the worlds and each other. Gilman, too, juxtaposes ordinary women with extraordinary tasks. In *Moonwise*, the two earthly characters, Sylvie and Ariane, spinsters and "silly sisters," have created in tandem and in a game, worlds and worlds, similar to the Gondal of the Brontës or the childhood creations of C. S. and Warnie Lewis. Gilman's Ariane, a spinster whose attitude toward questing recalls the decidedly mixed attitude of hobbits toward heroics, may be an unlikely quest hero, but she never denies her calling: "She had no idea how they were going, whether in or out of time, in dreams, in symbol, or on foot; they might be back by dark or never: there was no packing for such a journey" (97). Like Frodo and Bilbo, Ariane must obey the summons, though the road ahead is dark. In the Secondary World of Cloud, she encounters another unlikely quest hero. Nameless till the end of the novel, he is both tinker or traveler and sacrifice or numen. Because gender does not determine destiny in this sub-creation, the active questing principle is embodied in the female and the passive nurturer in the male.

Delia Sherman's first published novel, *Through a Brazen Mirror*, retells "The Famous Flower of Serving Men," from Francis James Child's enumeration of English and Scottish ballads (#106), in an otherworld that somewhat resembles fourteenth-century Britain. Sherman's version brings to the surface the ballad's gender-bending subtext. In her novel, the cross-dressed quest hero Eleanor Flower does not fall in love with the King, while the King loves her only when he believes she is a man. In Sherman's fiction, women are powerful without being anachronistic, unlike the current crop of Amazons and other heroine barbarians, called by Gilman in a 1998 telephone interview "trousers-role fantasy."

McKillip's recent work shows more overt influences from the classic fairy tales and Medieval ballads than from Tolkien. Her heroes are not twentieth-century women, but they are strong. In *Winter Rose* she retells "Tam Lin" in language as plain and poetic as that of the original ballad, focusing on the quest of a daring and self-sufficient woman. Rois Melior has otherworldly powers, manifested in visions and herb-lore. In an archetypal reversal, she is the quest hero who saves the enchanted prince. She rescues her Tam Lin (called Corbet Lynn) from the Queen of the Wood, not, as in the original ballad, to claim a father for her child—she is virginal—but to find herself, to give him freedom, to save her sister, and to find her own mother. As Rois muses, late in the story, "I did not know who I had rescued from the wood: Laurel, or Corbet, or all of us, or if, in the end, I had only rescued myself" (McKillip, *Winter Rose* 248). In all of McKillip's work, empowerment is the reason for and the result of the female hero's quest.

A second premise accepted by most of these writers is that fantasy depends upon the magic of words, and that sub-creation entails inventing a history and languages for the Secondary World. The success of the sub-creator in suspending the reader's disbelief depends upon establishing the authenticity of the Secondary World's languages and history.

Gilman believes that her most conscious debt to Tolkien is in this assumption that the language comes first, the names, and then the story. Gilman is, like Tolkien, a philologist, remaking her world through language, unlike many who have been inspired by his vision but not his method of creation. She builds her world of words as stones: as she notes, "I think philologically; when I use a word I'm conscious of everything it's ever meant." Her prose style is absolutely *sui generis*; her linguistic inventiveness encompasses Yorkshire dialect, metaphysical conceits, and contemporary vernacular. In addition, Gilman notes that the Shire, with its evocation of the English Midlands, was a potent influence on *Moonwise*: "[I]t was always hobbits for me, not elves, because they were rooted in the English landscape." She praises what Ursula Le Guin once called "the rocking horse rhythm" of the hobbits' journey from safety into danger, alternating between the comfort of the homely houses and the stark perils of the wild. Above all she appreciates the appendices, the true history of an imaginary world.

Rosemary Edghill is less influenced by Tolkien's way with words, his invented languages and neomedieval locutions derived, perhaps, from William Morris's saga-language. At the furthest extreme of *clinamen*, she insists upon the necessity of contemporary idiom in contemporary fantasy. She states, "I suppose a lot of my own writing is a response to the 'forsoothly' nature of Tolkien's storytelling" (e-mail communication). Her elves are capable of neomedieval high speech, but the effect is always undercut by slangy comments from the human characters. At the climax of *The Sword of Maiden's Tears*, the skeptical Jane and the elf Melior roam Manhattan's abandoned subway tunnels in search of the *grendel*. Melior speaks:

> 'It is past midnight ... and those who travel are safe within doors. It is time for
> us to travel, Mistress Jane.' . . . .'Whassamatter you guys? Ya wanna live
> forever?' Jane quoted, getting to her feet. (203)

In similar postmodern fashion, Gilman and Edghill's human characters live in
secondary worlds that include *Hobbit* and *LR*. *Moonwise* has many affectionate
references to Tolkien and George MacDonald. Ariane puns endlessly, reminding
us that behind her quest lies that of the hobbits, "the odd ring of power" (11). In
Edghill's Books of the Twelve Treasures, it is clear that the human characters also
know their Tolkien. When Rohanan Melior of the House of the Silver Silences
appears on a street in Manhattan, the novel's protagonist Ruth can place him easily:
"If I said I thought he was a Tolkien elf, you'd say I was crazy. There isn't any
such thing as an elf" (*Sword* 22). Another elf, Gauvain Makindeor, looks "like a
refugee from some alternate planet where Ralph Lauren had collaborated with
J.R.R. Tolkien on the set design for *Lord of the Rings*" (*Cloak* 126).[9]

A third premise accepted by all four writers is that the Secondary World of epic
fantasy, like that of Classical epic, is ruled by Fate, its plots determined by prophets
and oracles speaking in riddles. As William Dowie notes in "The Gospel of
Middle-Earth," "instances of prophecy" such as gnomic verses are common in
Middle-earth, "implying the existence of a transcendent realm outside ordinary
time and power" (281). Within the greater history of the Four Ages of Middle-
earth, the plot of *LR* looks both backward and forward through dreams and
prophecies. McKillip believes the greatest influence of *LR* on her writing is in the
importance of prophecies and destiny in determining character, revealed in the
Riddle-Master books through the archetype of the prince in hiding. As with
Gilman, riddles are key to McKillip's worlds, especially in the Riddle-Master
trilogy, whose magic system is modeled on the orally transmitted lore of the Celtic
Triads and the Anglo-Saxon riddles. As the young Riddle-Master Morgon notes,
explaining his persistence in a perilous quest, "Riddles are often dangerous, but an
unanswered riddle may be deadly" (*The Riddle-Master* 106). The riddle-game
between Bilbo and Gollum in *Hobbit* (chapter 5, "Riddles in the Dark") is clearly
the model here. Tolkien based his riddles on the "style and method" of the Anglo-
Saxon originals (*Letters* 110, 123); as he hinted, jovially, to the editor of *The
Observer*, "I should not be at all surprised to learn that both the hobbit and Gollum
will find their claim to have invented any of them disallowed" (*Letters* 25, 32).
Gilman evokes the same riddle-game in *Moonwise*, in punning fashion, as Ariane
attempts to solve the witch Malykorne's impossible riddles: "What then? Wind and
riddles . . . Thy burden's light, said Malykorne. A soul for hallows' sake. . . .
What *has* it got in its 'pocalypse then? String, or nothing" (267).

Although the women fantasists accept some of Tolkien's premises, they differ
strongly with him on the subject of women's roles. The most obvious "anxiety"
for women writers results from the presumption that female characters in the
Secondary World must be restricted to the roles played by women in our primary
world's medieval romances—object of the quest, mother, temptress, witch—or else

absent, as in epics such as *Beowulf* or the *Song of Roland*. The late twentieth-century writers are unanimous in believing that Tolkien *should* have swerved from this presumption in his attitude toward women, whether expressed overtly in characters such as Rosie Cotton or Arwen, or implicitly by their absence. They ask: Where are the Dwarf women? Must the Companions of the Ring be male? Gilman notes that from her first reading of *LR*, she was disappointed in Tolkien's women, but adds, "he's English—it's what you have to take." She finds his treatment of women in the trilogy mild compared with the treatment she received as a student at Cambridge University in the 1970s. Instead of following Tolkien and creating an order of male wizards, Gilman derives her eccentric witches from Mary Poppins and from Irene's grandmother in MacDonald's Goblin books. Even as a child, she realized that for these women, power came from wisdom, not from sexuality, and definitely not from reproduction! Gilman notes she was particularly hurt when she first learned that "the Entwives weren't Ents," but beings of lesser power and wisdom. Her female protagonists and antagonists (and her woods) swerve precisely from this aspect of the tree-loving Tolkien.

McKillip, too, sees the role of women as the point of departure of her work from Tolkien's. She notes: "Even in college I thought I should write at least one volume from a woman's point of view—as LeGuin did in the *Earthsea* trilogy —because there were no women *for me* in Tolkien." This volume became *Heir of Sea and Fire*, the middle work in the Riddle-master trilogy. In this book, the king's daughter Raederle, instead of waiting to be found and claimed, takes her destiny in her own hands and goes in quest of self-knowledge and her prophesied beloved. She finds her heritage of magical power and comes into her kingdom; in the process she becomes as strong and vital a character as Morgon, the Star-Bearer who is the Riddle-Master. Like an earthly witch, Raederle can bind and loose, compel the stones and the sea, but Prospero-like, she also masters the words and names of the male-dominated school of wizardry.

Some of the women fantasists also swerve from another premise of medievalizing fantasy: the unquestioned acceptance of medieval ideals of kingship and class structure. On the page or on the Internet, neomedieval fantasy posits a great chain of being with everyone—human, hobbit, dwarf, or elf—in their proper places. This intensely traditional nature of modern fantasy has been much decried, but the fact remains: somehow, fantasy readers cannot accept, for instance, "The Senator from Elfland's Voters" or "The Return of the Union Organizer" in their Secondary Worlds.

Whereas the other women are less disturbed by the conservative politics of the genre, Rosemary Edghill finds Tolkien's assumptions about the "natural aristocracy" of the elves most disturbing. Her satirical urban fantasies, which contain their own Secondary World of Elphame, represent a major divergence, constantly foregrounding the evils of aristocratic Elves. Their behavior is precisely what one might expect of a race possessing limitless power and near-immortality. Their treatment of humans is beyond fascism—they simply do not care what happens to these serfs, whom they call "mud-born." In an e-mail communication, eluki notes:

> I honestly am surprised at the leftist revolutionary tone of the series [the Twelve Treasures]; it's in some sense a response to the real-world lesson that paternalistic pseudo-benevolent governments just don't work. The rebels are emblematic of a traditional oppressed class, a peasantry deprived both of the traditional amenities of life, but also barred from access to a technology that would improve their quality of life, since their overlords (who are explicitly of both a different class and species) have no use for it.

Tolkien himself was not unaware of the dangers inherent in any world where mortals and immortals coexist. He notes in a letter to Naomi Mitchison that reviewers who dismissed his work as "a plain fight between Good and Evil" missed the implied criticism of the elves who remained in Middle-earth during the Third Age.

> They wanted to have their cake and eat it: to live in the mortal historical Middle-earth because they had become fond of it (*and perhaps because they there had the advantages of a superior caste*), and so tried to stop its change and history, stop its growth, keep it as a pleasaunce, even largely a desert, where they could be 'artists'—and they were overburdened with sadness and nostalgic regret. (*Letters* 197; my emphasis)

A final Tolkienian assumption, common to all fantastic literature, is that in the Secondary World, magic works. In some ways, *LR* is about the end of magic, the fading of wonder from the world. With the Ring destroyed, magic must pass from Middle-earth, the wizards and other guardians must leave, and the dominion of Man begin, "for the Third Age was over, and the Days of the Rings were passed, and an end was come to the story and song of those times" (*RK* 383). At the end of *RK*, the Elves are already nothing but a "story" to many in Middle-earth; the War of the Ring is receding quickly into legend. Like Bilbo before him, Frodo could have used the Ring to become a mage, rivaling Sauron or Saruman, but he rejects that path and renounces the Ring of Power. Then, like the Elves, he must leave his world and seek solace in another.

Although the women fantasists accept this assumption—all write about magic—in reality this is another point of "clinamen." A central theme of all their novels is the difficulty of learning magic, of becoming a mage, which in turn is intimately connected with becoming a writer. The normal resolution for the mode of romance is a dynastic marriage, restoring harmony in the Secondary World. At the close of *LR*, Aragorn and Arwen are wed, and even the warrior-maiden Eowyn accepts a new role as healer and wife of Faramir. In the Secondary Worlds of the women fantasists, however, rather than follow the traditional marriage plot, the female protagonists and antagonists prefer living as witch, wizard, or sorcerer to living happily ever after as wife. Only a few characters—mostly McKillip's —manage to do both. Another aptly named Sybel, protagonist of McKillip's first adult fantasy novel *The Forgotten Beasts of Eld*, achieves self-knowledge and wizardly power, yet also weds the handsome, insightful Prince Coren.

Delia Sherman's historical romance *The Porcelain Dove*, set in an eighteenth-century France that juxtaposes the magic of Perrault's fairy tales with the Reign of Terror, represents the triumph of two women—the wizard-maid Linotte, and the *femme de chambre* Berthe Duvet, who becomes a writer and a mage herself—and marriage is not a desired outcome for either one. Linotte achieves the story's quest and becomes an accomplished sorcerer, but Berthe learns wisdom through becoming a writer:

> When first I picked up this quill, the things I did not know and understand filled my soul with a regret as sour as wine hoarded long past its prime. Writing, I have poured them all out upon this paper, and find . . . that their bitterness has leached away. I'm left with the paper itself . . . covered with what I know and understand. And the sight of it makes me feel as light and clear as an empty bottle waiting to be filled with new wine. (399)

Like all of Sherman's work, this novel has a strong lesbian subtext. Berthe may never consummate her relationship with her aristocratic employer Adele, but she is faithful to her through revolution and magical vicissitudes, and so transforms Adele to "her best self" (391). By writing the tale, Berthe transcends her class and her sex and becomes something altogether new.

Gilman's *Moonwise* is in its entirety a meditation on wisdom and craft, the arts of magic and of letters. Her Ariane and Sylvie, human women, are mirrored in the Otherworld by Mally and Annis, not good and bad witches but aspects of the moon, of life, of death. At the novel's comic resolution—a wedding, though not that of any of the principals—Ariane realizes that she has become a witch: "She was the witch, the other. *One is one, and all alone*" (369). She experiences an epiphany; in this instant of understanding, she sees the object of her quest, "stone and soul and thorn, within her" (373) all the time, forever.

The mode of romance, inherently optimistic, in these novels expresses the anxiety of being doubly marginalized. These women are doubly outsiders, writing outside the literary mainstream and outside the academic world as well. Without Tolkien, however, they might have had no careers except as "children's writers," further marginalized and unable to explore adult issues in complex language. In an e-mail communication, eluki bes shar notes:

> [I am] distressed by authors who emulate the surface of *LR* without understanding the deep structure of the book; their work doesn't have anything for me. Since the publication of *LR*, fantasy has become a genre which models its standard on *LR*, which has an effect on everyone writing genre fantasy. The stories we want to tell all have to fit into that mold, for good or ill, but it's important to remember

that a lot of our Tolkienesque assumptions have been filtered through TSR [manufacturers of Dungeons and Dragons™ and its infinite spin-offs].[10]

While we may lament the proliferation of faded copies of Middle-earth, Tolkien's achievement is in no way diminished by those who have flattered through imitation. In addition, Tolkien's unexpected commercial success must be thanked for allowing these voices to be heard in print—though perhaps not by the appropriate audience! As Gilman notes, "interesting fantasists get caught in the commercial net like dolphins" and like dolphins, their works may struggle and die of neglect for want of amenable souls, willing to enter into quirky Secondary Worlds and follow different paths to transcendence. In their own ways, inspired by yet questioning his premises and "dialoguing with his assumptions," these writers have succeeded in emerging from Tolkien's shadow.

NOTES

1. Bloom defines "swerve" or "clinamen" *in The Anxiety of Influence* as "poetic misreading or misprision proper; I take the word from Lucretius, where it means a 'swerve' of the atoms so as to make change possible in the universe. A poet swerves away from his precursor, by so reading his precursor's poem as to execute a 'clinamen' in relation to it. This appears as a corrective movement in his own poem, which implies that the precursor poem went accurately up to a certain point, but then should have swerved, precisely in the direction that the new poem moves" (14).

2. Other 1960s Tolkien fans have become scholars, editors, and critics, while never losing their love of literary fantasy. I am in the latter category: in 1967, I wrote a musical version of *LR*—an act of hubris possible only for a teenager unaware of copyright law. This opus was actually produced at a coffeehouse, The Thorn, in Norwich, Connecticut, in 1969. Greer Gilman, born in 1951, had not read the trilogy when I cast her as Elrond (we were short of men); she had resisted reading Tolkien precisely because he was a "campus craze." Then as now, she sternly resists anything trendy. After that, as she notes "it was hobbits for me."

3. I have used these terms in presentations and articles including "Medieval Revival Societies and Writers of Medievalizing Fantasy" (*The Year's Work in Medievalism* 1989) and "Current Medievalist Writing Groups" (*The Year's Work in Medievalism* 1991).

4. See William Howard Green, *The Hobbit: A Journey into Maturity*, who links Coleridge's literary theory to Tolkien through I. A. Richards.

5. This collection of portraits and interviews with contemporary fantasists demonstrates the many different voices and visions of those who have followed Tolkien—and those who have swerved.

6. Gregorian, like Gilman, was a graduate of Wellesley. Before her untimely death, she published a complete trilogy set in Tredana. The other volumes are *The Broken Citadel* (1975) and *The Great Wheel* (1987). These novels, while following Tolkien closely, incorporate Oriental landscapes and myths, drawing on Gregorian's Armenian heritage.

7. Tolkien was always careful to differentiate his invention of languages from the philological game playing with which his critics charged him (e.g. *Letters* 374–75).

8. Rosemary Edghill is the writing name of eluki bes shahar, her chosen name. I will use the former name when referring to her publications, the latter when referring to interviews and e-mail communication.

9. In an e-mail communication, eluki bes shahar elaborated on the reading habits of her characters: "Nic is a MAJOR Tolkien fan (far more so than his author); he read LOTR in Vietnam as a kid, and it really resonated with him. Ruth read parts of it in High School, but is mostly picking up on the references to it in other (more contemporary) fantasy works. Philip has heard of it and has seen the movies, but isn't fond of fantasy. Holly Kendal and Rook, of course, have both read it in their high school days—it's sort of part of the gamer/SCAdian's core curriculum."

10. I must note that on her Web site, eluki bes shahar disclaims membership in the club of strong poets; she is proud to be called a "genre writer who writes to the market," and so "as James Cameron (my hero!) says: 'It's a timing thing. I don't care whether it has any organic validity or not.' And that, for my money, is the difference between genre and mainstream fiction."

WORKS CITED

Bloom, Harold. *The Anxiety of Influence: A Theory of Poetry*. New York: Oxford UP,1973.
——. *A Map of Misreading*. New York: Oxford UP, 1975.
Coleridge, Samuel Taylor. *Biographia Literaria*. Ed. George Watson. London: J. M. Dent, 1956.
Dowie, William. "The Gospel of Middle-Earth." *J.R.R. Tolkien, Scholar and Storyteller: Essays in Memoriam*. Ed. Mary Salu and Robert T. Farrell. Ithaca: Cornell UP,1979. 265–85.
Edghill, Rosemary. *The Cloak of Night and Daggers*. Twelve Treasures #3. New York: DAW, 1997.
——. *The Cup of Morning Shadows*. Twelve Treasures #2. New York: DAW, 1995.
——. *The Sword of Maiden's Tears*. Twelve Treasures #1. New York: DAW, 1994.
——. "The Official Rosemary Edghill Website." <http://www.sff.net/people/eluki>.
eluki bes shahar. E-mail correspondence with the author. December 1997 and January 1998.
Gilman, Greer Ilene. *Moonwise*. New York: Roc (NAL), 1991.
——. Personal interviews. 1969–1998.
——. Telephone interview. July 1998.
Green, William H. *The Hobbit: A Journey into Maturity*. New York: Twayne, 1995.
Gregorian, Joyce Ballou. *Castledown*. New York: Atheneum, 1973.
——. *The Broken Citadel*. New York: Atheneum, 1975.
——. *The Great Wheel*. New York: Ace, 1987.
Manlove, Colin. *Modern Fantasy: Five Studies*. Cambridge: Cambridge UP, 1975.
McKillip, Patricia A. *The Book of Atrix Wolfe*. 1995. New York: Ace, 1996.
——. *The Forgotten Beasts of Eld*. 1974. New York: Avon, 1975.
——. *Harpist in the Wind*. 1979. New York: Ballantine, 1980.
——. *Heir of Sea and Fire*. 1977. New York: Ballantine, 1978
——. *The Riddle-Master of Hed*. 1976. New York: Ballantine, 1978.
——. *Winter Rose*. 1996. New York: Ace, 1997.
——. Telephone interview with the author. 4 January 1998.
Perret, Patti. *The Faces of Fantasy*. Intro. Terri Windling. New York: Tor, 1996.
Sherman, Delia. *Through a Brazen Mirror*. New York: Ace, 1989.

———. *The Porcelain Dove, or Constancy's Reward.* New York: Dutton, 1993.

Shippey, T. A. "Creation from Philology in *The Lord of the Rings.*" *J.R.R. Tolkien, Scholar and Storyteller: Essays in Memoriam.* Ed. Mary Salu and Robert T. Farrell. Ithaca: Cornell UP, 1979. 286–316.

———. *The Road to Middle-earth.* London: Unwin, 1982.

13

Loss Eternal in J.R.R. Tolkien's Middle-earth

W. A. Senior

Accepting J.R.R. Tolkien's own pronouncement in his letters, Verlyn Flieger in *A Question of Time: J.R.R. Tolkien's Road to Faerie* notes that the central focus of *The Lord of the Rings* is death and immortality (89). Charles W. Nelson has acknowledged this assessment and notes its validity but comments that others, given the depth and complexity of the Tolkien canon, might propose various other central concerns. Tolkien's detractors, such as Edmund Wilson, Catharine Stimpson, Christine Brooke-Rose[1], to whom both Flieger and Nelson are in part replying, see Tolkien's oeuvre as much ado about nothing, dismissing it since it does not fit into their (often political) restrictive and theoretical models of literature and fantasy (or the fantastic). Tolkien's proponent—among them T. A. Shippey, Richard West, Jared Lobdell, Paul Kocher, Richard Purtill, Randel Helms, and many others—discuss the function and importance of realism, narration, time, nostalgia, biography, medieval romance, Anglo-Saxon and Norse literature, and a host of other certainly applicable constructs and elements of Tolkien's fiction. However, I would like to propose one concept that subsumes many of the others and that concomitantly provides Tolkien with his most pervasive and unifying component of atmosphere and mood: the sustained and grieved sense of loss, of which death is but one form, that floods through the history of Middle-earth.

To begin, the word "loss" and its variously related linguistic forms occur with such frequency, particularly in *LR* and *Silm*, that they fairly shout for attention. Furthermore, the revealingly titled volumes of "Lost Tales," which followed the publication of *Silm* and the fifth posthumous collection, *The Lost Road and Other Writings*, continue to develop Tolkien's dominant theme. And, consistently enough, references to loss pervade the arguments of many critics. For instance, in reviewing Tolkien's early life, Flieger uses the term over and over (e.g., 13–14) to refer to the misfortunes of Tolkien's childhood. R. J. Reilly observes:

> The Third Age is, for the reader, old beyond measure, but the beings of this age
> tell stories out of ages yet deeper "in the dark backward and abysm of time," and
> in fact often suggest that these stories recount only the events of relatively recent
> times . . . and that the oldest things are lost beyond memory. (139)

Reilly's view is instructive for, in fact, the loss reaches back far before the Third
Age into the earlier ages of Middle-earth and its mythic past. Thus, in the article
on "Thinning" in the *Encyclopedia of Fantasy*, John Clute states that *LR* "comes
at the end of aeons of slow loss" (942). Even Colin Manlove treats the idea—albeit
dismissively—at length and claims of *LR* that "nothing is at risk, nothing can be
lost" (184). In his discussion of Galadriel's elegiac song on the banks of the
Silverlode in Lórien, Manlove complains that the "whole passage is not about loss
simply, but a loss so bejewelled that it is a pleasure to contemplate"; and he feels
further that there "is no real pain here" (188). It is also notable that Rosemary
Jackson derides much fantasy as "a literature of desire, which seeks that which is
experienced as absence and loss" (3). However, Jared Lobdell insists that the idea
of maintaining "the past alive in the present," whether in language, story, myth, or
history, is really "the heart of Tolkien's world" (21, 48, and 74–75); any such
attempt must deal with what has gone before and is no more.

Taken in extended definition, "to lose" and "loss" become elevated from
simple, reductive definition to a structuring component of Tolkien's
Weltanschauung. J. R. Clark Hall offers several applications of the Anglo-Saxon
weak verb "losian," the avuncular ancestor of the modern term: Alfred's
translations of Boethius and Gregory's "Pastoral Care" use it to mean "to be lost,
perish, fail," and in Ælfric it signifies to "escape, get away" (cf. Klaeber's *Beowulf*,
lines 1392, 2062); and in the Lindisfarne version of the Gospel of St. Luke it even
means to destroy (222). The *OED* weighs in further to suggest, based in part on
Old Norse usage, that the "etymological sense may be rendered by 'dissolution'";
and it cites early nominal uses as "perdition, ruin, destruction; the condition or fact
of being 'lost,' destroyed, or ruined." Given Tolkien's knowledge of Norse and
Germanic language and etymology, it would seem likely that he, too, was aware
of the weight of the word in its various possibilities and thus consistently and
consciously used it in the construction of the history of Middle-earth. Certainly,
the connotation implicit in the preceding definitions describes the falling world
paradigm into which the entire Middle-earth saga—taken again in its Norse
sense—fits.

Seen from such a perspective, the incendiary arguments of those who would
indict Tolkien for the literary heresies of nostalgia and escapism lose both smoke
and fire. Surely, anyone trying to "escape" through the magic portal of "fantasy"
would not insist, in volume after volume, tale after tale, on the incalculable
devastation and annihilation faced by the denizens of Middle-earth from Fëanor to
Frodo. Similarly, it is hard to imagine that anyone seeking to hang onto the past
—whether it be the Edenic period of the First Age or the Edwardian era of

Tolkien's own early life—would persist in chronicling, often in passages redolent of the bleakest of Norse fatalism, such appalling destruction across the mythic ages.

Nor will the accusation of irrelevance, the lack of reflection of real world events hold, for although much of Tolkien's work has its roots in medieval literature and languages, it is equally indebted to the upheaval of his own time, in which he could see earlier history reenacted. Flieger argues for the cultural context of Tolkien's fiction, referring to "a substrate of darker, flintier material, stained and spotted by the Age of Anxiety in which Tolkien lived and out of which he wrote" (7). This central theme of loss, with all its various etymological associations, may well encapsulate the defining ethos of the first half of the twentieth century with its two world wars, burgeoning technology, and cultural "dissolution." In one of his best known poems "The Second Coming" (1920), W. B. Yeats offers a mirror to Tolkien's viewpoint, in contemporary historical terms:

> Things fall apart; the centre cannot hold;
> Mere anarchy is loosed upon the world,
> The blood-dimmed tide is loosed, and everywhere
> The ceremony of innocence is drowned.
>
> (401–2)

A more apt descriptor of the world of "the lost generation" following the Great War there is not.[2] And in the Dead Marshes before Mordor lie reflections of the skeletons of the fields of Flanders and the unimaginable trenches of the Front, what the eyewitness Tolkien himself termed "the carnage of the Somme" (*Letters* 53).

In his useful overview of World War I, *The War in the Trenches*, Alan Lloyd describes the first charge on July 1, 1916: "Wave upon wave of infantry was shattered. Following echelons saw those ahead mown down; leading groups, clinging to desperately won positions, waited in vain for reinforcements, which had, in turn, been massacred" (94). This appalling carnage resulted in almost 58,000 British casualties in one day of fighting, and within the entire attacking force one out of every two men was either killed or wounded (95). After a month of such butchery, which yielded virtually no British or French advances, Commander-in-Chief General Haig wrote that such losses would not be "sufficient to justify any anxiety as to our ability to continue the offensive" (99). It does not require a long leap from Haig's statement to the Witch King of Angmar, Lord of the Nazgûl, driving his own troops to slaughter before the walls of Minas Tirith and trampling them as he approached (*RK* 119).

Moreover, during the generation before World War I most of Europe was preparing for the coming conflict, and as a result an entire literary sub-genre arose (what Frank McConnell calls "the tale of invasion"), reflecting the "massive buildup of personnel" in all the major European armies except England's (131).[3] As early as 1871, Sir George Chesney wrote *The Battle of Dorking* (the immediate source of H. G. Wells *War of the Worlds*) about a German blitzkrieg attack outside of London.[4] In 1906, Field Marshall Moltke (the younger) told the Kaiser that the war would be "a long wearisome struggle with a country that will not be overcome until its whole national force is broken, and a war which will utterly exhaust our own people, even if we are victorious" (Tuchman 22). In the wars of Middle-earth, which flame up anew seemingly without end and cause its ruin as changes in its boundaries and lands are carved into its face, we see Europe's parallel devastation during the first half of the twentieth century. In Elrond's tale to the Council in Rivendell there is a wistful echo and reminder of this wasting strife: "I have seen three ages in the West of the world, and many defeats and many fruitless victories" (*FR* 318). Galadriel later reiterates this point when she tells Frodo and the others of her near-timeless involvement in the struggle: "I have dwelt with him [Celeborn] years uncounted; for ere the fall of Nargothrond or Gondolin I passed over the mountains, and together through the ages of the world we have fought the long defeat" (*FR* 463).

Thus, we must turn particularly to *Silm*, specifically to the period of the First Age, which Tolkien considered the most important part of the history of Middle-earth, for the bloody chronicle of this ageless perdition, to return to a root meaning of "loss" in unyieldingly dark terms. In just two dozen short chapters, Tolkien uncompromisingly narrates the course of hundreds of years of war against Morgoth that laid waste parts of the world and destroyed the princes and peoples of the Noldor. We witness the destruction of Beleriand, Gondolin, Nargothrond, and Doriath; the violent and often horrible deaths of Finwë, Fingolfin, Finarfin, Fëanor and all his sons, Finrod, Fingon, Beleg, Glorfindel, Turgon, and Elenwë, to mention but a few; the destruction of Barahir, Hador, Beren, Tuor, Húrin, Galdor, Huor, and countless others among men, elves, and dwarves. Morgoth's butchery of the noble houses of the Noldor, leaving only Galadriel behind, recalls again the slaughter of two generations of British men in the two world wars, a loss that bled the empire white and led to its gradual dissolution, which even today is changing the map of the world.

All this devastation began when Ungoliant and Melkor blasted the two trees, Telperion and Laurelin, and the latter stole the Silmarils. Beyond the grief and anger of the Valar and lesser angelic orders for this horridly senseless depredation comes an event that introduces one of Tolkien's most moving and constant themes: the loss of a parent or child. The theft of the Silmarils moves Fëanor to curse Melkor, but it is the loss of Finwë, King of the Noldor, that drives him to raging madness, "for his father was dearer to him than the Light of Valinor or the peerless works of his hands; and who among sons, of Elves or of Men, have held their fathers of greater worth" (*Silm* 93). Fëanor storms out of Taniquetil hell-bent on revenge; yet, "his loss was not his alone" (93), a prophetic comment indeed in view of the Kinslaying and Fëanor's betrayal of Fingon and his followers during the crossing of the ice when "Elenwë the wife of Turgon was lost, and many others perished also" (106). From this division of the Noldor, only more devastation would ensue, for in battle after battle, their numbers would diminish, as would those of their allies.

After Fëanor's initial assault on Angband and his resultant death, the Noldor would fight four major battles over these dark ages. The eighteenth chapter of *Silm* on the fall of Beleriand is particularly redolent of Norse resignation and grim acceptance of a twilight world of encroaching shadow. During this "fourth of the Great Battles, Dagor Bragollach," for instance, the siege of Angband is ended by Morgoth's sweeping offensive, which scatters the Noldor as those elves who survive flee south or into the hidden land of Doriath. Two of Finarfin's sons, Angrod and Aegnor, fall in battle; Finrod himself is surrounded and saved only by the heroics of Barahir and his men, but all "cut their way out of battle with great loss" (*Silm* 181–82). Of his father Fingolfin's death in single combat with Morgoth before Angband, no elf ever made a song, "for their sorrow is too deep" (185). The breaking of the leaguer and alliance, the deaths of so many in this symbolic trench warfare, doom the Noldor.

Still, the greatest of the tales of rue is ahead, and the following chapter tells the story of Beren and Lúthien, perhaps the heart of *Silm*. Like Fëanor's, Beren's tragedy begins with the loss of his father, Barahir, and a hazardous, painful journey through snow and winter to seek vengeance. After entering Menegroth, Beren, who has followed Lúthien from glade to glade after the initial bliss of their first meeting, vows his love for this daughter of Thingol and Melian, a Maia, in words that resonate of Fëanor's love of his father: "And here I have found what I sought not indeed, but finding I would possess forever. For it is above all gold and silver, and beyond all jewels" (*Silm* 200). Beren and Lúthien's quest together encompasses the deaths of many, including those of Finrod and the hound Huan, and indirectly brings about the fall of Doriath. After Beren's death, Lúthien forsakes Valinor to rejoin him, and the chapter ends on the emphatic note of the unending sorrow of the Eldar for "Lúthien the beloved, whom they have lost" (225). Of her mother, from whom she would be parted beyond the end of the world, we learn that "no grief of loss has been heavier than the grief of Melian the Maia in that hour" (226). The final chapters of this first section, in unflinching detail, recount the tumultuous devastation that this seemingly endless war wreaks in both the world seen and unseen. Katharyn Crabbe summarizes the impact of the last chapters of the "Quenta Silmarillion": "[T]he loss of the Silmarils dominates the final pages, and the reader is left with the sense of that loss and the sense of a world disfigured" (125).

A review of the two short chapters that close *Silm* exhibits Tolkien pursuing the same demons. "The Akallabêth" is, in fact, subtitled "The Downfall of Númenor." Amandil, Elendil's father, sacrifices himself and leaves his son in an attempt to get help against Sauron from the Valar. In his last counsel to his son, he advocates waiting and watching because in the war to come, "you shall lose all that you have loved, foretasting death in life, seeking a land of exile" (332). After Ar-Pharazôn claims Aman and the Valar call upon The One, the shape of the world is again changed, and Amandil's prophecy holds true (338–39). Morgoth's power and malice have been removed, yet his lieutenant Sauron remains, a menace to those descendants of elves and men who follow the golden age of the Noldor and their allies. Ultimately, the fate of the Last Alliance punctuates Tolkien's theme:

"Then Gil-galad and Elendil passed into Mordor and encompassed the stronghold of Sauron; and they laid siege to it for seven years, and suffered grievous loss by fire and by the darts and bolts of the Enemy" (354); both then, of course, fall in combat with Sauron himself, ending the Second Age of Middle-earth with the supposed losses of the Palantiri, the Tree, and the rings of Power, especially the One Ring.[5] Jared Lobdell finds in the stories of Númenor a "paradise lately lost —but not, witness Aragorn, entirely lost" (52).

However, many of those who have lambasted Tolkien had no opportunity to read *Silm* or any of the ensuing volumes since these latter tomes had not been published. Thus their chief torment has been *LR*, for which they did not have the context of the earlier works in the chronological history of Middle-earth; and one other particular violation for which Tolkien has stood in the dock is his putative reluctance to kill off his main characters—even though virtually no central character survives *Silm*. In *LR*, the Nine Walkers set out against the Nazgûl, the Nine Riders, but only one of the former dies, whereas all of the latter are destroyed; Gandalf falls in Moria but returns resurrected; Bill the pony finds his way back to Barliman Butterbur; Éomer, Faramir, and Aragorn survive all battles; Éowyn and Merry destroy the Lord of the Nazgûl; and the hobbits are all reunited. Boromir does die (albeit heroically) as a result of his hubris and covetise, but otherwise only secondary characters such as Halbarad the Ranger are killed, prompting Colin Manlove to grumble that Tolkien "is simply not prepared to allow any telling loss . . . into the book" (185); similarly, Kathryn Hume complains that "the fellowship is too little damaged. . . . Heroism that exacts no price loses its meaning" (47). In another vein Mark Roberts criticizes *LR* for not being governed by "an understanding of reality which is not to be denied" (459). Yet it is important to recall that Tolkien fully understood the reality of modern warfare and the destruction it entails; he comments that a "real taste for fairy-stories was wakened by philology on the threshold of manhood, and quickened to full life by war" (*Essays* 135). Perhaps we can see in the survival of eight of the company Tolkien's heartfelt desire to keep the bonds of fellowship of which the war deprived him. After the death in World War I of Rob Gilson, one of his close friends from school, Tolkien wrote: "So far my chief impression is that something has gone crack. . . . I don't feel a member of a complete little body now" (*Letters* 10). Much has been made of Tolkien's membership in a series of literary clubs, culminating of course in the Inklings, and the rupture and loss of such groups with their accompanying intellectual and personal solace exerted a telling and permanent effect on Tolkien.

Still, the indictment of softheartedness will not entirely stand, particularly if one examines the end of *LR* closely. As in *Silm*, the relationship between parent and child continues as a central concern. Denethor's tragic self-immolation is caused by an extreme sense of loss and guilt; his "intelligence, spurred by pride and desire, degenerates into madness out of grief over his son's loss" (Chance 93). Similarly, "Éowyn's restoration depends, then, on a psychological bridging over her despair over the loss of Theoden and in a sense of Aragon, just as Faramir's restoration depended on the bridging of grief over the loss of his father" (Chance

97). At one point Merry feels he should smoke pipeweed no more because of the death of Théoden, of whom he once claimed: "As a father you shall be to me" (*RK* 54). One of Sam's major fears issues from the vision of the Gaffer, trudging forlornly away from Bagshot Row, which he saw in Galadriel's mirror (*FR* 471).

And there are more forms of loss than that of life. Frodo loses a finger, which is symbolic of a greater suffering and deprivation, and he also loses the Ring, the weight of which will never leave him. As Brian Attebery ironically notes, "Frodo is rewarded, at the end of *LR*, with pain and exile, while Sam faces a diminished world bereft of elven magic" (15).[6] Sam also loses Frodo, the master whom he has followed essentially to hell and back. In recognition of Sam's heartfelt bereavement, Ursula K. Le Guin has commented that in reading the final lines of *LR* to her children, "I know I will have to put on a stiff frown so that little Ted will not notice that I am in tears" (176). As the Fourth Age begins, the living reminders of the past themselves fade one by one, lost to "them greediest paws of time" in keeping with Tolkien's theory of the "Eucatastrophe," which relies on the idea of "sorrow and failure" of loss (*Essays* 153). Shippey observes that the "good side in *LR* does win, but its casualties include, besides Théoden and Boromir, beauty, Lothlórien, Middle-earth, and even Gollum. Furthermore, the characters are aware of their losses all the time, and bear a burden of regret" (143). Elrond, Galadriel, and most of the high elves depart as the world changes and they lose their place in Middle-earth. The great forests begin to fail as do the Ents, and even Tom Bombadil, "the spirit of the (vanishing) Oxford and Berkshire countryside," will vanish (*Letters* 26).[7] Tolkien was well aware of such consequences of the upheavals of time; Auden astutely observes, "In our historical existence even the best solution involves loss as well as gain" (60).[8] The same frequently applies to fantasy, despite the vociferous complaints of its detractors.

What sets Tolkien apart from later fantasists (and particularly his inferior imitators) is, in great part, the depth of such loss and his constant reaffirmation of its power and effect. Stephen R. Donaldson labels the mood that overlies all of Tolkien's work as a "nostalgic patina" but also says he has never desired to try to reproduce it in the Covenant novels (Senior 226), and it might be pointed out that this theme of loss goes far deeper than a patina. His powerful epic fantasy, like Ursula K. Le Guin's Earthsea novels, looks more forward than backward, away from a destructive past and toward a healing future; Le Guin has, in fact, stated that if she had read Tolkien before writing her own work, she would have been paralyzed. In many such authors' works, the importance of the mythic past is acknowledged, but the claims of the future override it. Even Guy Gavriel Kay's Fionavar trilogy, probably the major work closest in tone and mood to Tolkien's, uses contemporary figures translated into the magic realm as his focus, as well as characters taken from Shakespeare and others. As a result, the evocation of a nostalgic past lacks the cohesion that Tolkien provides.

Many important contemporary fantasists turn the issue in other directions; often they address loss in the primary world. Tim Powers's highly original and idiosyncratic fantasies place a modern poker playing Fisher King in Las Vegas, imagine Percy Bysshe Shelley as the relative of a vampire, and summon up the ghost of a cranky Thomas Edison in a teenager's head. The issue of loss informs but does not infiltrate the entire narrative. Charles de Lint's urban fantasies, such as *Dreams Underfoot*, are often metaphorical accusations against the poverty of contemporary life in which the homeless and down and out are pictured as ogres, odd monsters, and assorted magical creatures almost invisible on the periphery of middle-class perception; the loss he signals is radically different than that in Tolkien's world. Robert Holdstock's Mythago novels more often than not paint the return to the mythic past as an individual quest to recover something or someone. Michael Bishop's World Fantasy award winner, *Unicorn Mountain*, parallels the plight of a herd of diseased unicorns that seem to appear out of nowhere with those stricken with AIDS.[9] Among others, the problems of the loss of faith, community bonds, tolerance, and even common sense drive Bishop's criticism. And yet, there is a connection to Tolkien in all of their work, for as he phrased it, "As far as we can go back, the nobler part of the human mind is filled with the thoughts of *sibb*, peace and goodwill, and with the thought of its *loss*" (*Letters* 110; emphasis in text). If we consider many of these recent fantasists, however, the sense of loss that comes through in their works emanates from recent history and events; rarely does it go back beyond a generation or two. Many of these fictions are thus both topical and immediate in their application of fantasy's traditional themes and concerns.

The issue of loss, along with that of wonder, may in fact be deemed central to modern fantasy. In a review of Ellen Datlow and Terry Windling's annual *Year's Best in Fantasy and Horror* (St. Martin's, July 1996), Gary Wolfe puzzles that "Fantasy has never had an facile emotion [sic] tagline like SF's 'sense of wonder,' but one could easily come away from this collection with the impression that most modern fantasy, and much horror, is about a sense of loss" (65).[10] Tolkien would, no doubt, agree.

NOTES

1. Although he does not discuss Tolkien in particular, Tzvetan Todorov, for instance, disregards almost all modern fantasy as escapist and dismissable.

2. According to Robert Hendrickson in the *Encyclopedia of Word and Phrase Origins* (New York: Facts on File, 1977), M. Pernollet of the Hotel du Pernollet coined the phrase "une generation perdue" to Gertrude Stein to describe the young men who had gone to war, not been educated properly, and thus had been lost. The term was only later applied to the literary genre of the period and its practioners (420).

3. As another influence, Lobdell argues for the influence of the Edwardian adventure story on Tolkien and suggests that the lost world motif (to use Conan Doyle's title) lies at its center (17–21).

4. That a war would occur was generally taken for granted. In fact, no less an authority than Bismarck himself had predicted that "[s]ome damn foolish thing in the Balkans" would renew the seemingly constant European internecine strife (Tuchman 71). The Germans had been building toward confrontation for more than a generation.

5. Tolkien himself explains and wonders at the powerful emotions that he is trying to create: "one that moves me supremely and I find small difficulty in evoking: the heart-racking sense of the vanished past (best expressed by Gandalf's words about the Palantir)" (*Letters* 110).

6. In his response to Edmund Muir's simplistic criticism, Shippey concurs, although from a different perspective: "When all is over Frodo for one is neither 'well,' 'triumphant,' nor even 'happy.' And he only exemplifies a much stronger theme in the work as a whole the failure of the good" (139).

7. The last chapters of *LR* witness the return of the four hobbits to a Shire laid waste by logging and pollution, and any reader of Tolkien can immediately detect his love of trees and his ecological concerns. For Sam the worst of the depredation is the destruction of the Party Tree (*RK* 360), a scene that echoes Tolkien's anguish over the cutting down of many of the old trees in the Oxford area. In the introductory note in an early edition of *Tree and Leaf*, Tolkien explains one of the major influences for the story "Leaf by Niggle":

> One of its influences was a great-limbed poplar tree that I could see even lying in bed. It
> was suddenly lopped and mutilated by its owner, I do not know why. It is cut down now,
> a less barbarous punishment for any crime it may have been accused of, such as being large
> and alive. I do not think it had any friends, or any mourners except myself and a pair of
> owls. (5)

8. In a letter to Rayner Unwin in 1958, Tolkien commented: "I met a representative of Het Spectrum, and saw a good deal of the depressing World of ruined and half-rebuilt Rotterdam. I think it is largely the breach between this comfortless world, with its gigantic and largely dehumanised reconstruction, and the natural and ancestral tastes of the Dutch, that has (as it seems) made them in R[otterdam] almost intoxicated with hobbits" (*Letters* 265).

9. In fact, almost none of the winners of the IAFA Crawford Award, which has been given since 1985 to the year's best first fantasy novel, uses the ethos of loss as Tolkien does. The list includes de Lint, Elizabeth Marshall Thomas, Jeanne Larsen, Jonathem Lethem, Sharon Shinn, and Mary Doria Russell.

10. This "sense of loss," in fact, is part of the concept of eucatastrophe and demands a corrective, which Tolkien defines as one of the three quintessential functions of fantasy: "Recovery (which includes return and renewal of health) is a regaining" (*Essays* 146).

WORKS CITED

Attebery, Brian. *Strategies of Fantasy*. Bloomington and Indianapolis: Indiana UP, 1992.

Auden, W. H. "The Quest Hero." In Isaacs and Zimbardo. 40–61.

Chance, Jane. *The Lord of the Rings: The Mythology of Power*. New York: Twayne, 1992.

Clark Hall, J. R. *A Concise Anglo-Saxon Dictionary*. 4th ed. Cambridge: CambridgeUP, 1975.

Clute, John, and John Grant, eds. *The Encyclopedia of Fantasy*. New York: St. Martin's, 1997.

Crabbe, Katharyn W. *J.R.R. Tolkien*. New York: Frederick Ungar, 1981.

Flieger, Verlyn. *A Question of Time: J.R.R. Tolkien's Road to Faerie*. Kent, OH: Kent State UP, 1997.

Hume, Kathryn. *Fantasy and Mimesis: Responses to Reality in Western Literature*. New York and London: Methuen, 1984.

Isaacs, Neil D., and Rose A. Zimbardo, eds. *Tolkien and the Critics: Essays on J.R.R. Tolkien's Lord of the Rings*. Notre Dame and London: U of Notre Dame P, 1968.

Jackson, Rosemary. *Fantasy: the Literature of Subversion*. New York: Methuen, 1981.

Klaeber, Fr., Ed. *Beowulf and the Fight at Finnsburg*. 3rd ed. Lexington, MA: D. C. Heath, 1950.

Le Guin, Ursula K. "The Staring Eye." *The Language of the Night: Essays on Fantasy and Science Fiction*. Rev. Ed. Susan Wood. New York: HarperCollins, 1989. 173-176.

Lloyd, Alan. *The War in the Trenches*. New York: David McKay, 1976.

Lobdell, Jared. *England And Always: Tolkien's World of the Rings*. Grand Rapids, MI: Eerdmans, 1981.

Manlove, C. N. *Modern Fantasy: Five Studies*. Cambridge and New York: Cambridge UP, 1975.

McConnell, Frank. *The Science Fiction of H. G. Wells*. New York: Oxford UP, 1981.

Purtill, Richard L. *J.R.R. Tolkien: Myth, Morality, and Religion*. San Francisco: Harper, 1984.

Reilly, R. J. "Tolkien and the Fairy Story." In Isaacs and Zimbardo. 128–150.

Roberts, Mark. "Adventures in English." *Essays in Criticism* 6 (1956): 450–59.

Senior, W. A. *Stephen R. Donaldson's Chronicles of Thomas Covenant: Variations on the Fantasy Tradition*. Kent, OH: Kent State UP, 1995.

Shippey, T. A. *The Road to Middle-earth*. Rev. ed. London: Grafton, 1992.

Tolkien, J.R.R. *Tree and Leaf*. London: Unwin, 1964.

Tuchman, Barbara. *The Guns of August*. New York: MacMillan, 1962.

Wolfe, Gary K. "Reviews." *Locus* 36.6 (June 1996): 15+.

Yeats, W. B. *The Variorum Edition of the Poems of W. B. Yeats*. Ed. Perry Alt and Russell K. Anspach. New York: MacMillan, 1966.

14

Orcs, Wraiths, Wights: Tolkien's Images of Evil

Tom Shippey

One of Tolkien's least noted but most significant ironies in *LR* occurs almost at the end of *TT* in "The Choices of Master Samwise." Sam here, wearing the Ring, which he has taken from Frodo's apparently dead body, overhears the conversation between the two orc captains, Shagrat of Cirith Ungol and Gorbag from the Tower of Minas Morgul—one of six occasions in *LR* when we hear orcs talking. Gorbag tries to convince Shagrat that Frodo cannot be the only interloper in the area: someone else must have cut the cords on the body and stabbed Shelob. "I'd say there's a large warrior loose, Elf most likely ;"this someone else, this "large warrior" (actually Sam himself) is the real danger, and the "little fellow," Frodo, may be relatively insignificant: "The big fellow with the sharp sword doesn't seem to have thought him worth much anyhow—just left him lying: regular elvish trick" (*TT* 438-9).

There is no mistaking the disapproval in Gorbag's last three words. Like other characters in *LR* (not all of them on the side of Sauron), "elvish" to him is pejorative. It is clear that he regards abandoning one's comrades as contemptible, and also characteristic of the other side. And yet only a page later it is exactly what characterizes his own side. Shagrat responds to Gorbag's argument by pointing out "there's a lot you don't know," and one of the things the Morgul captain does not know is that a sting from Shelob is not necessarily fatal (*TT* 439):

> "She's got more than one poison. When she's hunting, she just gives 'em a dab in the neck and they go as limp as boned fish, and then she has her way with them. D'you remember old Ufthak? We lost him for days. Then we found him in a corner; hanging up he was, but he was wide awake and glaring. How we laughed! She'd forgotten him, maybe, but we didn't touch him—no good interfering with Her." (*TT* 440)

Regular orcish trick, one might say, to abandon one's comrade to a particularly horrible and fully conscious death, and furthermore to laugh about it, and expect the laughter to be shared. It might be argued that it is one orc who condemns desertion and the other who practices it, but in this respect, at least, Shagrat and Gorbag seem to be of one mind. Shagrat sees nothing wrong with Gorbag's use of "elvish," and Gorbag has no quarrel with Shagrat's sense of humor.

The subtle irony furthermore makes a point that is repeated again and again in the orcish conversations we hear, and which was in its wider implications also important enough for Tolkien to stress again and again. It can be stated very simply, though its implications then take a good deal of drawing out (and cost Tolkien a good deal of later concern). Briefly, what the episode with Shagrat and Gorbag reveals is that orcs are moral beings, with an underlying morality much the same as ours. But if that is true, it seems that an underlying morality has no effect at all on actual behavior. How, then, is an essentially correct theory of good and evil corrupted? If one starts from a sound moral basis, how can things go so disastrously wrong? It should require no demonstration to show that this is one of the vital questions raised with particular force during the twentieth century, in which the worst atrocities have often been committed by the most civilized people. Tolkien deserves credit for noting the problem, and refusing to turn his back on it, as so many of his more canonical literary contemporaries did.

Tolkien's general attitude to the problem of the orcs is in *LR* both clear and orthodox. He insists in several places that evil has no creative power.[1] It "mocks" and does not "make." Treebeard states to Merry and Pippin as the Ents march on Isengard (*TT* 107), and Frodo repeats it to Sam as they prepare to leave the Tower of Cirith Ungol (*RK* 227):

> "I don't think it [i.e. the Shadow] gave life to the orcs, it only ruined them and twisted them; and if they are to live at all, they have to live like other living creatures. Foul waters and foul meats they'll take, if they can get no better, but not poison. . . . There must be food and water somewhere in this place."

The orcs cannot live on poison, and they cannot live on a basis of total amorality, though of course neither their food not their moral sense may be what one would wish to share. The importance of these very clear statements is moreover drawn out in several places by C. S. Lewis, a more discursive writer than Tolkien, in a way with which his friend would probably have had no fundamental disagreement. In his many defenses of Christianity, Lewis was several times concerned to repeat the argument against Dualism, or Manichaeanism, an old heresy with which he evidently had some sympathy (e.g., he saw it as reappearing in the heroic mythology of Scandinavia), but which he also regarded, rather surprisingly, as dangerous because it was all too capable of revival.[2] But, he insists in *Mere Christianity* (45–46), the old heresy does not ultimately make sense. No one "likes badness for its own sake . . . just because it is bad." They like it because it gives them something, whether that is sensual gratification (in the case of sadists), or something else, "money, or power, or safety." But these latter are all good things in themselves. Wickedness is always, according to Lewis, "the pursuit of some good in the wrong way." But since "[g]oodness is, so to speak, itself" while "badness is only spoiled goodness," then it follows that the two equal and opposite powers of the Dualist worldview cannot exist. The evil power, the Dark Power in which Lewis firmly believed, must be a mistake, a corruption, not an independent and autonomous force.

This opinion is of course very firmly built into Tolkien's whole mythology.[3] But the critical element, for practical purposes and indeed for understanding of Tolkien's and Lewis's contemporary world, must have been (and must remain) the question of how this ancient and mythological corruption would show itself in daily life. Much of Lewis's reputation, for instance in *The Screwtape Letters* (a work dedicated to Tolkien), derives from the acuteness with which he connects theological speculation to what one might call "the psychopathology of everyday life."[4] Tolkien made no attempt to compete with him here. But one can see certain parallels with Lewis, and a certain shared Inkling attitude to the problem of evil, even evil in daily life, if one looks at Tolkien's highly original and provocative images of evil: not just evil characters, such as Sauron and Saruman, but generic evil, in the shape of the orcs, the wraiths, and the wight(s).

To repeat, there are six orcish conversations in *LR*, and all make very similar and consistent points. Orcs are marked above all by a strong sense of humor. Almost the first thing Pippin notices as he comes round in "The Uruk-hai" (longest of the orcish conversation-pieces) is an orc laughing at his struggles. The orcs laugh again when Uglúk picks him up by his hair, and "hoot" with mirth when Merry struggles against Uglúk's medicine. In speech they make jokes continually, from the yellow-fanged guard's "Lie quiet, or I'll *tickle* you with this" (my emphasis), to the orcish spectators', "Can't take his medicine" or Uglúk's sarcastic reply to the Northern orcs' question, "Go on running. . . . What do you think? Sit on the grass and wait for the Whiteskins to join the picnic" (*TT* 59). Common words in orcish mouths are "sport," "play," "fun." There is a characteristic orcish joke in the slavedriver uruk's proverb adaptation near the end of "The Land of Shadow": "'There now!' he laughed, flicking at their legs. 'Where there's a whip there's a will, my slugs" (*RK* 250). Of course orcish "fun" usually derives from torture, their jokes are aggressively sarcastic, and their mirth comes from seeing others (including their own comrades, like "old Ufthak") suffering or helpless. But these are all components of human humor, too, loath as one may be to admit it. Even hobbits understand it enough to join in, as Merry does with his defiant, "Where do we get bed and breakfast?" (*TT* 58). The orcs may be well down, or even off, the scale of humorous acceptability, but it is the same scale as our own; and humor is, in conformity with Lewis's opinion above, a good quality in itself, though like all good qualities it can be perverted.

Orcs indeed are quite ready to use the word "good," as the slavedriver uruk does. He follows up his proverb with the threat, "you'll get as much lash as your skins will carry when you come in late to your camp. *Do you good.* Don't you know we're at war?" (*RK* 250; my emphasis). When Grishnákh the Mordor orc rejoins Uglúk's company in the chapter "The Uruk-hai," he, too, says that although he could not care less about Uglúk, "[T]here were some stout fellows with him that are too good to lose. I knew you'd lead them into a mess. I've come to help them" (*TT* 62). Grishnákh is lying, of course—he has come back in search of the Ring —but it is the kind of thing orcs say, and they are not always lying. Orcs in fact put a high theoretical value on mutual trust and loyalty. "Rebel" is another of their pejorative words, used both by Shagrat (of Gorbag in "The Tower of Cirith Ungol") and by the soldier orc to the tracker orc in "The Land of Shadow." Snaga says to Shagrat, "I've fought for the Tower against those stinking Morgul-rats," which shows a kind of limited loyalty (*RK* 217). Another favorite word among the orcs is "lads," a word that implies male bonding and good fellowship. Gorbag proposes to Shagrat that "you and me'll slip off and set up somewhere on our own with a few trusty lads." "[L]et the lads play!" says Shagrat just a little earlier (*TT* 436, 435). Surrounded by the Riders of Rohan, Uglúk says to his followers that there is one thing the Riders do not know, "Mauhúr and his lads are in the forest, and they should turn up any time now" (*TT* 66). It should be pointed out that while Gorbag and Shagrat soon fall out, and their ideal of being "trusty" is ironic because as Shagrat says, "I don't trust all my lads, and none of yours; nor you neither, when you're mad for fun" (*TT* 441); nevertheless, Mauhúr and his lads *do* turn up and do make an attempt at a rescue. The orcs furthermore—to say the best one can of them—understand the concept of a parley, in the chapter "Helm's Deep," and even obey the rules of war with their warning, "Get down or we will shoot you from the wall" (*TT* 178). Saruman's orcs show group pride in their boast, many times repeated, "We are the fighting Uruk-hai." Although all orcs appear to be man-eaters, they do not regard this as cannibalistic, but reserve that accusation for orcs who eat other orcs, hence Grishnákh's accusation: "How do you folk [the Northerners] like being called *swine* by the muck-rakers of a dirty little wizard? It's orc-flesh they eat, I'll warrant" (*TT* 55).

It would be tedious to point out the ways in which all these claims are systematically disproved or ironized, as by the Ufthak vignette mentioned above. But the point remains: the orcs recognize the idea of goodness, appreciate humor, value loyalty, trust, group cohesion, and the ideal of a higher cause than themselves, and condemn failings from these ideals in others. So, if they know what is right, how does it happen that they persist in wrong? The question becomes more pressing in that orcish behavior is also perfectly clearly human behavior. The point could be argued from *LR* itself, but it is confirmed by Tolkien's "very finished essay on the origin of the Orcs" to be found in *Morgoth's Ring*, which Christopher Tolkien sums up as "my father's final view of the question: Orcs were bred from Men" (421). Long before that, however, in *Hobbit* (69), Tolkien had suggested a connection between the goblins of that work and the agents of technological "advancement" in human history; and though he became increasingly concerned over the implications of the orcs in his story, and tried out several explanations for them, their analogousness to humanity always remained clear.[5]

The slavedriver uruk's cry, "Don't you know we're at war" is also one that almost all Europeans of the earlier twentieth century must have heard in daily life, in whatever language, too many times. But if orcs represent only an exaggerated form of recognizably human behavior, the question remains: in all reality, how do people get like that?

The issue of the process of corruption in what was originally good seems to have been a topic among the Inklings, considered both theologically and mythologically (as in *Mere Christianity* or *LR*), but also in straightforwardly human terms, the latter especially by Lewis. The third volume of his Space trilogy, *That Hideous Strength*, often seems, indeed, to be a translation into a more realistic setting of the kind of thing that Tolkien was describing in fantasy: one might say, simultaneously describing, for though *That Hideous Strength* came out nine years before *LR*, in 1945, Lewis was always much quicker to publish than his friend, and both works were in gestation during the same period—a period in which the two authors were moreover in constant contact.[6] Be that as it may, one can see in the death of Frost the arch-materialist at the end of chapter 16 of Lewis's book an attempt to write an account of something, in a human, which might be seen as the analog of being turned to stone, in a troll. At the start of chapter 6 the language of Wither, the unbelievably dreary Deputy Director of N.I.C.E. (the National Institute for Co-ordinated Experiments) has strong overlaps with that of Saruman. And if one reverts to orcs, there is a classically orcish conversation in Lewis's novel between two humans, Len and Sid, who come upon Mr Bultitude the bear in chapter 14. They are in fact looking for animals for N.I.C.E.'s experiments; they know that this one cannot be theirs, nor have they been sent to catch it, but they drug and steal it anyway. Their conversation follows exactly the same lines as the orcs' rhetoric of cooperation covering mutual distrust and fear, along with their heavy use of sarcastic humor (though rendered less realistic, as was also the case with Tolkien, by Lewis's refusal to allow obscenity):

> "You're a bucking good mate to have," said Len, groping in a greasy parcel [for something to put dope on, Sid having refused to let his dinner be used]. "It's a good thing for you I'm not the sort of chap to split on you." "You done it already," said the driver [Sid]. "I know all your little games." (382)

The two men talk about being "mates," refer to each other's "little games," just like orcs, but their motivation is naturally easier to understand. Sid at least does not like what he is doing—"Get out? . . . I wish to hell I knew how to"—and Len's silent expectoration may well indicate agreement along with resignation. They have got into their state as willing cooperators with evil through initial weakness or necessity, reinforced by fear, and made to seem palatable or even admirable by the steady, dulling use of a rhetoric of smartness and shrewdness. The process is traced in much more detail throughout Lewis's book in the career of the ambitious, feeble, superficially clever university don Mark Studdock (though Studdock ultimately saves himself, in chapter 15, in a scene that also has Tolkienian connections).

A further slant on the process of corruption comes moreover from another work by Lewis of almost exactly the same period, *The Great Divorce*, first published in 1946. In this work Lewis takes up the question of the nature of hell, something that forms a natural challenge, as Lewis saw, to the whole thesis of "badness" being only "spoiled goodness." After all, if all evil creatures were good in the beginning, as even Sauron was, according to Elrond, what justice is there in condemning them irrevocably to perdition? Could there not be some way of saving them? Tolkien never took up the challenge of finding some way of educating or "rehabilitating" orcs, though he was aware of it (see note 5 above), and though he did spend considerable time on the possibility of rehabilitating Gollum, not to mention Saruman and even Gríma Wormtongue. But Lewis tackles the issue of justice straightforwardly in *The Great Divorce*, with a succession of easily recognizable human types, all marked, however, by intense self-absorption and refusal to admit an initial error: the Spoiled Poet, the Atheist Bishop, the Dwarf Tragedian, and others. Lewis's point is simply that these people are not condemned to hell by some outside power, but by their own selfishness. The doors to hell are locked indeed, but only on the inside.

This was a theme of some importance to Lewis, to be returned to in several works and re-imaged in several ways, and one need not assume that Tolkien always agreed with him, or approved what may have been Lewisian borrowings. However, the overlap between the works of the two men in the 1940s and 1950s is enough to suggest that they shared some views. Orcish behavior, whether in orcs or in humans, has its root not in an inverted morality, which sees bad as good and vice versa, but in a kind of self-centeredness that sees indeed what is good—like standing by one's comrades or being loyal to one's mates—but is unable to set one's own behavior in the right place on this accepted scale. It has another root in a ready tolerance of evil as long as it is made into a kind of joke (*Screwtape Letter* no. 11 has a good deal to say about this). And there is a third root in the effect of the steady corruption of language. Lewis returned to this theme also again and again, in his comments on the work of "the Philological Arm" in *Screwtape*, in the scene in which Haldanian arguments about the inevitability of progress prove untranslatable into a sensible tongue in *Out of the Silent Planet* chapter 20, in the reworking of the Tower of Babel myth at the climax of *That Hideous Strength*, p. 435—"'*Qui Verbum Dei contempserunt, eis auferetur autem Verbum hominis*' ('They that have despised the Word of God, from them shall the word of man also be taken away')." Tolkien did not present similar images of negative language, but he spent enormous amounts of effort trying to create language that was aesthetically and morally more pleasing than that of everyday. He would surely have agreed entirely with Lewis (and with their other contemporary Orwell) that although foolish thoughts give rise to foolish language, a feeble or perverted language, or rhetoric within that language, makes it difficult if not impossible not to have foolish and perverted thoughts. The orcs' constant sarcasm is in this view a major and not just a superficial problem.

To summarize: there is in Tolkien's presentation of the orcs (as much more obviously in Lewis's gallery of the dupes and the self-deluded) a quite deliberate realism. Orcish behavior is human behavior, and their inability to judge their own actions by their own moral criteria is a problem all too sadly familiar. The orcs and their human counterparts are, however, an ancient problem and an ancient type. Just as the word "orc" is in origin Anglo-Saxon (see *Morgoth's Ring* 124, 422), so the creatures themselves would fit or could find counterparts in old epic or fairy tale. Yet in Tolkien's lifetime it must have seemed to many that an entirely new species of evil had come upon the world, one that also had its origin in perversion or corruption of the good, but one which was even more insidious, familiar, and threatening, not least to academic minds. For this, too, Tolkien found an image and a word, and in this too he was echoed and glossed by his friend Lewis. Tolkien's second major generic image of evil is the "wraith," or "Ringwraith."

The image itself is strikingly original: there is nothing like it in any early epic, not even *Beowulf*. Yet as with so many of Tolkien's creations, light is shed on the "wraiths" by the exercise of looking up the meaning of the word in the *Oxford English Dictionary*, on which Tolkien worked in his youth and with which he so often openly or tacitly disagreed. The entry on "wraith" in the *OED* shows a rather characteristic self-contradiction. Meaning 1 offers this definition: "An apparition or specter of a dead person; a phantom or ghost," giving Gavin Douglas's 1513 translation of the *Aeneid* as its first citation. As sense b, however, and once again citing Douglas's *Aeneid* in support, the *OED* offers, "An immaterial or spectral appearance of a living being." Are wraiths, then, alive or dead? The *OED* editors accept both solutions, for which (since the contradiction occurs in their source text) they cannot be blamed. On the other hand the *OED* has nothing at all to say about the word's etymology, commenting only of "obscure origin"—just the kind of puzzle that repeatedly caught Tolkien's attention (see *The Road to Middle-earth* 51–64 and *passim*). Both the contradiction as to meaning and the uncertainty about derivation seem in fact to have had some bearing on Tolkien's creation of the "wraiths": he integrated the former and solved the latter.

To take the issue of etymology first, an obvious suggestion to anyone with Tolkien's background would be to take "wraith" as a Scottish form derived from Anglo-Saxon *wriðan*, "to twist" or "to writhe." If this verb had survived in full into modern English, it would have had the same conjugational pattern as, for instance, the common verbs "ride" or "write," giving "writhe – wrothe – writhen" as its principal parts, parallel to "ride – rode – ridden," "write – wrote – written." This has not happened. Verbs of this kind, however, commonly create nouns associated in meaning but differentiated by vowel change, as with "road" from "ride," or "writ" from "write." The *OED* cites both "wreath" and "wrath" as deriving from "writhe," the first rather obviously (a twisted thing), the second less obviously, but paralleling, for instance, Old English *gebolgen*, "angry, swollen with rage," from a verb deriving from the same root as "belly"—wrath, then, a twisted emotion as anger is a swollen one. Could "wraith" not be from the same root as "writhe?"[7] That Tolkien thought so is suggested by a word that Legolas uses in

"The Ring Goes South." There the Company's attempted crossing of Caradhras is frustrated by snow and the malice of the elements, and Legolas goes forward to scout out their retreat. He returns to say that the snow does not reach far, though he has not brought the sun with him: "She is walking in the blue fields of the South, and a little wreath of snow on this Redhorn hillock troubles her not at all" (FR 381). By "wreath" here, Legolas clearly means something like "wisp," something barely substantial, and though the OED does not record it, that is also a meaning of "wraith"—a wraith of mist, a wraith of smoke, a wreath of snow.

Wraiths then are not exactly "immaterial," rather something defined by their shape (a twist, a coil, a ring) more than by their substance. In this they are like shadows, and indeed the 1b citation from Gavin Douglas offers the two words as alternatives, a "wrath or schaddo" of Aeneas. And just as they are ambiguous as regards substance, if you see one, you cannot be sure (according to the OED) whether it is alive or dead. All these points are taken up by Tolkien; and indeed, not very much is added, for though the Ringwraiths appear some thirty or forty times during LR, we are in fact told very little about them. They were once men, says Gandalf early on, who were given rings by Sauron, and so "ensnared. . . . Long ago they fell under the dominion of the One [Ring], and they became Ringwraiths, shadows under his great Shadow, his most terrible servants" (FR 78). The Lord of the Nazgûl, we learn very much later, in "The Siege of Gondor," was once the sorcerer-king of Angmar, a realm overthrown more than a thousand years in the past (RK 107). He should, therefore, be dead, but is clearly alive in some way or other, and so positioned neatly between the two meanings given by the OED. He is also in a sense insubstantial, like a shadow, for when he throws back his hood at the end of "The Siege of Gondor," there is nothing there; yet there must be something there, for "he had a kingly crown; and yet upon no head visible was it set" (RK 120). He and his fellows can act physically, carrying steel swords, riding horses or winged reptiles, the Lord of the Nazgûl wielding a mace. But they cannot be harmed physically, by flood or weapon—except, coincidentally, by Merry's blade of Westernesse, wound round with spells for the defeat of Angmar: it is the spells that work, not the blade itself. The Ringwraiths share something, then, with mist and smoke, something also physical, even dangerous or choking, but at the same time effectively intangible.

None of these etymological points, however, helps with the most important questions about the Ringwraith concept: how do you become one, and how persuasive, or suggestive, is the process implied? Probably Tolkien himself developed answers to these questions only slowly. The Ringwraiths, or Black Riders, appear many times in the first book of LR, and in the first chapter of the second book, but seem relatively undeveloped, having little tangible impact except in the attack on Weathertop. Three times they encounter hobbits or men—Gaffer Gamgee, Farmer Maggot, Barliman Butterbur—and try in a rather straightforward way to get information from them. Several times they are seen as shadows or shapes, sniffing or crawling. They raid the house in Buckland and the inn in Bree, again in straightforwardly human ways. In FR (apart from Weathertop and the account given of the Morgul-knife by Gandalf in "Many Meetings"), it is really only in the brief account of them given by Boromir in "The Council of Elrond" that there is much sign of the meanings and the impact that they develop later.

What Boromir says is that Gondor was defeated in Ithilien not by numbers but by a "power . . . that we have not felt before"; Boromir describes this (as usual) as "a great black horseman, a dark shadow under the moon," but adds that wherever "he came, a madness filled our foes, but fear fell on our boldest" (*FR* 321). This is to be the leading characteristic of the wraiths from the moment they begin to reappear (now on winged steeds in the sky) after the Fellowship has emerged from Lothlórien. After that there are perhaps a dozen occasions in *LR* when a Nazgûl passes overhead, over Sam and Frodo, or over Gondor, or over the Riders, and the description is usually a combination of the same elements: shadow, cry, freezing of the blood, fear. Typical is the moment when Pippin and Beregond hear the Black Riders and see them swoop on Faramir in "The Siege of Gondor" (*RK* 93):

> Suddenly as they talked they were stricken dumb, frozen as it were to listening stones. Pippin cowered down with his hands pressed to his ears; but Beregond . . . remained there, stiffened, staring out with starting eyes. Pippin knew the shuddering cry that he had heard: it was the same that he had heard long ago in the Marish of the Shire, but now it was grown in power and hatred, piercing the heart with a poisonous despair.

The last word is a critical one. As *LR* develops, it becomes clear that though the Ringwraiths do have physical capacities, their real weapon is psychological: they disarm their victims by striking them with fear and despair.

This at least is a suggestive concept. Many people during the course of the twentieth century, and authors as different from Tolkien and from each other as Alexander Solzhenitsyn and William Golding, have been surprised, even baffled, by the strange passivity of the Western world (a phrase Tolkien would have accepted) in the face of deadly dangers coming out of the East. Whole communities seem again and again to have gone to their deaths in a sleepwalking state, abandoning thoughts of resistance when it would have been entirely feasible.[8] In contests between the strong and the weak, the weak (the wraiths) have often won. This thought is not entirely unconnected with suspicions about how one becomes a wraith. It can happen as a result of a blow from outside, as Gandalf points out, if the splinter of the Morgul-knife had not been cut out of Frodo: "You would have become a wraith under the dominion of the Dark Lord" (*FR* 291). But more usually the suspicion is that people make themselves into wraiths. They start off with good intentions; they accept rings from Sauron (as Lewis would have said) not with any commitment to "badness," but with the intention of using them for some purpose that is in essence good, for power or security or knowledge. But then they start to cut corners, to eliminate opponents, to believe (as has so often happened during the twentieth century in literature and in life) in a "cause" that justifies anything they do. The spectacle of the person eaten up by the cause is familiar enough to give the wraith-idea plausibility.

Once again, Lewis seems to have developed the wraith concept in a more realistic mode in *Hideous* (almost certainly under the influence of Tolkien, the concept, like so much mentioned in this essay, must have been a topic of Inkling conversation). The obvious wraith in Lewis's book is Wither, the Deputy Director of N.I.C.E. On one level he is an obvious example of the bureaucrat, that characteristic twentieth-century figure. His language is elaborate, polished, utterly evasive. He is a master of getting his own way and of forcing weak people like Mark Studdock into disastrous situations, without committing himself to any statement at all. It is impossible to argue with him since he never says anything that contains any substance; nor does he appear to remember anything he has said before. All this is familiar enough to those who work in large organizations. But Wither turns out to be something very like a wraith on a nonrealistic level as well. At a critical moment in chapter 9, when Mark Studdock has made up his mind to resign from N.I.C.E. and leave, he walks into the Deputy Director's office without an appointment. He thinks for a moment that he has found a corpse, but Wither is breathing, and is even awake and conscious. He seems, however, to be in another world: "What looked out of those pale, watery eyes was, in a sense, infinity—the shapeless and the interminable. The room was still and cold: there was no clock and the fire had gone out. It was impossible to speak to a face like that" (230). Wither tells Studdock to go away, his nerve breaks, and he runs out. But as fast as he runs and reaches the edge of N.I.C.E's grounds, he sees a figure before him, "a tall, very tall, slightly stooping figure, sauntering and humming a little dreary tune; the Deputy Director himself" (231). Studdock loses courage and turns back to slavery and self-betrayal. What he has seen must be a wraith in the second sense given by the *OED*, a "sending" or an "eidolon" of a living person. But Wither is a wraith in all the senses so far accumulated: he hovers between life and death, he can be both real and insubstantial, if you see him you cannot be sure it is him, he creates a kind of existential despair, and he has been eaten up by his job and his professional bureaucrat's idiolect.

We do not meet anyone quite like Wither in *LR*, and anyone like him would be an anomaly in Middle-earth. Nevertheless the Withers of this world and the Ringwraiths have a certain "applicability" to each other, to use Tolkien's word from the foreword to the second edition of *LR* (*FR* 12). Saruman approaches the bureaucratic style and idiom, and can be imagined as a Ringwraith in the making. When he dies, at the end of "The Scouring of the Shire," his near-wraith status is revealed, as a "grey mist" gathers round his body, rises "like smoke," is "dissolved into nothing," and leaves behind a corpse shrunken by "long years of death" (*RK* 365). Like a wraith, he has been effectively dead for many years, but without realizing it. Something similar might be said about the fleshless Gollum, but many of the characters in *LR* show the first signs, or are aware of the first risks, of becoming a wraith: Bilbo (with his petulant anger at Gandalf), Frodo (starting to become transparent), Gandalf himself (refusing to touch the Ring). The image is a fantastic one in Tolkien, and hovers between fantasy and realism in Lewis, but most people with much experience of "the psychopathology of everyday life" will find it easy to translate into a non-fantastic mode. Screwtape makes the transition neatly at the end of letter 12 when he remarks that Christians describe God as the One "without whom Nothing is strong." They speak truer than they know, he declares:

> Nothing is very strong: strong enough to steal away a man's best years not in sweet sins but in a dreary flickering of the mind over it knows not what and knows not why, in the gratification of curiosities so feeble that the man is only half aware of them . . . or in the long, dim labyrinth of reveries that have not even lust or ambition to give them a relish. (64)

Or, he might have added, in watching daytime television. When Frodo says just before Weathertop that if the "short commons" and the "thinning process" continues, "I shall become a wraith," he expresses a fear which extends outside Middle-earth, and it is no wonder that Strider rebukes him "with surprising earnestness" (*FR* 248). If one should want to read the autobiography of a wraith, set in a world somewhere between medieval allegory and working in a modern office, a classic example is (or should be) Gene Wolfe's novella "Forlesen," a work written in ironic celebration of Labor Day. Tolkien, Lewis, and Wolfe demonstrate between them that one of the major advantages of fantasy in the modern world is that it effectively addresses the major threats of the modern world, like work, tedium, despair and bureaucracy, so often a closed book to modern mainstream authors without real-life work experience.

Orcs and wraiths do, finally, share one quality. In both one can see, if faintly, an element of goodness perverted, of evil as a mistake, something insidious. Neither image contradicts the orthodox, anti-Manichaean, Lewisite/Boethian view that evil is an absence, not an independent force or "mighty opposite." Yet Tolkien's imagination was in some respects wider than Lewis's, and less controlled by abstract reasoning. There is one generic image in *LR* that raises a doubt about the whole thesis outlined above, which is that of the "Barrow-wight." The wight appears only once, and it is in any case a hangover from a period before Tolkien conceived *LR* (see *Road to Middle-earth*, 95–100); it could be left aside as merely an anomaly. Still, it is a disturbing anomaly, if one considers all the details given.

In "Fog on the Barrow-downs" the four hobbits are caught by the Barrow-wight, dressed in white, and laid out in the barrow with "many treasures" about them; there is a sword across the necks of all but Frodo; the wight's arm then comes in and reaches for the sword, evidently intending to sacrifice its victims; Frodo cuts the arm off and calls on Tom Bombadil, who appears, banishes the wight, and revives the other three hobbits. As Merry wakes up, he cries: "The men of Carn Dûm came on us at night, and we were worsted. Ah! the spear in my heart!" (*FR* 196). Tom distributes some of the treasures, piles most of them on the grass to break the spell, and keeps one for himself and Goldberry: "Fair was she who long ago wore this on her shoulder. Goldberry shall wear it now, and we will not forget her!" (*FR* 198).

Some puzzles emerge even from the paraphrase above. The easiest explanation of a "Barrow-wight" is to say that it is a *draugr*, in Old Norse, a "drow" in later Orkney dialect, that is to say a ghost or an animated corpse that haunts the barrow in which it has been buried, and especially the treasure in the barrow. But this cannot be the case with the wight. The treasure clearly belonged to the "Men of Westernesse," as Tom calls them, and he remembers them benevolently. That is why he takes the brooch for Goldberry. The men of Westernesse, meanwhile, are the enemies of Carn Dûm, the country ruled by the sorcerer-king who would in time become Lord of the Nazgûl. While Merry is asleep he seems to have been possessed by the spirit of a man of Westernesse, and he relives the latter's death agony when he wakes. The wight, then, does not come from the people buried in the barrow, and what it seems to be doing, in some way or other, is trying to relive an earlier triumph, by turning the hobbits once again into the people buried in the barrow (through the influence of the clothes and the treasure), and then once again killing them. But this does not explain where the wight itself comes from.

There is as so often in Tolkien a rather similar problem in *Beowulf*, in lines 2233–77, in which we are told that long ago the survivor of a noble race hid treasure in the ground, in a barrow (*beorh*). He then died, "the surge of death ran to his heart," and—the poem follows on without a break—a dragon found the hoard "standing open" (*opene standan*). This does not make much sense in *Beowulf*, for the main point about burying a treasure is of course to conceal it, not leave it standing open: many have thought that the Last Survivor and the dragon are one and the same creature. Like several heroes of Norse saga, and like Eustace Scrubb in Lewis's children's book *The Voyage of the Dawn Treader*, the Last Survivor "lay down on his gold" and turned into a dragon. If this latter idea were to be accepted for *LR*, the wight would indeed have to be the spirit or the undead body of one of those interred in the barrow, the "Men of Westernesse." But the unwelcome corollary of that solution is that in death a foe of the Dark Lord had been turned into one of his allies, if not servants—perhaps embittered and corrupted by ages of greed and loneliness. Alternatively, the *Beowulf* poet could have the story right after all. The treasure was deposited, but the barrow left open. Then something came in from outside, from the place to which Tom returns it: "*Where gates stand for ever shut, till the world is mended*" (*FR* 195). But even this view contains a certain inner contradiction, for Tom also calls back the sleeping hobbits, on the same page, with the words "*Dark door is standing wide . . . and the Gate is open.*" The gate could be open for the hobbits and shut for the wight, but not then "for ever shut." The two disturbing suggestions here are, first, that the wight really is a "drow" or a dragon, the spirit of a buried person; but in that case good can be turned to evil even after death, as in some branches of Classical mythology, which suggest that the dead all hate the living, even their own dearest relations, simply out of jealousy of life.[9] Alternatively, the wight is just an alien power, perhaps created by the spells of Angmar, which has made its way into the barrow; in that case it seems that persecution can be carried beyond the grave, to be visited on the person whose spirit is briefly reanimated in Merry. Neither view is entirely satisfactory, but both of them suggest that there are some things not accountable by Lewisite or Boethian philosophy. Goodness may be omnipotent, but it has its own reasons for not intervening.

And in the meantime (which may be millennia) humans and hobbits are in effect in a Manichaean world in which one does not have to have the seeds of evil in one's heart to become a victim, and in that "Nothing is strong" in ways which Screwtape did not envisage. This world, alas, is the real world of the twentieth century and of Tolkien's own lifetime, a lifetime in which many things which had been rendered apparently impossible by "the progress of civilization" returned to confound optimists: state-authorized torture, death camps, genocide, "ethnic cleansing." Such actions must have been carried out, one might think, by "orcs," but there is every evidence that they were planned by "wraiths"—and Tolkien's point, which he repeats again and again, that no one is secure from the prospect of becoming a "wraith" is one that no one, not even the most *bien pensant* of his critics, can afford to ignore. It could be argued with some logic that if these were the real-life points that Tolkien (and Lewis) wanted to make, then they should have set them in real-life contexts without the veil or, for some, the distraction of fantasy. To this one can only reply that the topic of the origins of evil is one which several of their contemporaries, including the most distinguished (Orwell, Golding, Vonnegut, LeGuin, T.H. White), were able to handle only through media in one way or another non-realistic.[10] We do not know why this should be so, but the pattern is consistent enough to suggest that the fantastic element is not a whimsy but a necessity.

Furthermore, there can be little doubt that the reason for the massive appeal of Tolkien in particular does not lie merely in an appetite for whimsy, but in a feeling that his work addresses serious issues that demand a response not forthcoming from the official spokesmen of his and our culture. During most of Tolkien's professional and creative life the literary environment of England was dominated by groups such as the "Bloomsberries" centered on Virginia Woolf, E. M. Forster and Bertrand Russell, or the *Sonnenkinder* of Evelyn Waugh. These had their own themes and their own merits, but if one asks what a reader was likely to learn from any of them about the origins of evil, say, or the balance between freedom and responsibility in political power, then the answer must be, "very little."[11] One of the most apparent features of all those writers mentioned is their severe concentration on private morality. Those inhabitants of the twentieth century, however, who did not have the luxury of a private income, "a room of one's own," freedom from conscription, or the ability to avoid political choices such as service (or the refusal of service) in Vietnam, have consistently found in Tolkien an integration of private with public morality that commands their attention, and often their imitation. It is not an accident that Tolkien has in effect created a new mass-genre, the epic fantasy trilogy; nor that his works are consistently to be found on barricades and among protesters in England, the South Seas, Russia, and across the world.[12] His and his friends' theorizings about the nature and sources of evil may have seemed recondite or atavistic at the time, but they combined fantastic speculation with a wide and painful experience, and a certain hard realism, notably absent from the works of more professional and more sheltered philosophers, not to mention psychologists. Middle-earth certainly has an appeal based on its landscape, its characters, its revival of romance; but this would be purely superficial (as it is in the works of some but not all of its imitators) without its animating themes of power, evil, and corruption. Sauron and the Ringwraiths, Big Brother and the Party, the pig's head and the choirboys: these have been the defining images of evil—wholly original, highly varied, oddly consistent—for a culture and a century which have had too close a contact with evil for more traditional images of it to seem any longer entirely adequate.

NOTES

1. For more extended comment on this point, see my *Road to Middle-earth*, 128–33.

2. Besides the passage cited below, see for instance the short article "Evil and God" in *God in the Dock: Essays on Theology and Ethics*, 21–24. The reviving relevance of a kind of Manichaeanism was another point at which Tolkien and Lewis were in agreement, see Tolkien, *"Beowulf*: the Monsters and the Critics" (*Essays* 26).

3. The most perceptive statements of the differences between the good and evil sides in *LR*, and the most convincing refutation of complaints about their similarities, come in W. H. Auden's 1956 review and 1968 article.

4. I take the phrase from Sigmund Freud's *Zur Psychopathologie des Alltagslebens*. As a guide to events in everyday life the book is almost comically disappointing. Lewis repeatedly drew attention to the inadequacies of Freud's views of human evil (and everyday life) throughout his works.

5. Tolkien's shifting views over the origin of the orcs can be seen in several places, notably *Letters* (187–95, 355), and *Morgoth's Ring* (123–24, 408–24). Were they bred from elves or from humans? Could they interbreed with humans? How did they reproduce? Were they of "mixed origin?" Were some of them perhaps in origin Maiar? The horns of the dilemma that Tolkien found all but impossible to resolve were these: on the one horn, the inability of the evil powers (Melkor, Sauron) to create, forced on Tolkien by Lewis's orthodox argument summarized above, meant that they must be a corruption of something pre-existing; but if this were so, then on the other horn they must in theory be not "irredeemable," unlikely as this seemed, and impossible as it might be for elves or men to carry out see *Morgoth's Ring*, (419). For further comment see my *Road to Middle-earth* (207–8).

6. The first volume of the Space trilogy, *Out of the Silent Planet*, was published in 1938, the third volume, *That Hideous Strength*, in 1945. Lewis published an abridged edition of the latter in 1955, which omits some of the passages cited here.

7. In view of the early Scottish provenance, the obvious derivation would be from the past tense of the verb *wráð* in Old English. This would give *wrothe in standard modern English, but Scots and Northern English dialects did not round Old English long -*á*, creating doublets such as home (standard) / hame (Northern), or stone (standard) / stane (Northern). Gavin Douglas's "wraith," from *wríðan*, would then be an exact parallel to "raid," from *rídan*, the latter introduced into standard English from Scottish by Walter Scott. Its etymology is exactly parallel to standard "road," and both derive from Old English *rád*, as

(in my view) "wraith" does from *wráð.*

8. Solzhenitsyn muses on the failure to resist extermination squads in *The Gulag Archipelago*, 11–15; Golding's hero Ralph in *Lord of the Flies* is marked not by lack of courage, but lack of aggression: his passivity leads to the death of Piggy. Parallels might easily be drawn in the post–war periods (*Lord of the Flies* came out in the same year as the first volume of *LR*, 1954) with the failure of the League of Nations twenty years before.

9. Lewis puts this belief into the mouth of the Un-man in chapter 13 of the second volume of the Space trilogy, *Perelandra*. The Un-man here could also be cited as a kind of "wraith." The body of the scientist Weston is clearly possessed by the devil, but sometimes (as in chapter 13) reverts to being itself; unless this is a trick, or only a "dying psychic energy" like the one that animates Merry for a moment.

10. I discuss the relationship between some of the members of this group in Shippey (1993).

11. One can, for instance, read the much-praised and ambitiously titled work *Principia Ethica* by G. E. Moore (a leading "Bloomsberry") from beginning to end without finding anything that has any practical bearing on the issues that were to dominate the century. I take the term *Sonnenkinder*, meanwhile, from Martin Green's account of the Waugh circle, *Children of the Sun*. The relationship between the Inklings and the Bloomsbury group has yet to be studied, but it seems clear that Lewis at least was responding to some of the latter (Forster, Russell) in several of his works.

12. A point made with great force by Patrick Curry's *Defending Middle-Earth*, especially pp. 54–56.

WORKS CITED

Auden, W. H. "At the End of the Quest, Victory." *New York Times Book Review* 22 Jan. 1956: 5.

———. "Good and Evil in *The Lord of the Rings*." *Critical Quarterly* 10 (1968): 138–42.

Curry, Patrick. *Defending Middle-Earth: Tolkien, Myth and Modernity*. New York: St Martin's, 1997.

Freud, Sigmund. *Zur Psychopathologie des Alltagslebens.* Karger: Berlin, 1904. Trans. Alan Tyson. *The Psychopathology of Everyday Life*. New York: Norton, 1965.

Golding, William. *Lord of the Flies*. London: Faber and Faber, 1954.

Green, Martin. *Children of the Sun: a narrative of "decadence" in England after 1918*. New York: Basic Books, 1976.

Lewis, C. S. *God in the Dock: Essays on Theology and Ethics*. Ed. Walter Hooper. Grand Rapids, MI: Eerdmans, 1970.

———. *The Great Divorce*. New York: Macmillan, 1946.

———. *Mere Christianity*. rev. ed. London: Collins/Fontana, 1952.

———. *Out of the Silent Planet*. London: Bodley, 1938.

———. *Perelandra*. London: Bodley, 1943.

———. *The Screwtape Letters*. New York: Macmillan, 1943.

———. *That Hideous Strength: a Modern Fairy-tale for Grown-ups*. London: Bodley, 1945.

———. *The Voyage of the Dawn Treader*. London: Geoffrey Bles, 1952.

Moore, George Edward. *Principia Ethica*. Cambridge: Cambridge UP, 1903.

Shippey, T.A., *The Road to Middle-earth*. New ed. London: HarperCollins, 1992.

———. "Tolkien as a Post-War Writer." *Scholarship and Fantasy: The Tolkien Phenomenon*. Ed. Keith J. Battarbee. University of Turku Press: Turku, 1993: 217–36. Reprinted in *Proceedings of the J.R.R. Tolkien Centenary Conference, 1992*. Ed. Patricia Reynolds

and Glen H. GoodKnight. Milton Keynes: Tolkien Society and Altadena: Mythopoeic
       Press, 1995, 84-93.
Solzhenitsyn, Alexander. *The Gulag Archipelago*. Trans. Thomas P. Whitney. Glasgow:
       Collins/ Fontana, 1974.
Wolfe, Gene. "Forlesen." *Gene Wolfe's Book of Days*. Garden City, NY: Doubleday, 1981.

Selected Bibliography

For comprehensive listings of Tolkien's works published up to 1992, see Wayne G. Hammond's and Douglas A. Anderson's *J.R.R. Tolkien: A Descriptive Bibliography* or Humphrey Carpenter's Tolkien biography. Below are detailed the editions of Tolkien's books used in this collection and other notable publications. The sheer volume of critical reviews, articles, books, theses, and other such materials on the author is far larger than many readers and critics might think. Listed here is a selection of the many significant pieces of scholarship on Tolkien.

PRIMARY WORKS

Tolkien, J.R.R. *The Hobbit, or There and Back Again.* 1937. 3rd ed. London: Unwin, 1981.

——. *Farmer Giles of Ham.* 1949. London: Grafton, 1993.

——. "The Homecoming of Beorhtnoth Beorhthelm's Son." *Essays and Studies* 6 (1953): 1–18.

——. *The Fellowship of the Ring: Being the First Part of The Lord of the Rings.* 1954. 4thed. London: Unwin, 1981.

——. *The Two Towers: Being the Second Part of The Lord of the Rings.* 1954. 4th ed. London: Unwin, 1981.

——. *The Return of the King: Being the Third Part of The Lord of the Rings.* 1955. 4th ed. London: Unwin, 1981.

——. *The Adventures of Tom Bombadil and Other Verses from the Red Book.* 1962. London: Grafton, 1993.

——. *Tree and Leaf.* 1964. 2nd ed. London: Unwin, 1988.

——. *Smith of Wootton Major.* 1967. London: Grafton, 1993.

——. *The Road Goes Ever On: A Song Cycle.* Music by Donald Swan. London: Unwin, 1968.

——, trans. *Sir Gawain and the Green Knight, Pearl and Sir Orfeo.* 1975. Ed. Christopher Tolkien. London: Unwin, 1979.

——. *The Silmarillion.* 1977. London: Grafton, 1992.

——. *Letters.* Ed. Humphrey Carpenter. 1981. London: Unwin, 1990.

——. *Unfinished Tales of Númenor and Middle-earth.* London: Unwin, 1982.

——. *Finn and Hengest: The Fragment and the Episode.* 1982. Ed. Alan Bliss. London: HarperCollins, 1998.

——. *The Monsters and the Critics and Other Essays.* 1983. Ed. Christopher Tolkien. London: HarperCollins, 1997.

——. *The Book of Lost Tales, Part I.* Ed. 1983. Christopher Tolkien. London: Grafton, 1994.

——. *The Book of Lost Tales, Part II.* Ed. 1984. Christopher Tolkien. London: Grafton, 1992.

——. *The Lays of Beleriand.* 1985. Ed. Christopher Tolkien. London: Unwin, 1987.

——. *The Shaping of Middle-earth: The Quenta, the Ambarkanta, and the Annals.* 1986. Ed. Christopher Tolkien. London: HarperCollins, 1993.

——. *The Lost Road and Other Writings: Language and Legend before The Lord of the Rings.* 1987. Ed. Christopher Tolkien. London: HarperCollins, 1993.

——. *The Return of the Shadow: The History of The Lord of the Rings Part One.* 1988. Ed. Christopher Tolkien. London: Unwin, 1990.

——. *The Treason of Isengard: The History of The Lord of the Rings Part Two.* 1989. Ed.

Christopher Tolkien. London: HarperCollins, 1993.
——. *The War of the Ring: The History of The Lord of the Rings Part Three.* 1990. Ed. Christopher Tolkien. London: Grafton, 1992.
——. *Sauron Defeated: The End of the Third Age, the History of The Lord of the Rings Part Four.* 1992. Ed. Christopher Tolkien. London: HarperCollins, 1993.
——. *Morgoth's Ring: The Later Silmarillion Part One, The Legends of Aman.* 1993. Ed. Christopher Tolkien. London: HarperCollins, 1994.
——. *The War of the Jewels: The Later Silmarillion Part Two, The Legends of Beleriand.* 1994. Ed. Christopher Tolkien. London: HarperCollins, 1995.
——. *The Peoples of Middle-earth.* 1996. Ed. Christopher Tolkien. London: HarperCollins, 1997.
——. *Roverandom.* Ed. Christina Scull and Wayne G. Hammond. London: HarperCollins, 1998.
Tolkien, J.R.R. and E. V. Gordon, eds. *Sir Gawain and the Green Knight.* Oxford: Oxford UP, 1925.

SECONDARY WORKS

Algeo, John. "The Toponymy of Middle-Earth." *Names* 33.1–2 (1985): 80–95.
Allan, Jim, ed. *An Introduction to Elvish.* Hayes, Middlesex: Bran's, 1978.
Attebery, Brian. *The Fantasy Tradition in American Literature: From Irving to Le Guin.* Bloomington: Indiana UP, 1980.
——. *Strategies of Fantasy.* Indianapolis: Indiana UP, 1992.
Auden, W. H. "The Hero is a Hobbit." *New York Times Book Review* 31 Oct. 1954: 37.
——. "A World Imaginary, but Real." *Encounter* 3 (1954): 59–62.
——. "At the End of the Quest, Victory." *New York Times Book Review* 22 Jan. 1956: 5.
——. "The Quest Hero." *Texas Quarterly* 4.4 (1961): 81–93.
——. "Good and Evil in *The Lord of the Rings.*" *Critical Quarterly* 10 (1968): 138-42.
Barbour, Douglas. "'The Shadow of the Past': History in Middle Earth." *University of Windsor Review* 8.1 (1972): 35–42.
——. "J.R.R. Tolkien." *Supernatural Fiction Writers: Fantasy and Horror.* Ed. E. F. Bleiler et al. 2 vols. New York: Scribner, 1985. 1: 675–82.
Beagle, Peter S. "Tolkien's Magic Ring." *Holiday* June 1966: 128,130,133–34.
Beatie, Bruce A. "The Tolkien Phenomenon: 1954–1968." *Journal of Popular Culture* 3.4 (1970): 689–703.
Becker, Alida, ed. *The Tolkien Scrapbook.* New York: Grosset, 1978.
Begg, Ean C. M. *The Lord of the Rings and the Signs of the Times.* London: Greaves, 1975.
Blissett, William. "The Despots of the Rings." *South Atlantic Quarterly* 58 (1959): 448–56.
Bradley, Marion Zimmer. *Men, Halflings and Hero Worship.* 1961. Baltimore: T-K Graphics, 1973.
Brogan, Hugh. "Tolkien's Great War." *Children and Their Books: A Celebration of the Work of Iona and Peter Opie.* Oxford: Clarendon, 1989. 351–67.
Brooke-Rose, Christine. *A Rhetoric of the Unreal: Studies in Narrative and Structure, Especially of the Fantastic.* Cambridge: Cambridge UP, 1981.
Burger, Douglas A. "Tolkien's Elvish Craft and Frodo's Mithril Coat." *The Scope of the Fantastic—Theory, Technique, Major Authors.* Ed. Robert A. Collins and Howard D. Pearce. Westport: Greenwood, 1985. 255–62.
Burns, Marjorie. "J.R.R. Tolkien: The British and the Norse in Tension." *Pacific Coast Philology* 25.2 (1990): 49–58.

Carpenter, Humphrey. *J.R.R. Tolkien: A Biography*. 1977. London: Grafton, 1992.

——. *The Inklings: C. S. Lewis, J.R.R. Tolkien, Charles Williams, and Their Friends.* London: Unwin, 1978.

Carter, Lin. *Tolkien: A Look Behind The Lord of the Rings*. New York: Ballantine, 1969.

——. *Imaginary Worlds: The Art of Fantasy*. New York: Ballantine, 1973.

Chance, Jane Nitzsche. *Tolkien's Art: 'A Mythology for England'*. London: Macmillan, 1979.

——. "Tolkien and His Sources." *Approaches to Teaching Sir Gawain and the Green Knight.* Ed. Miriam Youngerman Miller and Jane Chance. New York: MLA, 1986. 151–55.

——. *The Lord of the Rings: The Mythology of Power*. New York: Twayne, 1992.

Chance, Jane, and David Day. "Medievalism in Tolkien: Two Decades of Criticism in Review." *Studies in Medievalism* 3.3 (1991): 375–87.

Clausen, Christopher. "*Lord of the Rings* and "The Ballad of the White Horse'." *South Atlantic Bulletin* 39.2 (1974):10–16.

Colebatch, Hal. *Return of the Heroes: The Lord of the Rings, Star Wars and Contemporary Culture*. Perth: Australian Institute, 1990.

Collins, David R. *J.R.R. Tolkien: Master of Fantasy*. Minneapolis: Lerner, 1992.

Crabbe, Katharyn W. *J.R.R. Tolkien*. 1981. New ed. New York: Continuum, 1988.

Curry, Patrick. "Why Tolkien is for the Real Grown-ups." *New Statesman* 31 Jan. 1997: 47.

——. *Defending Middle-earth: Tolkien, Myth and Modernity*. New York: St. Martin's, 1997.

de Camp, L. Sprague. *Literary Swordsmen and Sorcerers: The Makers of Heroic Fantasy*. Sauk City, WI: Arkham, 1976.

DeSpain, Jerry Lynn. "A Rhetorical View of J.R.R. Tolkien's *The Lord of the Rings*." *Western Speech* 35.2 (1971): 88–95.

Dubs, Kathleen E. "Providence, Fate, and Chance: Boethian Philosophy in *The Lord of the Rings*." *Twentieth Century Literature* 27 (1981): 34–42.

Elgin, Don D. *The Comedy of the Fantastic: Ecological Perspectives on the Fantasy Novel*. Westport, CT: Greenwood, 1985.

Ellison, John. "From Innocence to Experience: the 'naivete' of J.R.R. Tolkien." *Mallorn* 23 (1986): 10–13.

——. "'The Legendary War and the Real One': *The Lord of the Rings* and the Climate of its Times." *Mallorn* 26 (1989):17–20.

Ellwood, Gracia Fay. *Good News from Tolkien's Middle Earth: Two Essays on the 'Applicability' of The Lord of the Rings*. Grand Rapids, MI: Eerdmans, 1970.

Epstein, E. L. "The Novels of J.R.R. Tolkien and the Ethnology of Medieval Christendom." *Philological Quarterly* 48.4 (1969): 517–25.

Evans, Robley. *J.R.R. Tolkien*. New York: Warner, 1972.

Everett, Caroline Whitman. "The Imaginative Fiction of J.R.R. Tolkien." M.A. thesis. Florida State U, 1957.

Flieger, Verlyn. "Medieval Epic and Romance Motifs in J.R.R. Tolkien's *Lord of the Rings*." Diss. Catholic U of America, 1977.

——. *Splintered Light: Logos and Language in Tolkien's World*. Grand Rapids, MI: Eerdmans, 1983.

——. "Naming the Unnameable: The Neoplatonic 'One' in Tolkien's *Silmarillion*." *Diakonia: Studies in Honor of Robert T. Meyer*. Washington, D.C.: Catholic UP of America, 1986. 127–132.

——. *A Question of Time: J.R.R. Tolkien's Road to Faerie*. Kent, OH: Kent State UP, 1997.

Flieger, Verlyn and Carl F. Hostetter, eds. *Tolkien's Legendarium: Essays on The History of Middle-earth*. Westport, CT: Greenwood, 2000.

Friedman, Barton R. "Fabricating History: Narrative Strategy in *The Lord of the Rings*." *Clio* 2.2 (1973): 123-144.

——. "Tolkien and David Jones: The Great War and the War of the Ring." *Clio* 11.2 (1982): 115–36.

Fry, Carrol L. "Tolkien's Middle-Earth and the Fantasy Frame." *Studies in the Humanities* 711 (1978): 35–42.

Fuller, Edmund. *Books with Men Behind Them*. New York: Random, 1962.

Gardner, John. "The World of Tolkien." *New York Times Book Review* 23 Oct. 1977: 1, 39–40.

Giddings, Robert, ed. *J.R.R. Tolkien: This Far Land*. London: Vision, 1984.

Giddings, Robert, and Elizabeth Holland. *J.R.R. Tolkien: The Shores of Middle-earth*. London: Junction, 1981.

Glover, Willis B. "The Christian Character of Tolkien's Invented World." *Criticism* 13 (1971): 39–53.

Green, William Howard. "*The Hobbit* and Other Fiction by J.R.R. Tolkien: Their Roots in Medieval Literature and Language." Diss. Louisiana State U, 1969.

——. *The Hobbit: A Journey into Maturity*. New York: Twayne, 1995.

Greene, D. M. "A Study of the Fictional Works of J.R.R. Tolkien." M.Litt. thesis. Oxford U, 1988.

Grotta, Daniel. *J.R.R. Tolkien: Architect of Middle-Earth*. 1976. Philadelphia: Running, 1992.

Hall, Robert A. Jr. "Tolkien's Hobbit Tetrology as 'Anti-Nibelungen'." *Western Humanities Review* 32 (1978): 351–59.

Hammond, Wayne G. and Douglas A. Anderson. *J.R.R. Tolkien:A Descriptive Bibliography*. Winchester: St. Paul's, 1993.

Hammond, Wayne G., and Christina Scull. *J.R.R. Tolkien: Artist and Illustrator*. Boston: Houghton, 1995.

Harvey, David. *The Song of Middle-earth: J.R.R. Tolkien's Themes, Symbols and Myths*. London: Unwin, 1985.

Hayes, Norren, and Robert Renshaw. "Of Hobbits: *The Lord of the Rings*." Critique 9 (1967): 58–66.

Helms, Randel. *Tolkien's World*. Boston: Houghton, 1974.

——. *Tolkien and the Silmarils*. London: Thames, 1981.

Hieatt, Constance B. "The Text of *The Hobbit*: Putting Tolkien's Notes in Order." *English Studies in Canada* 7.2 (1981): 212–24.

Hillegas, Mark, ed. *Shadows of Imagination*. 1969. 2nd ed. Carbondale: Southern Illinois UP, 1979.

Hood, Gwenyth Elise. "The Lidless Eye and the Long Burden: The Struggle Between Good and Evil in Tolkien's *The Lord of the Rings*. Diss. U of Michigan, 1984.

Hunnewell, Gary. *Tolkien Fannish and Scholarly Activities and Publications 1993*. Arnold, MA: New England Tolkien Society, 1995.

Huttar, Charles A. "Tolkien, Epic Traditions, and Golden Age Myths." *Twentieth-Century Fantasists: Essays on Culture, Society, and Belief in the Twentieth-Century*. Ed. Kath Filmer. New York: St. Martin's, 1992. 92-107.

Hyde, Paul Nolan. "Linguistic Techniques Used in Character Development in the Works of J.R.R. Tolkien." Diss. Purdue U, 1982.

Irwin, W.R. "There and Back Again: The Romances of Williams, Lewis, and Tolkien."

Sewanee Review 69 (1961): 566-78.

Isaacs, Neil D. and Rose A. Zimbardo, eds. *Tolkien and the Critics: Essays on J.R.R. Tolkien's The Lord of the Rings.* Notre Dame: U of Notre Dame P, 1968.

———. *Tolkien: New Critical Perspectives.* Lexington: UP of Kentucky, 1981.

Johnson, Judith A. *J.R.R. Tolkien: Six Decades of Criticism.* Westport, CT: Greenwood, 1986.

Kilby, Clyde S. "The Lost Myth." *Arts in Society* 6.2 (1969): 155–63.

———. *Tolkien and The Silmarillion.* Wheaton, IL: Shaw, 1976.

Kirk, Elizabeth D. "'I Would Rather Have Written In Elvish': Language, Fiction and *The Lord of the Rings.*" *Novel* 5 (1971): 5–18.

Knight, Gareth. *The Magical World of the Inklings: J.R.R. Tolkien, C. S. Lewis, Charles Williams, Owen Barfield.* Longmead, UK: Element, 1990.

Kocher, Paul H. *Master of Middle-earth: The Fiction of J.R.R. Tolkien.* Boston: Houghton, 1972.

———. *A Reader's Guide to The Silmarillion.* Boston: Houghton, 1980.

Le Guin, Ursula K. *The Language of the Night: Essays on Fantasy and Science Fiction.* 1979. New ed. London: Women's, 1989.

Lewis, C. S. "A World for Children." *Times Literary Supplement* 2 Oct. 1937: 714.

———. "The Gods Return to Earth." *Time and Tide* 14 Aug. 1954: 1082–83.

———. "The Dethronement of Power." *Time and Tide* 22 Oct. 1955: 1373–74.

———, ed. *Essays Presented to Charles Williams.* 1947. Grand Rapids, MI: Eerdmans, 1968.

Little, Edmund. *The Fantasts: Studies in J.R.R. Tolkien, Lewis Carroll, Mervyn Peake, Nikolay Gogol and, Kenneth Grahame.* Amersham, UK: Avebury, 1984.

Lobdell, Jared, ed. *A Tolkien Compass.* La Salle, IL: Open Court, 1975.

———. *England and Always: Tolkien's World of the Rings.* Grand Rapids, MI: Eerdmans, 1981.

Mack, H. C. "A Parametric Analysis of Antithetical Conflict and Irony: Tolkien and *The Lord of the Rings.*" *Word* 31.2 (1980): 121–49.

Manganiello, Dominic. "The Neverending Story: Textual Happiness in *The Lord of the Rings.*" *Mythlore* 18.3 (1992): 5–14.

Manlove, C. N. *Modern Fantasy: Five Studies.* Cambridge: Cambridge UP, 1975.

Mathews, Richard. *Lightning From a Clear Sky: Tolkien, the Trilogy, and The Silmarillion.* San Bernardino: Borgo, 1978.

McLellan, Ruth Elizabeth. "Form and Content in *The Lord of the Rings.*" M.Phil. thesis. U of Toronto, 1968.

Miller, Miriam Youngerman. "'Of sum mayn . . . .': *The Lord of the Rings* and *Sir Gawain and the Green Knight.*" *Studies in Medievalism* 3.3 (1991): 345–65.

Monsman, Gerald. "The Imaginative World of J.R.R. Tolkien." *South Atlantic Quarterly* 69 (1970): 264–78.

Monteiro, Maria do Rosario. "Númenor: Tolkien's Literary Utopia." *History of European Ideas* 16.4–6 (1993): 633–38.

Montgomery, John Warwick, ed. *Myth, Allegory, and Gospel: An Interpretation of J.R.R. Tolkien, C. S. Lewis, G. K. Chesterton, Charles Williams.* Minneapolis: Bethany, 1974.

Montgomery, Marion. "The Prophetic Poet and the Loss of Middle Earth." *Georgia Review* 33 (1979): 66–83.

Moorcock, Michael. *Wizardy and Wild Romance: A Study of Epic Fantasy.* London: Gollancz, 1987.

Morse, Robert T. *Evocation of Virgil in Tolkien's Art: Geritol for the Classics.* Oak Park, IL: Bolchaz-Carducci, 1986.

Moseley, Charles. *J.R.R. Tolkien*. Plymouth, UK: Northcote, 1997.

Murray, Robert S. J. "A Tribute to Tolkien." *Tablet* 15 Sept. 1973: 879–80.

Neimark, Anne E. *Myth Maker: J.R.R. Tolkien*. New York: Harcourt, 1996.

Nelson, Charles. "Courteous, Humble, and Helpful: Sam as Squire in *Lord of the Rings*." *Journal of the Fantastic in the Arts* 2.1 (1989): 53–63.

Noad, Charles E. *The Trees, the Jewels, and the Rings*. Harrow, UK: Tolkien Society, 1977.

Noel, Ruth S. *The Mythology of Middle-earth*. Boston: Houghton, 1977.

———. *The Languages of Tolkien's Middle-earth*. Boston: Houghton, 1980.

Obertino, James. "Moria and Hades: Underworld Journeys in Tolkien and Virgil." *Comparative Literature Studies* 30.2 (1993): 153–69.

O'Hare, Colman. "On the Reading of an 'Old' Book." *Extrapolation* 14.1 (1972): 59–63.

O'Neill, Timothy R. *The Individuated Hobbit: Jung, Tolkien, and the Archetypes of Middle-earth*. Boston: Houghton, 1979.

Parker, Douglass. "'Hwaet We Hobytla . . . .'" *Hudson Review* ((1956): 598–609.

Patterson, Nancy-Lou. "Tree and Leaf: J.R.R. Tolkien and the Visual Image." *English Quarterly* 7.1 (1974): 11–26.

Pearce, Joseph. *Tolkien: Man and Myth*. San Francisco: Ignatius, 1998.

Perret, Marion. "Rings off their Fingers: Hands in *The Lord of the Rings*." *Ariel* 6.4 (1975): 52–66.

Petty, Anne C. *One Ring to Bind Them All: Tolkien's Mythology*. Tuscaloosa: U of Alabama P, 1979.

Phillips, David Calvin. "Uses of Celtic Legend and Arthurian Romance in J.R.R. Tolkien's *The Lord of the Rings*." M.A. thesis. East Texas State U, 1993.

Provost, William. "Language and Myth in the Fantasy Writings of J.R.R. Tolkien." *Modern Age* 33.1 (1990): 42–52.

Purtill, Richard. *Lord of Elves and Eldils: Fantasy and Philosophy in C. S. Lewis and J.R.R. Tolkien*. Grand Rapids, MI: Zondervan, 1974.

———. *J.R.R. Tolkien: Myth, Morality, and Religion*. New York: Harper, 1984.

Ready, William. *Understanding Tolkien and The Lord of the Rings* (Original title: *The Tolkien Relation*). New York: Warner, 1969.

Reckford, Kenneth J. "Some Trees in Virgil and Tolkien." *Perspectives of Roman Poetry: A Classics Symposium*. Ed. G. Kark Galinsky. Austin: U of Texas P, 1974. 57–91.

Reilly, Robert. J. "Tolkien and the Fairy Story." *Thought* 38 (1963): 89–106.

———. *Romantic Religion: A Study of Barfield, Lewis, Williams, and Tolkien*. Athens: U of Georgia P, 1971

Reinken, Donald. L. "*The Lord of the Rings*: A Christian Refounding of the Political Order." *Christian Perspectives* (1966): 16–23.

Resnik, Henry. "An Interview with Tolkien." *Niekas* 18 (1967): 37–47.

Reynolds, Patricia, and Glen H. GoodKnight, eds. *Proceedings of the J.R.R. Tolkien Centenary Conference 1992*. Milton Keynes, UK: Tolkien Society, 1995.

Roberts, Mark. "Adventures in English." *Essays in Criticism* 6 (1956): 450–59.

Rogers, Deborah Champion Webster. "The Fictitious Characters of C. S. Lewis and J.R.R. Tolkien in Relation to Their Medieval Source." Diss. U of Wisconsin, 1972.

Rogers, Deborah Webster, and Ivor A. Rogers. *J.R.R. Tolkien*. Boston: Twayne, 1980.

Rosebury, Brian. *Tolkien: A Critical Assessment*. London: St. Martin's, 1992.

Rossi, Lee. D. *The Politics of Fantasy: C. S. Lewis and J.R.R. Tolkien*. Ann Arbor: UMI, 1984.

Ryan, J. S. "German Mythology Applied: The Extension of Ritual Folk-Memory." *Folklore* 77 (1966): 44–57.

——. *Tolkien: Cult or Culture*. Armidale, New South Wales: U of New England P, 1969.

——. "Tolkien's Concept of Philology as Mythology." *Seven* 7 (1986): 91–106.

St. Clair, Gloria Ann Strange Slaughter. "Studies in the Sources of J.R.R. Tolkien's *The Lord of the Rings*." Diss. U of Oklahoma, 1970.

Sale, Roger. *Modern Heroism: Essays on D. H. Lawrence, William Empson, and J.R.R. Tolkien*. Berkeley: U of California P, 1973.

Salu, Mary, and Robert T. Farrell, eds. *J.R.R. Tolkien, Scholar and Storyteller: Essays in Memoriam*. Ithaca, NY: Cornell UP, 1979.

Sarti, Ronald Christopher. "Man in a Mortal World: J.R.R. Tolkien and *The Lord of the Rings*." Diss. Indiana U, 1984.

Schlobin, Roger C., ed. *Aesthetics of Fantasy Literature and Art*. Notre Dame: U of Notre Dame P, 1982.

Scriven, R. C. "Hobbits' Apotheosis: The World of Professor of Tolkien." *Tablet* 11 Feb. 1956: 129–30.

Senior, W. A. *Stephen R. Donaldson's Chronicles of Thomas Covenant: Variations on the Fantasy Tradition*. Kent, OH: Kent State UP, 1995.

Shippey, T. A. *The Road to Middle-earth*. 1982. New ed. London: Grafton, 1992.

——. "Goths and Huns: The Rediscovery of the Northern Cultures in the Nineteenth Century." *The Medieval Legacy: A Symposium*. Odense: Odense UP, 1982.

——. "Tolkien and 'The Homecoming of Beorhtnoth'." *Leaves from the Tree: J.R.R. Tolkien's Shorter Fiction*. London: Tolkien Society, 1991. 5–16.

——. "Tolkien as a Post-War Writer." *Proceedings of the J.R.R. Tolkien Centenary Conference, 1992*. Milton Keynes, UK: Tolkien Society, 1995. 84–93.

Shorto, Russell. *J.R.R. Tolkien: Man of Fantasy*. New York: Kipling, 1988.

Sirridge, Mary. "J.R.R. Tolkien and the Fairy Tale Truth." *British Journal of Aesthetics* 15 (1975): 81–92.

Spacks, Patricia Meyer. "Ethical Pattern in *The Lord of the Rings*." *Critique* 3 (1959): 30–42.

Spice, Wilma Helen. "A Jungian View of Tolkien's 'Gandalf': An Investigation of Enabling and Exploitative Power in Counseling and Psychotherapy from the Viewpoint of Analytical Psychology." Diss. U of Pittsburgh, 1976.

Stevens, C. D. "High Fantasy versus Low Comedy: Humor in J.R.R. Tolkien." *Extrapolation* 21 (1980): 122–29.

Stimpson, Catharine R. *J.R.R. Tolkien*. New York: Columbia UP, 1969.

Straight, Michael. "The Fantastic World of Professor Tolkien." *New Republic* 16 Jan. 1956: 24–26.

Sullivan, C. W. III. "Tolkien and the Telling of a Traditional Narrative." *Journal of the Fantastic in the Arts* 7.1 (1996): 75–82.

Syme, Margaret Ruth. "Tolkien as Gospel Writer." Diss. McGill U, 1989.

Thomson, George H. "*The Lord of the Rings*: The Novel as Traditional Romance." *Wisconsin Studies in Contemporary Literature* 8 (1967): 43–59.

Timmons, Daniel. "J.R.R. Tolkien's Genealogies: The Roots of His 'Sub-creation'." *Mallorn* 34 (1996): 7–11.

——. "Sub-creator and Creator: Tolkien and the Design of the One." *Between Faith and Fiction: Tolkien and the Powers of His World. Proceedings of the Arda Symposium at the Second Northern Tolkien Festival, Oslo, August 1997. Arda Special* 1 September 1998. 52–68.

——. "J.R.R. Tolkien: The 'Montrous' in the Mirror." *Journal of the Fantastic in the Arts* 9.3 (1998): 229–46.

Tolkien, Christopher. *The Silmarillion: A Brief Account of the Book and its Making.* Boston: Houghton, 1977.

The Tolkien Papers: Mankato Studies in English, No. 2. Mankato: Mankato State College, 1967.

Toynbee, Philip. "Dissension Among the Judges." *Observer* 6 Aug. 1961: 19.

Traversi, Derek A. "The Realm of Gondor." Month 15 (1956): 370–71.

Urang, Gunnar. *Shadows of Heaven: Religion and Fantasy in the Writings of C. S. Lewis, Charles Williams, and J.R.R. Tolkien.* Philadelphia: Pilgrim, 1971.

Watson, J. R. "The Hobbits and the Critics." *Critical Quarterly* 13.3 (1971): 252–58.

Waugh, Robert H. "Perilous Faerie: J.R.R. Tolkien in the Selva Oscura." *Studies in Weird Fiction* 15 (1994): 20–27.

West, Richard C. *Tolkien Criticism: An Annotated Checklist.* 1970. Kent, OH: Kent State UP, 1981.

Wilson, Colin. *Tree by Tolkien.* London: Village, 1974.

Wilson, Edmund. "Oo, Those Awful Orcs." 1956. *The Bit Between My Teeth: A Literary Chronicle of 1950-1965.* New York: Farrar, 1965. 326–32.

Wojcik, Jan. "Tolkien and Coleridge: Remaking of the Green." *Renascence* 20 (1968): 134–39, 146.

Zgorzalski, Andrzej. "Time Setting in J.R.R. Tolkien's *The Lord of the Rings.*" *Zagadenienia Rodzajow Literackich* 13.2 (1971): 91–100.

Index

About the Contributors

GEORGE CLARK is Professor Emeritus of English at Queen's University, Canada, where he specializes in Old English and Old Norse. He is the author of a book and several articles on *Beowulf* and has translated Old Norse–Old Icelandic sagas and tales. He has published articles on *The Battle of Maldon*, Robert Henryson, Chaucer, *The Alliterative Morte Arthure*, and William Golding. Clark is currently a consultant reader for academic journals such as *PMLA, Speculum,* and *English Studies in Canada.*

JONATHAN EVANS is professor of English at the University of Georgia. He has published articles on medieval dragon-lore in *Mythical and Fabulous Creatures: A Source Book and Research Guide* and the *Encyclopedia of Medieval Folklore.* Other articles have appeared in *Semiotica, Style, and Poetics Today, Journal of Folklore Research,* and *Medieval Perspectives.* He is the co-editor of *Semiotics and International Scholarship: Towards a Language of Theory.* Evans is currently working on *Introductory Old English* and *Old Norse Dragon-lore: Beowulf and Its Analogues.*

VERLYN FLIEGER is associate professor of English at the University of Maryland. Her research interests encompass medieval literature, fantasy, and comparative mythology. She is the author of *Splintered Light* (1983) and *A Question of Time* (1997), both of which examine the symbolism and imagery of Tolkien's works. Flieger has also published many articles on Tolkien, C. S. Lewis, E. R. Eddison, and Charles Williams. She is the co-editor of *Tolkien's Legendarium: Essays on The History of Middle-earth* (2000).

CHARLES W. NELSON is associate professor of language and literature at Michigan Technological University. He administers courses in fantasy literature and Tolkien, the latter of which has been run for more than twenty-five years. He is the division head of the Fantastic Literature in English for the International Association for the Fantastic in the Arts. Nelson has published articles on Tolkien and has a forthcoming book from Greenwood Publishing that examines the literary archetypes of Tolkien's works.

FAYE RINGEL is professor of Humanities at the U.S. Coast Guard Academy, Connecticut. Her doctoral work was in comparative literature, focusing on aspects of medieval romance in Morris, Dunsany, and Tolkien. She is the author of *New England's Gothic Literature: History and Folklore of the Supernatural from the Seventeenth through the Eighteenth Century* (1995). Ringel has been active in Tolkien organizations since the 1960s.

WILLIAM N. ROGERS II is professor of English and Comparative Literature at San Diego State University. His interests and specialization range from nineteenth–century British Literature to the fiction of modern China and Japan. A particular concentration is in Victorian works of exploration and travel, especially issues concerning the (mis)understandings inherent in cross-cultural encounters. Rogers's "Arabia Deserta and the Victorians: Past and Present" is published in *Explorations in Doughty's Arabia Deserta* (1987).

GEOFFREY RUSSOM is professor of English and chair of Medieval Studies at Brown University. He is the author of *Old English Meter and Linguistic Theory* (1987) and *Beowulf and Old Germanic Metre* (1998), which is volume 23 of *Cambridge Studies in Anglo-Saxon England.* Russom has also published articles on Old English literature, Old Norse literature, the history of the English language, and problems of poetic form.

DAVID SANDNER is a Ph.D. candidate in English at the University of Oregon. He is the author of *The Fantastic Sublime: Romanticism and Transcendence in Nineteenth–Century Children's Fantasy Literature* (1997). He has articles on fantasy literature and Tolkien in *Mythlore, Extrapolations,* and the *Journal of the Fantastic in the Arts.* Sandner's doctoral work involves the theory and practice of imaginative literature in the eighteenth century.

ROGER C. SCHLOBIN is professor of English (retired) at Purdue University. He has authored six scholarly books and edited more than fifty. He has published over 100 articles that deal with topics such as fantasy, science fiction, pedagogy, and medieval and Arthurian literature. He is one of the founders of the International Association for the Fantastic in the Arts and currently serves as an editor for the association's journal.

W. A. SENIOR holds his Ph.D. from the University of Notre Dame. He has published articles in various journals on medieval literature, science fiction, and fantasy. He is the author of *Variations of the Fantasy Tradition: Stephen R. Donaldson's Chronicles of Thomas Covenant* (1995). Senior is the past president of the International Association for the Fantastic in the Arts.

TOM SHIPPEY is the former holder of Tolkien's Chair of English Language and Medieval English Literature at Leeds University. He has authored *The Road to Middle-earth,* as well as many other articles and papers on Tolkien's works. He has published extensively on Old English and medieval literature. He has been the editor or co-editor of several critical and creative anthologies on fantasy and science fiction, including *The Oxford Book of Fantasy Stories* (1994). Shippey is the current holder of the Walter J. Ong Chair of Humanities at Saint Louis University.

DEBBIE SLY lectures in English at Worcester College of Higher Education (UK). Her conference papers include "Non-Violence in Shelley's The Revolt of Islam," and "Prime Suspect 1–3." She has a forthcoming article, "Natural Histories: Learning from Animals in T. H. White's Arthurian Sequences," in *Worldviews* (2000). Sly's research interests embrace poetry of the Renaissance, Seventeenth Century, and Romantic periods (Spenser, Milton, Shelley), and popular literature (detective fiction and fantasy).

C. W. SULLIVAN III is professor of English at East Carolina University and a member of the Welsh Academy. He is the author of *Welsh Celtic Myth in Modern Fantasy* (1989), editor of *The Mabinogi: A Book of Essays* (1996), *The Dark Fantastic* (1997), *Science Fiction for Young Readers* (1993), and *Today Becomes Tomorrow* (1974). He is the editor of the *Children's Folklore Review*, and a member of the editorial board of *Paradoxa: Studies in World Literary Genres*. Sullivan's articles on mythology, folklore, fantasy, and science fiction have appeared in a variety of anthologies and journals.

DANIEL TIMMONS holds his Ph.D. in English from the University of Toronto. His dissertation examines fantasy theory, the scholarship of Tolkien, and the critical history of the author's works. He has published articles in *English Studies in Canada*, *Mallorn* (Journal of The Tolkien Society), *The Tolkien Collector*, and the *Journal of the Fantastic in the Arts*. Timmons has given papers on Tolkien in Canada, the United States, Poland, and Norway, and has an essay in the proceedings to the Second Northern Tolkien Society Festival symposium.

MICHAEL R. UNDERWOOD is a lecturer and director of the writing tutor program at San Diego State University. He specializes in the teaching of rhetoric and writing, British literature before the 1800s, and the work of J.R.R. Tolkien. Underwood has presented several papers on Tolkien at the conferences of The Mythopoeic Society.

TANYA CAROLINE WOOD is a Ph.D. candidate in English at the University of Toronto. Her master's thesis was on the utopian thought of James Tiptree, Jr. She has given papers on Francis Bacon's *New Atlantis* and Thomas More's *Utopia*, Donna Harraway's cyborg mythologies, Margaret Cavendish's concept of subjectivity, and utopian writing by seventeenth–century women. Wood's doctoral work involves a comparison of Margaret Cavendish's sexual politics in her primary and secondary worlds. She has a forthcoming article on *Sir Gawain and the Green Knight* in *Notes and Queries*.